HOG FEVER

By Richard La Plante from Tom Doherty Associates

Hog Fever
Leopard
Mantis
Steroid Blues
Tegné

HOG FEVER

Richard La Plante

A TOM DOHERTY ASSOCIATES BOOK
NEW YORK

A Forge Book
Published by Tom Doherty Associates, Inc.
175 Fifth Avenue
New York, N.Y. 10010

Forge® is a registered trademark of Tom Doherty Associates, Inc.

Library of Congress Cataloging-in-Publication Data

La Plante, Richard.
    Hog fever / Richard La Plante.
        p.   cm.
    "A Tom Doherty Associates book."
    ISBN 0-312-85830-2 (pb)
    1. Motorcycling.   2. Motorcyclists—Psychology.
    3. Harley-Davidson motorcycle.   I. Title.
    GV1059.5.L3   1995
    796.7'5—dc20   94-42268
                                                            CIP

First hardcover edition: April 1995
First trade paperback edition: June 1997

Printed in the United States of America
0   9   8   7   6   5   4   3   2   1

Contents

THE AMERICAN RIDE

Acknowledgments

Martin Fletcher; Warr's of London, Waterford Road;
Martin Szlagowski; Southern Cycles; Ultimate Performance UK;
Alan Fisher; The Hells Angels Motorcycle Club; Ian of Reading;
Betina Soto Acebal; George Bone; Simon Gluckman; Mark Phillips; Rally and Race; P & D Services; Surrey Harley-Davidson;
Brian John Nye; Battistini's Custom Cycles; Jeff Duval; Rikki
and Dean Battistini; Johnnie Walker; John Williamson; R.M.D.
Motors; Garry Stuart; Keith R. Ball and "Easyriders"; Terence
Stamp; Jimmy Maloney; Dave Munkenbeck; The Club (you know
who you are); Amagansett Wines and Spirits; Gary Wagner; Peter
Mayle; Lynda La Plante; Robert Eyster, M.D.; Mike Ramsey;
Anesthesia in General; Wes and Blaine; Doctor Kator; Hollace
Shaffer; Bubbles T. Klown; those whose names have been
changed to protect their guilt, and a special thanks to Frank
Aliano, Captain Bandana, and Big Dog Custom Motorcycles.

Live hard, ride free, my tattooed friend.
Enjoy life's road till journey's end.
Let speed, not haste, that be a must,
Fear none but those you can not trust.
Lest as a friend, they will deceive,
        only oneself, should one believe!

                        Brian John Nye

Prologue

EXHIBIT A

Air Mail—Special Delivery

Mr. Roy La Plante
1436 Remington Road
Philadelphia 51, Pa.

ATTORNEY AT LAW
3376 PEACHTREE RD., N.E.
NORTH ATLANTA 19, GA.
CEDAR 7-8691

Dear Mr. La Plante:

I checked the case of your son, Richard, to the fourth Monday in December, as I had planned to so do. I feel the attitude of the Judge will be considerably tempered by the Holiday Season if I am unable to dispose of the case by conference prior to Christmas.

The police charges were numerous, including driving under the influence of alcohol to the extent of making it less safe for your son to have operated his motorcycle than it would have been if he had not allegedly been under the influence. According to Georgia law it is not necessary for one to be intoxicated or drunk as we commonly understand such term. However, I have investigated the matter and am convinced that your son was not then in violation of the O.U.I. law.

However, he had alcohol on his breath following the drinking of a beer and martini three or four hours prior thereto, his appearance and method of operating his motorcycle influenced the police to make the drunk driving charge and which the police will not withdraw.

The other charge pending is speeding 60 MPH in a 35 MPH speed zone, weaving from lane to lane and operating at an excessive rate of speed on private property.

If your son were not an Oglethorpe College student the foregoing charges would be more serious. However, I feel that the Judge will probably suspend his driving privileges for a few months and admonish him for being reckless, and with long hair giving an appearance not acceptable in this community, Richard has cut his hair to a reasonable length and I have talked with him about need for making the most of his educational opportunity. He assures me his grades in college are good and he will try to make the honor roll next term. I have a 20-year-old son in college and face similar problems.

During the next week I will talk with the Judge in an effort to dispose of this matter without trial. Rest easy—your son will probably benefit and mature greatly from this experience.

Sincerely,
Roland Nacson

PH:D

cc: Mr. Richard Scars, 311 Brodhead St., Easton, Pa.
        Mr. Richard S. La Plante, Oglethorpe College, Atlanta, Ga.
        Mrs. Elgin MacConnell, Dean, Oglethorpe College

This letter, mailed to my father in 1966, marked the end of my biking days, or so I thought. They had begun with a Cushman motor scooter presented to me by my grandfather on my sixteenth birthday. It was a red breadbox with handlebars that cornered like a milk float and reached a top speed of thirty miles an hour. I customized it with kitchen pipes in place of its factory-supplied standard exhaust system, and riding along the ocean roads of New Jersey with the *bap, bap, bap* of the "plumbing" against the asphalt and the sun and wind against my skin, I had that great feeling: adventure mixed with independence.

I replaced the Cushman two years later with a 400 cc Norton Electra with an electric starter. The English bike had all the adventure and independence of the scooter plus the sheer power and "danger" of a big motorcycle. I rode straight through the summer then in the fall from Philadelphia to Atlanta, Georgia, for my first semester at college. My identity as "the guy with the motorcycle"—long haired and nonconforming—carried me well into my first year down south. By the time I was arrested, two months after my arrival, I was guzzling "moonshine" whiskey, riding with a couple of townie bikers, racing cars up and down Peachtree Street and acting out my own variation of the outlaw motorcyclist . . . and, I might add, that is exactly how I was treated by the judge in the Atlanta courthouse. I was tossed out of the court room and given a mandatory haircut (I was scalped) for starters, and had it not been for my long-suffering family, I would have been slated for six months on the Stone Mountain chain-gang. . . .

By the time my driving licence was returned, the helmet laws in the state of Georgia had come into effect and I refused to ride my Norton with a lid on my head. No freedom, no style.

That was it. I sold the bike, used the money to buy a Triumph TR3, the type of vehicle real bikers refer to as a "cage" (in other words, a car), and proceeded to "make the most of my educational opportunity."

Twenty years later I realized something was missing from my life. Perhaps it was the onset of middle age; maybe it was the glimpse of the Harley-Davidson motorcycles in Fred Warr's showroom just off the King's Road. The American bikes drew me like a magnet: they were priceless artifacts from a culture of wide roads, big skies, and warm sun. My ex-culture.

I became a frequent visitor to Warr's. At first I got by on simply being an American, asking questions about parts and service and hinting that I had been a bit of a heavy biker where I came from, trying not to give away that I knew precious little about the bikes themselves and in fact didn't know a carburetor from a camshaft. Fred was always willing to answer questions about the bikes, but after several months of regular appearances I became embarrassed about continually asking the prices yet never buying a motorcycle.

The truth was I had become obsessed. The bikes had a hypnotic effect on me. I loved to look at them; there was something in their design that seemed perfect. In fact, during that period nothing seemed so nearly perfect as those steel and chrome motorcycles in Fred Warr's showroom. The fact that they actually ran was a secondary feature. I would have been satisfied to have one in my living-room as an *objet d'art*.

Then three things happened. First, I moved out of London— so I needed something to commute on, something easy in traffic. Second, I got my hands on a bit of money. And third, Harley-Davidson came out with the new reliable Evolution engine and the "affordable" 883 cc Sportster.

I ordered one, in black, then waited a month. I made nightly visits to Warr's showroom on Waterford Road, peeking through the iron-grated windows, trying to get a look at my motorcycle. For some reason I wanted to see it alone, just me and the bike. Very personal.

And one night it was there. I knew it was mine because it was the only black Sportster in the showroom, just out of the crate and freshly polished, like a tight, muscular steel horse.

I was thirty-eight years old and I felt like a kid at Christmas, tingling with electricity and dying to get my hands on the bike. . . . At ten o'clock the next morning I did.

Then the nerves hit hard.

Looking at it had been one thing, actually riding it was something else. In spite of my bravado with Fred, I had not actually ridden a bike in twenty years, and that was in another country. I didn't even have a British driver's license, for a car or a motorcycle. However, standing there, in front of Fred and the idling Sportster, there seemed no time for doubt. So I climbed into the saddle and started off.

Slow and wobbly, conscious that everyone was staring at me and convinced they all knew I was faking it, in my new leathers, helmet, and shades, I ambled down the King's Road, sitting at the tail end of the traffic at red lights, watching other bikes shoot out and up the side. I breathed exhaust fumes and wondered if I had ever wanted to actually ride the bike after all. Maybe my subconscious intention really was to mount the Sportster on a plinth in the center of my living-room. By the time I had crossed the bridge into Putney I was certain that people were pointing at me and thinking, "Flash bastard, look at him, he can't even ride." I kept my eyes front and concentrated. Dropping the bike would have been the ultimate in humiliation. When I hit the A3, about four miles from Warr's, I felt a semblance of my old riding skills returning. My body was no longer resisting the flow of the bike, no longer acting as a counterbalance as the Sportster leaned into the bends in the highway. It wasn't exactly a unity between man and machine, but at least it was no longer a battle.

I reached fifty miles an hour on the A3: Fred had said that fifty was the limit for the first five hundred miles, until the engine had run in. At fifty, my eyes were watering and there was a hurricane in the ear section of my full-faced helmet. Fifty seemed fast. Ten minutes later I was riding the Sportster into my garage and feeling a strange sense of accomplishment.

I phoned Fred when I got into the house, told him I'd made it home but the ride had been a touch shaky.

He laughed, then said something that struck me as incongruous with my report of shaky roadwork. "That little bike is only the beginning for you. You'll end up with a Big Twin"—1340 cc—"I can always tell."

"Nope, never. This Sportster's all I'll ever need," I answered. I thanked him, put down the phone, and hustled to the garage.

I polished every inch of that 883, even got a toothbrush to clean between the spokes.

Eight years and four Harleys later, I'm still polishing.

And Fred was right—well, almost. He was just a bit out on the cubic centimeters . . .

My latest piece of metal sculpture is a Springer Softail, purchased from Fred in 1989. The engine has been bored to 95 cu. in. (nearly 1600 cc) and the bike has been customized from top to tail. It registers 100 HP off the back wheel and does everything but fly.

And I still stand there, alone in my garage, looking at it, like a kid at Christmas.

The Beginning

The first Harley-Davidson motorcycle, constructed in Milwaukee, Wisconsin, in 1903, was the creation of Bill Harley and Arthur and Walter Davidson. Harley, the only college graduate of the group, designed the motorcycle, Arthur Davidson drew up the patterns, and Walter Davidson built the bike.

The prototype Harley-Davidson was a conventional single-cylinder 400 cc engine bolted beneath the crossbar of a strengthened bicycle frame. There were plenty of problems with this arrangement; the main one was the frame was unable to handle the power and vibration of the engine, and it kept breaking. Eventually, after several rebuilds, the wheelbase was extended for stability, heavier steering head and wheel bearings were used, the frame tubes and wheels were made thicker, and "final drive" was achieved by a leather belt uniting the engine with the rear sprocket, allowing the rider to control the speed of the bike by tightening or loosening it. Harley-Davidson had a motorcycle. By 1905, the Milwaukee factory was producing eight of them per year.

In 1906, orders mounted to forty-nine, and an American industry was born. By 1910, the oldest of the three Davidson brothers, William, had joined the team as Vice President and

Works Manager of the plant. Three thousand bikes were built and sold, and the original single-cylinder 3 HP engine was replaced by a V-twin, two cylinders mounted at a forty-five degree angle to each other, and upgraded to 5.35 HP.

The two-cylinder V-twin engine was, and still is, the heart of Harley-Davidson.

The company manufactured its V-twins in 45 cu. in. and 74 cu. in. engine sizes, (about 700 cc and 1200 cc), which were nicknamed Flatheads because of the flattened shape of the engine heads, and began to battle for sales, both domestic and military, with its arch rival, the Indian motorcycle company.

At times, Harley's marketing techniques were less than sportsmanlike. At one point they encouraged their dealers to scrap any non-Harleys which came into their shops as part exchange for a Harley-Davidson as a way of getting the Indians off the road, and only a decline in public image forced them to withdraw this "exchange" offer. Forced to look for advances in engineering and style in order to compete, Harley first added a "buddy seat," allowing the Harley man to travel with a "companion," then revolutionized the engine by manufacturing the 1000 cc, 61 cu. in. and 36 HP overhead-valve V-twin. It was nicknamed the "Knucklehead" because of the shape, like the prominent knuckles of a clenched fist, of its rocker covers (the covers above the engine heads).

The Knucklehead was the forerunner of the Harley fleet. It is the source of the general Harley nicknames Twin and Big Twin, and stands, even today, as a "classic" Harley, a very desirable "base" bike for many "complete restorations" or "customs." The Knucklehead had speed and it had style, but, unfortunately, it leaked oil. Lots of oil.

In 1949 Harley-Davidson manufactured the Panhead engine, with pan-shaped rocker covers. Built to solve the oil-leak problem by placing the previously external oil lines inside the engine casing and upgrading the oil pump to regulate pressure, the new Pan also featured aluminum engine heads for a lighter and cooler performance. This configuration, however, created a problem of its own: insufficient oil pressure (partially cured, in later models, by the factory). In the style department, Harley replaced the Springer forks, two large springs (shock absorbers) mounted on top of the front forks of the bike, with a hydraulic system (no springs). They christened their new bike the Hydra-Glide.

Through this combination of factory innovation and creative marketing, Harley buried the Indian in 1952, only to be met by new competition from England—Triumph, Norton, and BSA. The Milwaukee boys turned to the US government for help, petitioning to have a 40% import tax placed on all non-American motorcycles. They were turned down.

They were forced to compete; this time on the racetrack, with a 750 cc, 45 cu. in. Twin. This was a fiasco that was hard pressed to make 80 MPH on the straights and consequently lost every race. So Harley tried again, creating an all-aluminum engine bored out to 883 cc named the XL Sportster. The XL could do 100 MPH, and finally beat the Triumph on the oval, also earning itself a reputation as a red-hot "street bike." It was not, however, red hot enough in the sales department to keep the company from financial trouble, and in the mid 1960s Harley went public, selling just enough stock to finance an upgrade in their product. Believing that an electric starter would make their heavier bikes more accessible to the general buyer by doing away with the "kick," they built the Electra-Glide, then spent the remainder of their money revising the hydraulically temperamental Panhead engine, giving birth in 1966 to the Shovelhead, after which the company was once again broke.

Rescue (or disaster disguised as rescue) came in the shape of a leisure industry conglomerate called the American Machine and Foundry Company, or AMF. AMF bought Harley-Davidson for twenty-one million dollars, then proceeded to crank production up to fifty thousand motorcycles a year (about three times their previous production), too many machines to be effectively screened for quality control. The consequence was that Harley-Davidson got an even worse reputation for reliability, or lack of it.

At the same time, the Japanese invaded the American motorcycle market at the cruiser end with the Honda Gold Wing, and at the street-hot end with the Kawasaki 900 range. The Japanese product was fast, relatively inexpensive, and reliable.

In 1978, the AMF petitioned the Tariff Commission to slap heavy import duties on the Japanese bikes—as Harley-Davidson had attempted with the English bikes—and failed. Then, in a competitive effort, they increased the engine size of the big bikes to 1340 cc and added a five-speed transmission to the touring models, following that with the Sturgis, a sports bike with a Kelvar belt-driven motor replacing the chain named after the annual bike meet in the hills of South Dakota. It was anything to increase that elusive reliability factor and win the bike market back from the Japanese. It didn't work, and in 1981 the AMF bailed out, selling Harley-Davidson back to Harley-Davidson, or, specifically, to a management-based group led by Chairman Vaughn Beals. Beals took control just as his company was going under for the third time.

In a last-ditch effort, Beals (on behalf of the reorganized Harley-Davidson Motorcycle Company) petitioned the Tariff Commission, requesting high import duties on only those Japanese bikes over 700 cc. The Commission finally came through, giving Harley a five-year period over which tariffs on big Japanese bikes would start high then taper off. It was the breathing space Harley-Davidson desperately needed, time to go back to the drawing-board on both design and marketing.

In 1983, Milwaukee launched the V2 Evolution engine. Using aluminum alloy for both heads and cylinders and burning unleaded fuel, the Evolution was—for the first time in Harley's history—oil tight and reliable. Harley-Davidson had finally stepped into the future—or more accurately the present.

In the same year the Harley Owners Group (HOG) was

formed, a Harley club sanctioned by Milwaukee and open (in the USA) to anyone purchasing a new Harley-Davidson motorcycle. The idea behind HOG was to link the buyer to the manufacturer. Willie Davidson, grandson of William Davidson and head of the design department, began spending time with and listening to the people who rode his motorcycles. He understood their desire for the classic look of the old Harleys coupled with the reliability of the new Evo engine, and it was through this combination that Harley-Davidson truly found its feet.

The new Heritage Softail (the cruiser of the fleet) was an updated Hydra-Glide from 1949, and the Sportster (the racing bike, light and easy to handle) still looked as it did in 1952, but was now powered by a choice of either an 883 or 1100 cc engine (and now a 1200 cc engine). In 1988, eighty years from their inception, Springer forks were reintroduced to create the FXSTX Springer Softail—a factory custom.

For some buyers it may have been nostalgia; for others, including myself, it was just plain perfection.

In America they call the 883 the ladies' bike, because at 463 lbs. with an overall length of 87 in. it is nearly two hundred pounds lighter and half a foot shorter than any of the Big Twins. In theory, that makes it a lot easier to throw around—or in my case, after twenty years out of the saddle, to ride at all.

I say "in theory" because I believe a lot of my apprehension regarding the 1340s was psychological. They looked too big to ride. In fact, because the saddle height of a stock (factory-built) Springer Softail is actually two inches closer to the ground than that of a Sportster, thereby lowering its center of gravity, the bigger bike is arguably easier to balance. On top of this, I genuinely loved the looks of the Sportster, basically just a frame and an engine, like a skeleton draped with muscle. About as lean as a bike gets.

And then, of course, there was the money factor. When I bought the 883 the price on the road was a touch under £4,000, less than half the cost of a new Springer Softail and just about a third of an Ultra-Glide, the flagship of the Harley fleet, including radio-cassette player, intercom, CB radio, leg shields, and enough luggage space to take the wife and kids off for a week in St. Tropez—sort of an open-air caravan.

The Ultra-Glide was never my idea of a "lean machine." I couldn't get into the idea of wheeling along the highway while having a conversation, via the headset-style intercom, with the person behind me. "Ah, pilot to copilot, pilot to copilot, do you read me, over?" Then again, I've lost some of my best Raybans while twisting my neck at seventy miles an hour, trying to communicate with a passenger: the wind, after scattering my words and splattering my face with saliva, catches the outside rim of the shades and removes them from my nose, sending them up then down beneath the front tire of the inevitable truck in the middle lane, while I ride on . . . teeth gritted, wind pounding my bared eyeballs, and tears streaming down my cheeks.

Now that's real biking.

The Buddhist Prayer Position

I had the real bike. But not the real license. It both-
ered me, but not enough to swap the Harley for a moped with
an L-plate. That didn't fit my self-image at all.

So I worked out an elaborate story in case I was stopped; I
would flash my Pennsylvania license (a car, not a bike license)
and explain that I had been in England for less than six months
and was leaving within the year, which would put me inside the
statutory limit on applying for a British license. I figured I could
get away with this once or twice. At least until it was discovered
that I had been a resident for ten years.

It was risky, but now that I had the Harley I wasn't going to
give it up.

The object was not to get stopped in the first place. I couldn't
afford to look like a beginner on the bike.

I placed myself on a secret training program. Up every morning
at seven, leathered and on the road by seven-thirty. Straight
down the hill and into Richmond Park, coinciding my arrival
with the opening of the gates. Then around and around the

eleven-mile perimeter, practising my corners and emergency stops.

Everything was going fine till the day it rained.

The smooth road surface was like an ice rink, and I was into my second circuit when a six-point buck crossed in front of the bike. I hit the brakes hard, front and rear. Too hard. The back wheel slid out to the side and for a moment I was travelling sideways at twenty miles an hour. Then the front wheel banged into one of the wooden posts that separate the road from the grass shoulder. It caught and stopped the bike. I continued to travel—or at least my body did. The zippered bottom of my pants, a thermal-lined waxed rainsuit, somehow managed to wrap round the left foot peg of the motorcycle. By the time I hit the ground my pants were around my ankles and my bare ass was pointing upwards in the Buddhist prayer position.

"Are you injured, sir?" A female voice dragged me back to full consciousness.

I looked up, over my own bared buttocks, to see a mounted policewoman staring down. That she kept from laughing is a testimony of her self-discipline. I did start to laugh; I couldn't help it, it was a combination of unused adrenalin and acute embarrassment.

Worse was yet to come. As I tried to stand up, the pants went lower, leaving me cupping my traumatized genitalia in a last-ditch effort at dignity. She dismounted and walked to the bike. Bent down, turned the ignition off, then freed my pants from the foot peg.

I was now curled in a fetal position, grinning like an idiot, and passing cars were slowing down to take a look at the accident. Finally, standing, I got my pants up, which was better than I could do with the motorcycle. I couldn't get the leverage I needed to lift it. The policewoman stepped in again and together we hoisted the Harley.

"A deer ran in front of me and I skidded," I explained.

"Are you carrying your operator's license, sir?"

I was taller than her by half a head and probably ten years older, yet I felt like a little kid caught pissing in the swimming pool. I pulled my wallet from my pocket and flashed her the Pennsylvania license.

"I'm an American." I said it like it was the single credential I needed to excuse my incompetence. She nodded her head and waited.

"I'm only here for a few months."

She held my eyes a moment then glanced at the bike.

"I'm taking the motorcycle home with me, back to the States," I explained.

"It has a British number-plate," she noted.

"I bought it here. To ride while I'm in Europe."

She nodded, then asked, "Do you feel able to ride it now?"

"Sure."

She watched as I started the bike, clicked it into first, and rode cautiously away. I caught a last glimpse of her in my rear-view mirror, remounting her horse. Then I turned the slippery corner at the top of the rise—travelling at a near right angle to the road, steering the bike like a car—and slithered back to my garage. I checked the bike for damage (none), wiped it down, and decided that my apprenticeship in Richmond Park had just ended; I couldn't risk another roadside rescue by the mounted police.

The next dry afternoon I saddled up and headed into London. It was my maiden voyage to town, and my first experience with heavy traffic: stop lights, cars, buses, and motorcycle couriers.

If I had felt like a poser in Putney, then I felt doubly self-conscious on Regent Street. Everything about me was brand new, my engineer boots, my gloves, my flying jacket, my helmet and shades, and my shiny black and chrome motorcycle. Even my technique for navigating through traffic—pull out, gun it, then get back in line fast—was new. Everything except my face. That was decidedly not new. That had seen a good many more years than most of the Kawasaki-mounted couriers who pulled up beside me at the lights, looking over at the old guy on the new bike with what I interpreted as a mixture of curiosity and scorn.

"How much did that thing cost you, mate?" was the standard line from the collage of Darth Vader look-alikes in full-faced helmets and tinted visors.

"A few grand," I would answer, underplaying the money side of Harleying.

Darth would then reappraise my bike and nod his helmet knowingly. "Is it quick?"

"Fair . . ." I'd begin as the light changed and the Vader look-alike astride his rice-burner left me in a cloud of black exhaust. My image of the biking rebel (a hold-over from college) was deteriorating quickly. I was more like an economy version of the late Malcolm Forbes.

The other tough part about my weekly forays into London was that each time I headed out of the driveway I actually wondered if I would ever be coming home again. I found the constant barrage of stimulus of city riding a nightmare. Horns blaring, people shouting, lights changing, everything happening at once: I felt that sooner or later I was going to get hurt. Which is not exactly the best feeling to have at the beginning of a ride.

The feeling itself, a composite of danger and inevitability was not new to me. I had encountered it many years before, during my days on the Norton, when I used to ride the bike to the Philadelphia Karate Club. It wasn't the ride that made me anxious in those days; the streets outside the center of the city were long, wide, and straight, much less demanding than the Soho-Piccadilly area of London. It was the karate class itself: the constant barrage as the Japanese instructors barked orders as I attempted to block and counter their kicks and punches. That felt very dangerous, but I was determined to learn, so I stuck with it. For fifteen years I stuck with it, and if I learned anything, it is that beyond technique there is spirit, and beyond spirit is "zanshin."

Exactly the same as riding a motorcycle.

"Zanshin," translated loosely from Japanese, means "perfect posture," but it is not so much an attitude of the body as an attitude of the mind.

In the early days of the martial arts, when masterless Samurai wandered Japan, zanshin was the difference between life and death. It was a relaxed preparedness, a sort of professional paranoia; an acute awareness of potential danger from all sides and at all times. Many Samurai would never bathe; in fact, it is said that Musashi (16th century), the "sword saint" of Japan, did not take a bath or comb his hair once from the time he took up the sword. He would not permit himself the relaxation of the water, the vulnerability of his nakedness, or the lapse in concentration required to attend to his vanity. Other more hygienic warriors bathed with their long swords—razor-sharp single-edged weapons with blades between two and three feet in length—beside them in the tub. They were always prepared to defend themselves, and even sleep became a discipline of "relaxed body and alert mind." Death was everywhere.

Zanshin was viewed as the most important element of combat, whether armed or unarmed. After all, what was the use of having the fastest draw, cut, and parry in town if the other guy had already removed your head? The art of zanshin was to stay relaxed under pressure, and aware of all avenues of escape, evasion, and attack. "Calm under fire" would be a more Western definition.

Zanshin made its way into Western civilization via the old gunfighters of the Wild West. Watch Clint Eastwood in Sergio Leone's *The Good, the Bad and the Ugly* and see the attention to detail given the gunfights. The stillness, the concentration, and the resolve. The build-up, the tension, then *bang!* Somebody dies. Like a chess game where the stakes are flesh and blood.

So riding a bike required zanshin; it was dangerous. First of all, I, the motorcyclist, was exposed, more or less (a lot more than less). Most protective helmets have only been tested for impact at speeds of 4.5–5 MPH, and the strap beneath the chin has been known to strangle the fallen rider. Leathers are good to minimize abrasion but they sure as hell won't protect anyone from broken limbs, and neither will they keep a red-hot exhaust pipe from burning the leg to the bone. No one would put two boxers in the same ring if one weighed six stone and the other twenty-four stone, plus held a shield made of steel. Yet that's the difference between a bike and a car. The answer is: don't get hit.

And that's precisely where "perfect posture" came in. Because the essence of perfect posture was concentration coupled with relaxation. It was OK being aware of all the dangers of biking but I couldn't ride as if I had a hot poker jammed up my ass, rigid and waiting for something to happen. If muscles are tight, reaction time is slow.

Even a great set of legs in a short skirt was an enemy, as evinced by an early spring trip on the 883 down the King's Road after that first cold, wet winter.

It was as if I had rediscovered the female anatomy after a long spell in solitary confinement. There were hundreds of women, short ones, tall ones, and then there *she* was. . . . Not only with stockinged legs and high heels but with a killer ass, tight and round. She was walking out of Peter Jones's. I stared. I revved. I did everything but sing. She kept her eyes front and continued walking. I followed at an idle, giving her hindquarters full concentration as she headed for the zebra crossing. . . . Hell, I could just about make out a pantie line beneath her blue cotton skirt . . . When—

Whack!

Smack into the rear end of a Volvo estate.

Naturally there was no damage to the Swedish tank, just an ugly dent in my fender. And it was completely my fault. (Unless you want to blame it on a combination of testosterone and silk.)

Zanshin. . . . Vital.

Particularly when you ain't got a license.

* * *

Zanshin. The way I had learned about this relaxed alertness in the dojo was by perseverance. In other words, by continuing to train. There were no short cuts; I could read about it, talk about it, philosophize about it, but the only way to get it was by going to the training sessions and experiencing the pressure of the simulated combat, by visualizing my opponents' hands and feet as sharp-bladed weapons. I simply could not afford to get hit. On the 883, Piccadilly and Soho became the dojo and the cars, trucks, buses, and couriers my opponents.

I was going to town three times a week anyway, to train at the Marshall Street dojo, and always, rain or shine, I took the bike. The ride to town became a discipline in itself.

At first, almost every time I made the twenty-two-mile journey I would have a near miss. A skid in the wet, a narrow escape from a car door opening as I came up the inside lane, a vehicle turning right without indicating. Someone shouting at me, diverting my attention. The trip there used to tire me out more than the karate training. I felt like a guy with a psychological L-plate, self-conscious about my riding abilities and even more so about my shiny new motorcycle.

Then, gradually, by virtue of repetition, I got used to it, more relaxed, and the near misses decreased rapidly. I was beginning to anticipate better and read traffic situations before they happened. A sign that I was improving was my traffic-light conversations with other riders. They were still asking the same questions, "How much does it cost?", "How fast is it?", "Is it reliable?", but I was no longer intimidated. Because I was using the bike, I felt less pretentious about discussing it, and began to feel like just another guy on a motorcycle, and not the old boy with his new toy. And so after each of my trips I appreciated the 883 a little more. Not only did I own a beautiful bike, but the bike actually had a practical function.

Polishing became ritualistic. As soon as the engine and pipes cooled down, no matter how tired I was, I washed and polished the Sportster.

My first six months of Harleying were centered around riding the motorcycle in and out of town, using the bike like a commuter vehicle. No riding companions, no winding country roads. No biking scene. That was to come.

A Custom Hog and a Bit of Class

It was somewhere at the tail end of those first months that I picked up a copy of *Easyriders*. It was one of those magazines in a plastic wrapper which sit in the speciality section of the tobacconist's, somewhere between *Exchange and Mart* and *Health and Efficiency*. The name brought back memories of the classic film *Easy Rider*, and the "turn on, tune in, and drop out" morality of the late '60s. Two hippie drug dealers are on a one-way trip to "discover" America set against the best music of the decade. And the two heroes, Captain America (Peter Fonda) and Billy (Dennis Hopper), don't make it in the end. Their freedom is snuffed out by a couple of Louisiana rednecks in a pickup truck, via a twelve-gauge shotgun. And here was a magazine with a "Captain America" Panhead on its cover. . . .

I pulled *Easyriders* down from the shelf, bought it, stuffed it inside my jacket, and carried it home. Then spent the remainder of the day locked inside my home office, devouring it from cover to cover.

Easyriders was as much about biker lifestyle as it was about the motorcycles themselves: rallies and biker rodeos, wet T-shirt competitions and rock 'n' roll bands, motorcycle clubs and brotherhood.

The pictures of the wide, open roads, the bikes, and the people who rode them acted like a catalyst to me, bringing back a strange longing for "sex, drugs, and rock 'n' roll." I may have been thirty-eight years old but I still had some unlived fantasies. And I had never seen a wet T-shirt competition.

The other thing that *Easyriders* activated was my consciousness of bike-image. The more I studied the pictures the more it dawned on me that there were no stock (factory) motorcycles displayed. All the bikes had been customized, making each of them individual, like one-off works of art; creations of the people who owned them.

This realization took me one step beyond Fred Warr's showroom and my impression of the stock Harleys as symbols of the American dream. Now the stock bikes seemed only the basis for the dream.

Several more issues of *Easyriders*, and I had the beginnings of Hog Fever. I needed to create a bike that was individual. Then I needed to get on that bike and have a few adventures.

I returned to Fred Warr's and priced the new models. I still couldn't afford a Big Twin but there was a compromise. Harley was about to produce a 1200 cc Sportster.

"The fastest stock bike the factory has ever built," Fred explained, selling me with that single line. After all, speed seemed a solid basis for a custom motorcycle.

"When will they be in?" I asked, calculating how hard I could squeeze my overdraft.

"Early summer. I should get half a dozen."

"Right, put me down for one. But this time I want to change a few things: the paint work, the exhaust-pipes, maybe the handlebars."

"We can do anything you want, as long as we use Harley parts," Fred promised.

"How 'bout the 883? Can you shift it for me? It's only done two thousand miles."

"I can sell as many of those little ones as I can get my hands on."

I wrote out a check for £200 to show my good intentions, although Fred said it wasn't necessary, shook his hand, and headed back to Kingston.

With three months to prepare for the arrival of the 1200 I bought every issue of *Easyriders* I could get my hands on. I even discovered a new magazine, produced by the same Californian publishers, called *In The Wind*.

I spent hours reading these magazines and studying the pictures of the bikes and their riders.

Some of them included a spec sheet for the motorcycle pictured, detailing the work that had created it. It would usually begin with the year and model, then move on to a description of the engine: for example, "rebuilt 84 cu. in. Shovelhead, S&S pistons, Mikuni carb. with custom air cleaner, S&S solid lifters and Andrews B cam . . ." Then to transmission, frame, forks, wheels, accessories, and finish. I'd never had any aptitude mechanically so these technical features went right over my head: instead, I studied the paint work and visible accessories, and the clothes the "real" guys were wearing.

The whole *Easyriders—In The Wind* scene had all the fascination for me of an alien culture. It was my private trip. I had no one to discuss it with, in fact no one in my social circle even owned a motorcycle. Half the time I was supposedly locked into my upstairs office writing novels was actually spent scouring one of the magazines. I felt like a teenager, reading *Playboy* or *Penthouse*. I was listening for the sound of my wife's footsteps on the stairs, prepared to slam the pages shut and slide the mag under my chair. Guilty for spending working hours fantasizing about life "in the wind."

I remember when she picked up a copy of *Easyriders* from

my desk. It had a great Evolution custom bike on the cover, with a stretched (extended) front end and lacquered black tank with orange flames, and it was straddled by a tattooed lady with industrial-sized tits. "I buy it for the bikes," I said on reflex, the same way the guilty man explains his *Penthouse* collection. "I buy it for the interviews."

I got the color scheme for my new bike from the "Readers' Rides" section of *In The Wind*.

I saw a photograph, sent in by a reader, of his 1987 1100 cc Sportster. Very simple. Black and chrome, but the "peanut" gas tank, named because it bears a striking resemblance to a peanut—and holds about as much gas—had a thin gold line accentuating its shape and the words Harley-Davidson etched in small gold script on the side. Subtle. Plus a small gold eagle attached to the big round plate on the left side of the bike.

That was it. My idea of a "custom" motorcycle. I got right down to Fred's.

Dave Munkenbeck, who has been Warr's stores controller since 1978, was behind the counter. At that time he rode an Electra-Glide with over a hundred and ninety thousand miles on it. Probably his tenth in the thirty years he's been riding. I doubt if he ever washed any of them.

I showed him pictures of the paint work and attempted to describe the placement of the eagle, hoping that a man who didn't even wash his own bike would appreciate my need to "go custom."

He nodded, turned, and pulled a plastic-wrapped chrome plate off his wall-mounted accessory rack. Eagle already in place.

"Is this what you're talking about?"

"That's the one. What is it?"

"It's a Derby cover."

"What's that?"

"It covers the housing for the clutch."

"Right. Could you put that one aside for me?"

"No problem, we always keep a few in stock."

Terrific, I thought, now we're talking custom, right on the same wavelength. I studied the wall.

"And how about those exhaust pipes?" I pointed to a set of chrome tubes. The ends were slash-cut and turned outwards.

"They're loud," Dave said, clinching the sale.

"Can you get them put on the bike for me?"

"Ten-four," he confirmed.

Now that the look of the bike was settled I had to get my own image sorted out. It was the helmet that was the problem. I'd picked up a Bell full-face at a motorcycle trade show and it just didn't cut it. It may have been fine for the courier brigade but I sure as hell never saw anybody in *Easyriders* with a full-face helmet. In fact I rarely saw any of them with helmets at all. Either they had taken them off for the pictures or they were riding in states like California, which, until 1992, had no helmet law. When a "bro" was pictured in a "lid" it was usually minimal and had *Helmet Laws Suck* printed across the front. Besides, the full-face restricted my peripheral vision and when I went faster than sixty miles an hour the roar inside sounded like a wind tunnel. I hated the thing.

I was making a business trip to Los Angeles before the new bike was scheduled for delivery. The helmet would give me an excuse to do some bike-related shopping in California, the home of *Easyriders* and *In The Wind*.

Hollywood Bikers

LA has always been a strange place for me.
I'd spent a bit of time there in the early '80s, looking for a record deal for Revenge, my heavy-metal rock band, and I still have vivid recollections of standing with one of our succession of managers and my lead guitarist on the corner of Sunset and Doheny, following a meeting with a music-biz lawyer. Minutes before, the lawyer had promised our manager a half-million dollars for the five-song demo tape that our band had produced. I had stopped in a tobacco shop and bought three king-size cigars, "stogies," to celebrate. We puffed until we were dizzy, the guitarist and I. Our manager refrained, being a little wiser to the ways of showbiz. Six months later, there was no half-million dollar deal, not even a returned phone call, although I heard indirectly that a disco group had offered the lawyer a five hundred dollar buyout for the name of my band.

For me, LA's always been like that. I leave thinking I've got the world in the palm of my hand only to open it up and find it's empty. Maybe the whole place is an illusion.

But California is the heartland of motorcycling: the roads are dry, the women are beautiful, and the coke, the preferred leisure drug of Hollywood bikers, *c.* 1989, before the substance abuse groups began to replace both the singles bars and the Polo Lounge, is purer than the snow in Aspen.

I had had only one experience with a Hollywood biker. It was months before, outside Fred Warr's showroom. The guy was there to get his bike serviced; he had just had it shipped from Los Angeles, a Heritage Softail, painted white and professionally customized: everything from extra-wide flat handlebars with micro-control switches to a hand-tooled leather silver-studded saddle, and a cross-over exhaust system (a set-up with a pipe on either side of the motorcycle, a unique configuration for a Softail), plus a license frame that featured BARTELS, LOS ANGELES printed in chrome beneath the license plate. The LA custom was parked outside the shop and a small crowd had gathered around it: one fellow was on his hands and knees, staring up the left-side exhaust pipe, convinced that the pipe was a dummy. The owner was a cross between Michael J. Fox and the late Freddie Mercury, short but handsome, and done up in the hippest leather gear, including a jaunty flying scarf wrapped round his face. It was as if an alien space craft had landed.

I approached with due respect.

"That's a beautiful bike."

Michael J. Mercury grunted.

"You don't see many of those around," I continued.

He looked up. "Where I come from, Harleys are like assholes." His voice was labored and uninterested. But very resonant.

I met his eyes, waiting for the inevitable punchline.

"Everybody's got one."

I nodded and walked back to my 883, watching as the Hollywood biker climbed on board his asshole and turned left out of Warr's then right at the intersection, proceeding down the wrong side of the King's Road.

He probably had his on-board gyroscope set for Melrose Avenue.

He was, however, correct. It seemed that everybody in Los Angeles had a Harley. And all of them, bikes and riders, looked to me as if they'd roared straight out of the pages of *Easyriders* or *In The Wind.* I spent hours lunching at Sunset Plaza, adjacent to the Strip, watching the parade of Harleys cruise by, studying flashes of fast-moving chrome, trying to pick out the details on the bikes and the types of people riding them. There were even a few regulars, bikers who parked along the curb in front of the outdoor tables and ate lunch. Their bikes were beautiful, in the same factory-custom sense as the King's Road Softail, but the riders always looked as if they had stepped out of an Armani catalog for biker apparel: pre-ripped denim and designer T-shirts.

At that time, 1987, biking business was so good in southern California that a bike shop didn't need to sell motorcycles at all; fortunes were made schlepping the appropriate biker accessories, and towards the end of my stay I went shopping for a new helmet at one of these "accessories only" shops near Century City. It featured scarves and bandannas, "Red Baron" riding goggles, wraparound '50s-style shades, fingerless gloves, and jackets that resembled chain-mail armor. Boots of all styles, from the regulation engineer boots favored by Marlon Brando in *The Wild One* to the Billy Idol models, silver toecaps and heel-wrapped chains with matching spurs. There were even chrome oil tanks, specially made for the Sportster.

Helmets, however, were a different story. These totally uncool devices were relegated to a small section in the far corner, dark and out of the way, like the orthopedic section of a flash shoe store. I sneaked back and rummaged through a selection of black open-faced (minus the Darth Vader visor), models of Japanese origin. I didn't fancy trying one on in front of the other bikers so I grabbed a medium and headed for the register.

There, feeling like I was committing an act of betrayal to the LA bike scene, I explained to the long-haired guy at the cash till that I lived in England, where they have helmet laws, therefore making my purchase a mandatory one.

"England, wow, groovy. Yeah, England, man, I can hear it in your voice. The accent."

"Actually I'm American, Philadelphia."

"Unbelievable, yeah, I can dig Philadelphia. What kinda bike ya got?"

Now I came into my own. "I've got a twelve hundred Sportster."

"A little one, man, that's cool, that's cool. . . ."

Little one? That really hurt. It was as if I had just been demoted to the B-team.

I'd barely recovered when the long-hair slapped a plastic-wrapped set of Red Baron riding goggles down on the counter. "You oughta get these; they go good with the half-face."

Five minutes later, I had two helmets (one for potential passengers), three pairs of Red Barons (an extra in case of theft), two sets of fingerless riding gloves, and the chrome oil tank. All boxed up and ready to lug out of the shop.

Back in my hotel room I spent half an hour steaming the Japanese trademarks off the helmets, then unwrapped the Red Barons, put them on and fastened one of the helmets into position. I looked like a candidate for *Top Gun.*

The look wouldn't have cut it in LA but I felt well ahead of the scene in England.

Down to Warr's.

The Sportster's gas tank had come back from Dream Machines, the custom painters. Fred would exchange it with the 1200's when it arrived. It was sitting on a shelf in the back of the shop.

"Looks real good," Dave commented as I lifted the protective cloth. It did look good, and different from the stock range of color combinations. That was what was important; it was different.

I handed Dave the box containing my chrome oil tank and asked if he could get it put on the bike. He gave it the once-over. The tank looked like some sort of kitchen appliance.

"Have to ask John about that; he does all that kind of thing."

John, who the hell was John?

He pressed a button and a buzzer sounded in the back of

the shop, the section partitioned off from view. A minute later a stocky kid in grease-covered overalls entered through the adjoining door. He had fine blond hair and wide blue eyes, and a certain arrogance to him.

"John, this is Richard La Plante."

He held out a sturdy hand. "Pleased to meet you, I'm John Warr." He had a gruff voice for a kid. So that was it, the son of Fred; it was a family business.

"Richard's got a new 1200 Sportster coming in; he wants to know if you'll replace the stock oil tank with this one here," Dave said, extending the appliance. It now reminded me of a canteen, or a silver drinking flask.

Young John viewed it with a strange expression, somewhere between amusement and scorn. For a moment I thought he was going to refuse me the privilege of "going custom."

He relented with a suspicious smile, the kind that suggested he couldn't quite understand the need for a chrome oil tank.

"Sure, I can do that."

"Great!" I said it like I owed him one.

John departed and I said goodbye to Dave, turning to glance at the new additions to the wall-mounted photographs as I exited the shop. There were the ones I'd seen before, shots of Fred and Dave, mounted on their Hydra-Glides, just after the Second World War, and there were a couple of pictures I hadn't seen: photos of a young guy racing around a banked track, going so low on the bike that his padded knee was scraping the ground. The racer had a familiar face. "Is that John Warr?" I asked.

"Yes, sir, on a tuned Sportster," Dave answered.

"Must be a good rider," I commented. I had instant respect for anyone who could wheel around a racetrack in a near-horizontal position. Suddenly the gruff voice and somehow superior manner fell into perspective. "A real good rider," I added.

"He is. And a good mechanic too. Nobody can make a Harley go faster than John. He knows everything about tuning a Twin," Dave stated.

Tuning a Twin. The phrase stayed in my mind as I left the shop. Maybe, one of these days, I'd get young John, boy racer, to tune my Twin.

After he'd bolted on my chrome drinking flask.

It was early June, and I had just closed the door to my office, got out the latest *Easyriders*, and settled into my reading chair when the phone rang.

I recognized Dave's voice.

"It's here, isn't it?"

"Sitting right in front of me," he replied.

"You want me down there today?"

"John's still got to do the oil tank, how about first thing in the morning?"

"When's the earliest I can be there?"

Eight thirty and I was outside the back door to the workshop, helmet and Red Barons in hand: John swung the two big wooden doors open and there it was.

The 1200 was magnificent.

I walked round and viewed it from all angles.

Custom paint, gold-eagle Derby cover, and chrome oil tank.

"Run it in before we change the pipes," John instructed.

"Yeah, sure."

I kissed the 883 goodbye, slapped another few thousand on my overdraft, and hit the road.

The 1200 felt very different from the 883. First of all the handlebars were the "buckhorn" models, rising higher than the comparatively flat bars of the smaller Sportster, so my seated position was the classic Harley "sit up and beg" position, more like I was riding on top of the bike as opposed to leaning forward and straddling it. Also the saddle was longer, so I settled in with my tail bone pressed securely into the slight rise before the pillion section. Very comfortable and also secure, like my ass had merged with the frame of the bike.

Under strict instructions not to over-rev the engine for the first five hundred miles I kept an eye on the handlebar-mounted tachometer, a feature of the 1200, and goosed it enough to confirm, in John Warr's parting words, that the 1200 was "a bit nippy."

I was about a mile from the shop, heading south along the King's Road, towards the river. There was very little traffic so I twisted the throttle, just enough to give me a real surge of speed. And the engine began to sputter. I twisted once more and the bike coughed and died. Switching up into neutral I pressed the starter button; the engine turned over but it wouldn't catch.

"Fuckers didn't give me any gas," I muttered, free-wheeling to the curb. I twisted off the gas cap and looked inside. Full.

Oh, no ... My heart was sinking fast. I must have pushed it too hard and blown the engine. What did John say about over-revving? I turned the bike around and started pushing.

It was hot and the bike felt like it weighed a ton. My Red Barons were dripping with condensation and the engineer boots weren't made for walkin'.

I couldn't have blown the engine. Impossible, I kept thinking.

I was getting angry. They'd sold me a turkey. Maybe John wasn't such a red-hot tuning ace. Maybe he'd screwed up when he switched the stock oil tank for my chromed one.

I was sweating now, so I switched tactics. Instead of pushing, I sat on the bike, shoved, and coasted, rolling a few yards before I had to push off again. Other motorcyclists were passing me by, Kawasakis and Yamahas, BMWs and Honda Gold Wings. Fucking Harley-Davidsons, never were reliable. I'd heard it said, now I knew.

I rounded the corner of Waterstone Road in a fury, pushed the bike outside the twin doors and pounded with the back of my fist.

John answered.

I was livid. "Fucking thing just stopped. A mile up the road it sputtered and died."

He nodded his head, then squatted down beside the bike.

"Did you turn your fuel-supply valve on?"

I started to deflate.

"We always shut 'em off when we work on a customer's bike. You should shut it off, too, when you're not using the motorcycle."

I watched him throw the small switch beneath the fuel tank to on.

It wasn't that I didn't know about the valve; it was one of the first instructions Fred had ever given me, way back with the 883. I just never did it.

"Start her up now," John said.

I pushed the starter button and the bike turned right over.

"Sweet as a nut," he smiled.

I shook his hand, mounted up, and rode away, instantly forgetting the anger, sweat, and blistered feet that had accompanied my breakdown.

By the time I hit the A3, two miles from home, I felt like I had been absorbed by the motorcycle. We were suddenly a single entity. Some type of animal, half flesh and half steel, running along, at fifty miles an hour, less than two and a half feet above the flat black highway. The sun was pouring down, and as I hit the crest of the hill and started down, the air parted in front of me like a warm envelope, the wind lapping against my face. All sensation merged, the hum of the engine, the forward momentum of the bike, the warmth of the air, and it was as though I was suspended in time, hanging effortlessly by a silver thread, "in the wind."

The 1200

Most of my mileage, minimal as it was on the 883, had been done between Kingston and Soho, two or three times a week. This, augmented by the routine run to the local video shop and the occasional cruise to Hampton Court, all added up to about a hundred miles every seven days. Hardly respectable saddle time for a biker.

When the promotional tour for my first novel, *Tegne, Warlord of Zendow*, came, I decided to travel by Harley.

The tour actually consisted of a few book signings—those events in which the author usually sits like a prat in the back of the bookshop, behind a desk, and blocks the way for shoppers who wonder what the hell this guy is doing barricading the aisle—and several radio shows. The first signing was local, right down the hill, in Kingston. The 1200 proved a handsome accessory, parked outside the small bookshop; it drew more of a crowd than I did. Then came a radio show in Sussex, down towards Brighton. About eighty miles, round trip.

It wasn't that I had avoided long trips, in excess of forty miles both ways, on the bike; it was just that I really didn't have anywhere to go, and certainly no one to ride with. I had taken my wife for a few circuits of Richmond Park, even my mother-in-law, but I knew from the beginning that we were never going to be a family that biked together. My wife's biking days had peaked with a boyfriend in the '60s, and Flossie, my mother-in-law, claimed her last heavy biking took place in the side-car of her dad's Ariel, *c.* 1929. I really didn't care. I enjoyed the motorcycle as a solo event. It was my domain, my territory. And now I was going to ride on down the motorway for my radio interview.

The interview was scheduled for eleven so I took off at nine, in case I got lost. The sky was blue and there was a brisk breeze. I turned left at the bottom of Kingston Hill and headed down the A3, passed the turn-off for the A240 and kept going, out of the suburbs and on to the open road. The bike, by now, had over five hundred miles on the clock so I could go as fast as I wanted.

Seventy was fine, particularly since the brisk breeze was now blowing me all over the road, and still those Jap bikes kept whizzing by on the outside lane. Christ, they must have been doing a hundred, I thought.

A hundred. The famous "ton." I'd once done ninety-five on the Norton on a trip from Philadelphia to Atlanta, until the battery fried and the bike completed the journey in a U-Haul trailer behind the family car. I had planned to do the ton then, but that was a long time ago and I'd always doubted the Norton's speedometer.

Seventy in a gale felt a hell of a lot more dangerous. But then there were those Jap bikes, how were they doing it? I nudged the bike up to eighty and pulled into the middle lane. I was wearing the open-face helmet and my Rayban aviators, and my face had begun to feel like a rubber mask being molded into new and never before tried shapes.

At ninety I began to have a few doubts: the bike was vibrating like an electric dildo, and I was concerned that the engine might fragment. Sheer paranoia, hardly the Samurai's zanshin. Another Jap bike zoomed by. This guy had to be doing one twenty; he had a full pack on his back—no doubt a picnic lunch—and looked like he was heading for a day's outing in

Guildford, hardly aware that Harley's answer to Nigel Mansell was busy setting the land speed record one lane away.

I must have opened my mouth at this point because suddenly my lips separated and flapped uncontrollably, the upper smacking towards my nose while the lower stuck to the tip of my chin. Did Mick Jagger once ride a Harley? I had to decelerate to gain control of my mouth. Then twisted the throttle again and went for the big one. Ninety-five, ninety-eight (what was that about John Warr coming off at a hundred and ten and only ripping the seat of his pants?), one hundred, one hundred and three miles an hour! The wind was howling through the straps of my helmet, giving the term "in the wind" a new and far less ethereal meaning, and beneath the pillowed saddle the Sportster engine was providing my sphincter with the massage of the century. But I'd done it, the famous ton.

After that moment of personal glory the interview was an anticlimax. I kept wanting to allude to the fact that I had travelled to the radio station at speeds in excess of 100 MPH but couldn't quite find the opening. The disc jockey just didn't seem to be a Harley type of guy. . . .

Then came the Johnnie Walker interview on GLR.

I parked the bike in the back lot of the GLR building and walked inside. The general format was that the PR person from my publishing company sent in my book and a brief but magnified biography. The DJ then skimmed the book and used the biography to organize the questions for his interview. This was only my third radio interview and I still found the process of sitting in a soundproofed studio having a conversation with the DJ's resonant voice in headphones which was transmitted to thousands of listeners a bit unnerving.

Johnnie stepped out of his soundproofed booth to welcome me. He was very relaxed and although he hadn't actually read *Tegne, Warlord of Zendow*, he had studied my biography and prepared his questions.

"What was it like to live alone in a tent in Mexico for nine months, then walk barefoot to Boston?"

The episode he was referring to had occurred during the psychedelic phase of my career as a psychologist. I had been employed as a counsellor in a state mental hospital for four months, and, plying myself with marijuana and regular doses of LSD, I appeared to the administration to be relating too well to the inmates. I was relating so well, in fact, that a couple of them broke out of the lock-up and took up residence at my house. I didn't report them—in fact we all got on very well as room-mates—which caused a great deal of distress to the hospital and subsequently ended my career in mental illness. After that I thought that living alone in the Sonora Desert was the only route to self-enlightenment. I managed this self-imposed exile for six months before hitchhiking to San Francisco, falling in with a commune of yoga-practicing vegetarians, giving away my shoes, and then walking the thirty-two hundred miles back to Boston. What could I say to Johnnie Walker?

"Great, quite normal actually, after ingesting enough magic mushrooms in Mexico to convince myself that I was the reincarnation of an Indian holy man."

"And what about your rock band Revenge? Funny we never heard of it over here, in England," the DJ probed.

Revenge . . . another classic episode in my pre-Harley life. But at least closer to two wheels and an armful of ink than my "organic mystic" period. I mean, how many married men begin a career as a rock and roll singer at the age of thirty-three? And to a large extent succeed? At least get far enough to become the opening act for the re-formed Steppenwolf, drape myself in an American flag and wail my guts out to five hundred real outlaw motorcyclists who were standing on the tabletops of the Brandywine Club, out on Highway No. 1, south of Philadelphia, shouting for Steppenwolf to take the stage and sing "Born to be Wild"? My music career had peaked when I smacked my guitar player's brother in the nose at a New York City night club. He left via an ambulance while I made a more dignified departure, though handcuffed, in the back of a police car. And that was about it for rock and roll.

I spared Johnnie the gory details and answered: "No, not really, very few ever heard of it in America either."

And so we went on, till we got to the Harley. Then Johnnie's eyes lit up. We're talking megawatts.

"A Harley-Davidson?"

"A 1200 Sportster."

From there the interview was a breeze. Johnnie Walker was a latent Harley man. My time on the air extended till the end of his show, after which he trailed me to the parking lot. The Sportster was parked to the side of the building.

"Man, it's beautiful." Walker paid homage as he continued towards the bike.

"You ever ridden one?" I asked.

"Not since I was a kid, and never a Harley. . . . Always been a fantasy of mine to ride a Harley."

"You got a license?"

Johnnie shook his head sadly.

"Never stopped me," I said, handing him the keys.

"I don't know if I should," he answered, taking them from my hand.

As he circled the Sportster I had a moment of déjà-vu.

The Oglethorpe College parking lot in Atlanta, Georgia. Many years ago I had offered the keys of my Norton to a fellow student, only after he had sworn to me that he'd spent two years riding with a Florida-based motorcycle club, credentials enough to warrant a turn around the lot. Then I'd watched as he revved the bike and sat there looking puzzled. He didn't know the difference between the clutch and the brake lever. I'd just started my run towards him, to get him off the motorcycle, when he popped the clutch. The Norton took off and he held on, until the bike flipped on to its side and dragged the ex-Florida biker around the lot by the seat of his pants. He screamed like a stuck pig until the Norton ploughed into a parked car and stopped dead. Luckily the bike was only scratched. The would-be hard man took a few stitches in his gluteus maximus, following a confession that it was actually his brother who had been in the club.

Johnnie Walker, thankfully, was good to his word. Both cowboy boots dragging for extra stability, the ever young DJ piloted the Sportster around the GLR lot.

"I'm surprised at how well balanced it is, how well it handles," he called during a tight figure-eight.

I watched him navigate, thinking, this guy's a natural biker.

"If you ever want to sell it, phone me. I'd mortgage my house for a bike like that," he said, dismounting.

"I will, I promise," I answered. I was already considering the mortgage scam as a way toward a Big Twin.

Sometimes during a ride, even a short one, I get into a state of mind that is something beyond thought, when I link up with the motorcycle in such a way that there is an instinctive relationship between my body and the body of the machine, as if I am fused into a perfect harmony. It is zanshin plus "in the wind," and could be expressed as a state of "highway heaven."

I have occasionally tried to analyze this experience. I have broken it down into a combination of traction (well-balanced tires, correct air pressure against dry, well-surfaced roads), physical comfort (not hungry or in need of a desperate piss, properly dressed for the climate), a clear sky, a clear road, and having the bike running sweet as a nut. These basics allow me to truly relax, into a state of mind which obliterates all sense of time and makes me receptive to the smells in the air, the rush of the wind against my skin, and the almost hypnotic forward motion of the motorcycle. It is like riding into a space beyond the laws of time and physics, so linked up with the universe that it is impossible to make a mistake (although a sudden pothole or patch of ice does shatter the illusion). These peak moments addict me to motorcycling. Some part of my mind and body remembers the euphoria and yearns for the next time. Like a drug.

I was in this state of highway heaven after the Johnnie Walker show. I had had a bit of a post-interview buzz that needed burning off, so I took the Westway back to town, a few clear miles to juice the bike and listen to the roar of the new pipes. They were sweet as a nut when I rounded the bend by Robin Hood Gate and wound my way up the gentle rise through Richmond Park which runs parallel to Kingston Hill. It was late in the fall, and the smell of burning leaves hung like incense in the air. I was only doing about thirty-five miles an hour as the bike rolled into the bends and curves, then took off on the straights like a thoroughbred. The 1200 really did handle. I just didn't want to use my brakes; it would have destroyed the experience. So when I saw the back-up of cars ahead I whipped out and to the side, twisted the throttle, and flew on by. I spotted the uniformed policeman as I pulled back in front of the lead car; he was waving me to the side of the road. Standing beside him was another uniformed cop with a hand-held radar device that looked like a megaphone.

I pulled over and shut off my engine. The empty-handed policeman walked to my bike. He was wearing high riding boots and a military-looking leather jacket.

"That's a beautiful motorcycle, sir."

"Thanks," I answered, glancing toward the lawman's white BMW. I couldn't come up with a compliment; it reminded me of a two-wheeled conveyance for the Gestapo, all it needed was machine-gun mounts on the front fairing.

"Do you know how fast you were going?"

"I have no idea, sir," I replied, trying to sound concerned.

I learned a long time ago—in Georgia, as I was being searched and handcuffed, prior to the removal, by crane, of the Norton—that it pays to be polite to the police.

"Forty-four miles per hour," he stated.

I nodded. It didn't sound that fast to me.

'Do you know the speed limit through Richmond Park?'

As a matter of fact I didn't. "I was overtaking," I countered.

He shook his head. "The limit is thirty miles per hour. I could let you go at forty, but not at forty-four," he explained.

As if that critical 4 MPH was the difference between a juvenile delinquent and a felon.

I nodded again and kept my mouth shut.

"You do own the motorcycle?"

"I do."

"And you have a current driver's license?"

I was in trouble now and I knew it. "Yes."

He wrote out the ticket and handed it to me.

"You have forty-eight hours to produce your license at the police station nearest your home."

I took the ticket, rammed it in my pocket, and got on the bike. It was a slow ride home.

I had that sinking feeling as I closed the garage door.

I was going to have to get an English license.

First thing the next morning I reported to the local police station and handed over the ticket, along with my Pennsylvania driving license. The woman behind the desk stared at both of them.

"Are you a visitor?"

"Not exactly."

She looked at me as if to ask what "not exactly" was supposed to mean.

"I live between here and my home in Philadelphia."

"It appears that the vehicle you were operating is registered here," she replied, suspicious.

"My wife is English, I've never been here long enough at one time to apply for a British license," I lied.

"Yet the motorcycle is registered and insured?"

"Yes," I answered. It was true. I was insured, although in view of my ten-year residence without a British license I'd always wondered whether my insurers would stand behind a major claim.

"Ordinarily, this offense would mean three points on your license."

I held a somber expression, sensing victory.

She handed me back the Pennsylvania license.

"If you do intend to reside in the UK for any length of time I suggest you apply for a UK operator's license. . . ."

And I did, that same afternoon.

Not that I had any intention of giving up the Harley.

In fact, the application alone gave me an entirely new line of fabrication in case of further inconvenience from the law.

Somewhere between the arrival of my provisional license and my search for a rider training program that would guarantee me a quick pass on the driving test, Derek the film director showed up at my house. On a custom-painted red Springer Softail.

I hardly knew Derek; I had only met him once before, years ago, at a dinner party in Kensington. He was a very groovy guy. To tell the truth, because I had been trying for several years to get one of my scripts made into a movie and he had already made a highly acclaimed British feature film, I was slightly in awe of him.

I welcomed his completely unexpected visit with all the ceremony of a visiting ambassador from *In the Wind.*

"I heard you had a bike," was his opening line, as he shut off the engine of his Big Twin and pulled his leathered leg across his hand-tooled saddle.

"I've got a 1200 Sportster," I replied. No "Hi, how are you? Fancy seeing you after three years," or "What the hell are you doing here?" No, none of those formalities. This was biker business and bikers obviously had no need for social graces.

I was about to launch into the "fastest stock bike Harley's ever made" routine when Derek, dismounting, said, matter of factly, "Yeah, I've got one of them in LA."

His statement left me lost for groove, so I stood there staring at the Springer. The bike was beautiful; it appeared much lower to the ground than my Sportster and featured a two-into-one fish-tail exhaust system, six tail-lights, and a solo saddle. The front wheel was twenty-one inches in diameter and looked like a bicycle tire, a marked contrast to the sixteen-inch rear tire. A very radical ride. But the *pièce de résistance* was the front end: the unique Springer forks, two huge coiled springs, were highlighted by chrome. Behind them, buckhorned handlebars and three headlamps.

Derek provided the voice-over to my inspection. "They took the original Springer front end, copied it, then rebalanced by computer. Handles like a dream." I turned to take in the man himself.

Derek was a shade shorter than me, probably two stone lighter, but so heavily leathered that what he lacked in size he countered with sheer armor. He was even wearing a type of helmet that I had never seen, full-faced but contoured perfectly to his head. Had he actually had it molded? A custom helmet? Before I could ask him about it he drew my attention to his black jacket. "California Highway Patrol. A real one."

Fuck me, the bike, the gear; this guy was blowing me away. I was speechless. Then he slipped out of the helmet.

And, by virtue of his nose, became human. It was a sizeable piece of equipment to start with but, because of the cold weather, had turned a far less subtle shade of red than his Springer.

"Come on in, have a cup of coffee," I said, keeping an eye on his nose and accepting his helmet as if I was the flight attendant on an aircraft carrier and our top gun had just whipped in to refuel.

"Helicopter helmet, man, the real thing," he said as I carried it in.

Derek was possibly the most authentic guy I'd ever encountered.

We sat in the kitchen and talked Harley.

He was a few seasons ahead when it came to riding and style. He'd done a lot of film work in Los Angeles and was apparently part of the LA biker scene. He spoke of biker bars and group rides into the desert.

I could only imagine what it would feel like to ride with sixty other bikers; the roar of the combined engines and the feelings of camaraderie as, in formation, two by two, down Interstate 10, the "pack" headed into the California desert at sunset. A long way from a solo run to Soho on a rainy day.

His departure came as unexpectedly as his arrival.

"Ready to ride?" he asked, standing to pick up his helicopter helmet. His nose had normalized its color, like a barometer. Maybe that was how he knew it was time to hit the road.

"Sure," I answered. What else could I say?

I went to the back room and grabbed my Irvin flying jacket (bought years before but now designated as my cold-weather riding coat).

"Great jacket, man," Derek commented as we left the house.

So far, so good, I may have just found my first riding buddy, I thought, strolling towards the garage for the Sportster. But were my riding skills going to be any match for the LA biker?

I wheeled the 1200 out, noticing that even with the slash-cuts the Big Twin sounded a lot deeper; I pulled alongside Derek. He revved his engine; I revved back. Then he took off, with me hot in pursuit of his six tail-lights.

We were neck and neck as we exited the driveway, turned the corner, and headed down Kingston Hill. Towards the motorway.

I hadn't thought to ask where we were going.

Derek was obviously on maneuvers; he kept dropping behind, waiting for me (confused as to what he was doing) to slow down, then he'd pull alongside, shout "Ya-hoo!" and accelerate, vanishing in a cloud of white smoke. I was definitely not ready for the desert.

He took the lead. Up the A3, left down Roehampton Lane, blasting towards Hammersmith, in the direction of his flat. By now my Red Barons were fogged up and I still didn't know where we were going.

Derek seemed to cover the entire highway; if I slipped out from behind a line of cars, he was there, passing me on the outside. If I accelerated, he shot by as if he'd been fired from a slingshot. If I slowed down he was beside me, revving. We stopped at a red light, ten minutes from my house. Derek was still revving. I was several miles on the wrong side of highway heaven. "I'm going home!" I shouted above his engine. I felt like the kid who cried "uncle" in the wrestling match.

"Right, I'll call you!" he shouted back.

The light changed and he let out the clutch. I could hear an echoing "Ya-hoo!" as he disappeared round the next bend.

I meandered home, locked up, and broke out the Yellow Pages. Maybe a training program would not only secure me a license but teach me how to ride. . . .

The guy who answered the phone at CSM Rider Training sounded like a potential courier. A low nasal voice and very down-to-business tone that suggested many wet London miles. He perked up when I slipped in a mention of the Harley, making myself out to be a heavy American biker who just happened to be in need of a quick British license.

"No problem. We guarantee you a pass, part one and part two."

"Terrific," I answered.

"As soon as you get a test date call us, then we'll get you in and sort you out."

"How long does the training take?" I tried to sound impatient, as if I didn't really need training.

"A couple of days for part one. We do it on our own course; you know, figures of eight, emergency stops, that kind of thing." Figures of eight? This sounded serious. "Another five days on the road and part two should be a doddle," the voice of CSM assured me.

"All right, I'll get back to you. . . ." But not for a while. Christmas was coming, the weather was cold, and I did have my provisional license. Of course, one of the provisions was that I did not operate a motorcycle with an engine capacity of over 125 cc, but, then again, there was that Pennsylvania loophole.

Derek became a regular if unpredictable visitor, always unannounced and rarely in the same jacket twice. I began to think that the unmuffled exhaust-pipes of every motor vehicle that passed our house via Kingston Hill was the man himself. I'd be in the bath, on the loo, asleep, and the sound would begin. "Derek's here!" I'd announce, charging around the bedroom in search of my underwear, only to hear the roar disappear into the distance. I never thought of suggesting that he should telephone first; it would have been very un-bro like.

One day I managed a glimpse at his odometer. It read seventy-eight. I turned away before he could see that I'd clocked it. Obviously the only riding Derek was doing was from his flat off the Portobello Road to my place. No journeys into the desert.

He was, in spite of his lack of mileage, a very engaging guy. Loads of style and a great eye for fashion: scarves, boots, jackets, and formation tail-lights. He was also in demand as a director: between the commercials that earned him a fortune and trips to LA for feature film projects it was a marvel that he found time to ride at all.

By the New Year he was deeply involved in a *Top Gun* style feature film (maybe he'd worn the helicopter helmet to the pitch meeting): fast planes, aircraft-carriers, incredible stunts, and a great soundtrack. He was going to need to go to LA for a couple of weeks to set it up and was concerned about leaving his Springer unattended at his place. Did I have room for it in my garage? (Is the Pope Catholic?) Of course, he assured me, I could use it as much as I wanted. "Treat it like your own bike," were his exact words. I told him I'd be honored to look after it for him but I doubted if I'd ride it. I was still partial to the Sportster. At least that's what I was telling myself.

Derek departed by taxi and the red Springer remained.

I mentioned before that I don't have much, if any, natural aptitude for mechanics, and that I sublimated this inability to change a head gasket with an obsession for polishing the bike. It made me feel as if I was doing something to enhance the performance of the machine, like cutting down wind resistance, but aside from wind resistance and the compulsion to make the chrome, steel, and paint work shine, there was another, more practical, reason for a major polish: it familiarized me with every external nut, bolt, and joint.

All Harleys vibrate, varying with the speed they travel and

the amount of performance work they have undergone. Occasionally something comes loose, a wheel nut or an oil filter, and a major polish is a natural time to take inventory. An inexpensive set of graded ratchets and a tube of Lock-Tite made me feel less vain and a lot more mechanical about the countless hours I spent with a wash bucket, chamois cloth, bottle of Mer (a German car wax), and a toothbrush for the spokes.

The night the Springer arrived I decided to polish my bike. Half an hour later I had begun to feel guilty. I had applied the Mer to the 1200 and was about to leave the garage for the twenty minutes that it needed to set and harden when I looked at the Springer. Derek's bike was clean, but judging by the dull spokes and tiny spots of new rust on the chromed wheel rims, it had never received a major polish. Why the fuck should I risk my tennis elbow (a hazard of the major polish) on somebody else's bike? Yet Derek did say, "Treat it like your own."

I walked over to the Big Twin; it even had a new smell to it, a mixture of leather and the aroma of fresh engine seals bedding in, a strange burning plastic type fragrance. *Treat it like your own. . . .*

I bent down and began, rubbing the rust spots on the wheel rims with a very fine grade of steel wool. By the time I got to chamois-clothing the Mer from the paint work (seven coats of paint, two of lacquer) I was in love.

The Springer Softail really was a piece of metal sculpture; a perfect blend of the old-fashioned Harley and the sleek customized monsters I studied in *In The Wind.*

I walked around the garage, viewing both the Sportster and the Springer from various angles. I would have liked to have owned them both, started a fleet, but if I had had to settle on one it would, honestly, have been Derek's Springer.

It hurt to admit it. Mainly because when the obsession begins—I call it Hog Fever—I've learned that whatever it takes, remortgaging the house, extending the overdraft, loading the credit cards—I've got to have it.

"Yeah, but it's slow and probably handles like a truck," I told myself. Anything to break the mind-lock.

"Use it as much as you want. . . ." Wasn't that what Derek had said? I opened the garage door. It was already dark. Tomorrow, I'd ride it tomorrow.

My first time on the Big Twin: it did feel like a truck. I was relieved, maybe I didn't need one of these monsters anyway.

I rode slowly down Kingston Hill, left through Robin Hood Gate, and into Richmond Park. I was trying to ride it the same way I rode the 1200, which is a racing bike, sitting tall in the saddle and stiff in the lower back but it's a style of riding that doesn't work on a 1340 cc motorcycle built as cruiser that comes stock with highway foot pegs. Your riding position on the Springer is legs straight out and feet up to the front. All the brake and gear controls are positioned for the highway pegs, which place your feet in an almost direct line below your hands, as opposed to the bent-legged, feet below the saddle position of the Sportster.

At first I didn't trust it; it didn't feel safe, like I couldn't get my feet down fast enough in case of an emergency. By the straight bit of road at the top of the rise I felt better, letting my body slump forward and relaxing with the roll of the heavier bike. By my second circuit of the park I was at a new level of highway heaven; the Springer seemed to hum along at about an inch above the surface of the road, its center of gravity so low that I felt like I was riding a sled across hard-packed snow.

"Sled": I'd seen the term in both *In The Wind* and *Easyriders*, and now I knew why they used it. These Big Twins, with their saddles barely two feet above the ground, were like highway sleds.

Just before I exited the park I caught a reflected image of myself in the back of the middle one of the three chromed headlamps, like a distorted face in a Christmas ball. Behind my reflection, to either side, the road, trees, and sky converged into a single kaleidoscope image. I felt like the captain of the starship *Enterprise.*

* * *

By the time Derek reappeared the odometer had gone from seventy-eight to three hundred. I was embarrassed but addicted. I'd even taken the Springer to Soho.

He thanked me for the shine, claiming it was cleaner than the day he rode it from the showroom, and tried not to gulp when he noticed the mileage. I complimented him on his new Dennis Hopper fringed jacket. (Was it really the one that Dennis had worn in *Easy Rider?*) Then he took "my" motorcycle away; I watched him as if I was witnessing a theft that I was powerless to stop.

Getting back on the 1200 was as awkward as riding the bigger bike for the first time. The upright position felt completely unnatural and the Sportster seemed a mile off the ground; and because of the riding position there was no highway collage reflected in the back of the headlamp.

It took about a week to reconvince myself that I owned a Harley at all.

Nerves of Steel and a Rod of Iron: Terence Stamp

When I was a teenager I went to a cowboy film called Blue. The star was an English actor named Terence Stamp. He was the most handsome guy I'd ever seen; blond hair, ice-blue eyes, and softly chiselled features. In the film he wore Mexican shirts with billowing sleeves, leather chaps, turquoise scarves, and a great flat sombrero. I wanted to look like Stamp, the guy had some very serious style.

Terence Stamp was my first, and come to think of it my only, matinée idol. I followed his career in the United States from *Billy Budd* to *The Collector* to *Far From the Madding Crowd*. When I moved to London a friend introduced us at a dinner party at Zen, the Chinese restaurant in Chelsea Cloisters. We got on immediately. Yoga, meditation, the teachings of Lao Tsu, breathing exercises, tantric sex, the martial arts; Stamp was an encyclopedia of metaphysical knowledge. He still exercised vigorously and looked great.

Our discussions continued; he had known everybody in the '60s, from Jimi Hendrix to Jim Morrison. While I was out buying their records Stamp was wheeling around London with them in the back of a cab. He'd done all the major hallucinogenics and most of the major starlets. "Nerves of steel and a rod of iron," he said, sending himself up.

Then he began talking about about his bottle-green Norton and matching leathers. A biker? Stamp, a biker? "I used to lay across the tank and talk to it every morning to get it to start," he recalled. Not only a biker, but a metaphysical biker, I realized. "As the traffic around town got heavier and heavier my nerves of steel turned to water and I let the Norton go," he explained.

Two days later, I received a large brown envelope in the mail. Inside was a picture of Stamp, clad in a tight leather riding suit and seated on a fabulous looking motorcycle with short racing handlebars (customized to such an extent I still can't figure out the make or model—although I know it's not a Harley). The famous wide-set eyes and high cheekbones were visible beneath the raised visor of a full-face helmet with a large star decorating the area above his forehead.

The photograph was inscribed with a single sentence. *When one is young one tries innumerable things to get one's rocks off.*

I called him up, acknowledged receipt of the picture, and invited him out to the house for Sunday lunch.

"You ever ride pillion?" I joked.

"Absolutely," he replied. "I'll meet you behind my place at noon." He wasn't joking. Nerves of steel. I should have seen it coming.

I actually hate having a passenger on the back of my motorcycle, always have and always will. As far as I'm concerned it wrecks the balance of the ride. Besides that, I feel totally responsible for the passenger's safety, more so than if I'm driving a car. I've solved the problem now with a solo saddle, but in those days, before I understood custom, I still had the two-up pillowed saddle that had come with the 1200.

I arrived at Stamp's bachelor quarters at noon. The back door opened, and there he stood. I was speechless. . . . He was kitted out in *all* the gear. . . . Not exactly the racing suit from the photograph but jeans, high boots, leather jacket, and open-faced helmet. I did a double-take. It was biker gear but, true to his unique sense of style, I had never quite seen anything like it. He was a polo-playing motorcyclist, a combination of horse-man and biker.

I had definitely never seen a helmet like the one he was wearing. It was tight to his head, high on the sides—above his ears—and the outer rims turned up slightly at both front and rear. A Prussian war helmet, an original Viking piece? I felt very pedestrian by comparison and even old LA Derek would have been hard pressed to keep up with this act. I motioned for Terence to mount up. He did and we were off, wheeling slowly towards Regent Street.

Now Stamp is a pretty fair sized man, a hair over six feet tall and somewhere around twelve stone. On the back of the Sportster he felt like a giant.

He had already seen the bike and I had certainly gone on about its speed and maneuverability. Now I wanted to demonstrate my mastery of the beast. Instead I was nervous, and my abrupt starts and stops resulted in several clashes of helmets, the front of his into the back of mine.

By the time we made it to Hyde Park I was surprised he wasn't concussed; he must have certainly wondered what he'd let himself in for, but Stamp, Zen master and stoic, was saying nothing.

I, on the other hand, was delivering a one-man commentary on the essence of motorcycling, sort of a *Zen and the art of* monologue punctuated by the clash of fiberglass. (At least, my helmet was fiberglass; Stamp's, for all I knew, was a sixteenth-century alloy.)

Paranoia was neck deep as I travelled towards the Fulham Road. Not only did I have no license and very little experience with pillion passengers, but I was carrying precious cargo, a man whose face was literally his fortune. One slip of the clutch and my spiritual mentor and former matinée idol would be having his boat race rebuilt at the Pountnoy Clinic.

In martial arts, as in motorcycle riding, spontaneity is of the essence: the ability to react fluidly and without thought to any stimulus is the difference between life and death. My spontaneity had all but frozen solid by the time I crossed the Old Brompton

Road and proceeded up Onslow Gardens. The light turned green ahead and I swung a wide right on to the Fulham Road. We were going so slowly that my wheels had lost angular momentum (the law of nature that allows two-wheeled travel in the first place) and I was leaning too far over; the rod of iron now felt like the man of lead on the back. I felt the back tire begin to slide out. . . . Fear is a real heightener; I could feel every nut, bolt, and inch of rubber on that Harley. Particularly the section of rear tire that was sliding in the gravel on the road. I was certain we were going over. . . . I had a quick flash of us both laid out beside the fallen motorcycle, me with my shattered Red Barons and Stamp with a concaved Viking war helmet and a flat nose, while some passer-by asked: "Isn't that Terence Stamp, the actor?" My premonition was amplified by a simultaneous knowledge of the million-pound accident claim (to encompass reconstructive work at the Pountnoy Clinic) that my insurers would renege on because I didn't have a British license. . . . I reacted by banging my support foot hard into the street, the old Steve McQueen move for a power turn, thereby jamming the bike into an upright position. Then I twisted the throttle. We straightened up, wobbled for a few yards, then stabilized, we continued our journey in a Zen-like silence. I deposited Stamp at the front door of the house and rode sheepishly down the drive and into the garage.

Lunch was fine and Terence, always the gentleman, refrained from comment about the trip out. If there was any giveaway that the ride had not exactly been a smooth one, it was when I offered to take him back to town later in the afternoon.

His ice-blues thawed noticeably as he glanced toward his helmet.

"We'll take the Jeep," I added.

"Absolutely," he said, smiling.

A Unique Riding Style

I applied for my test in late February of the new year. A few weeks later I received a card from the Department of Motor Vehicles scheduling me for early April. Fine by me, the weather would be warmer and the roads, I hoped, dry.

Then I made the call to CSM. The next training course started in a week and if I wanted to ensure my place I should send off a deposit. Done.

In spite of the bare-assed episode in the Park, a couple of near-fatal King's Road skids in the wet, and the Stamp episode, I still felt like a heavy biker as I rode towards my first day of the course. I'd added another small eagle to the air-cleaner cover and increased my polishing time by fifty percent. (Derek's Springer had been successfully suppressed into memory. The man himself was in LA and, after the three hundred-odd miles I had added to his bike, had rented a garage.)

The offices of CSM were located in the back lot of an industrial estate in a single-story building. The once white exterior paint had faded to a dull gray, a perfect match for the sky above. I wasn't certain where to leave the Sportster so I pulled up outside CSM, right in front of a small group of 125 cc practice bikes, left the engine idling, dismounted, and pushed through the front door.

'Where can I leave my bike?'

A guy about fifteen years younger than me, clad in head-to-toe leathers—well worn—looked up from the registration desk. He cocked his head to the side and listened like a surgeon for a heartbeat. Suddenly the sound of the idling 1200 amplified in perspective.

"Ah, yes, the purr of twin cylinders," Mr. Leather sighed. "You must be the gentleman with the H-D. . . . Let's take a look at it."

We walked outside and beheld the 1200.

A strange thing happens whenever I view the bike with a second party. I seem to perceive it through the other person's eyes, as if looking at it for the first time. This is no doubt another factor in my obsession for polishing; I always want to show the machine at its best.

On that particular day the Sportster appeared like a great silver shark amidst a school of minnows. The Kawasaki 125s, with their road dirt and L-plates, looked frail and vulnerable before the Harley.

"What a beast!" Mr. Leather exclaimed.

"Fastest stock bike Harley ever built," I confirmed.

He nodded his head and circled the 1200.

"It's so clean you could eat off it," he added, reverently.

The other trainees were now arriving, either by car or by L-plated 125s. Each of them eyed the Harley as they passed into the building. One or two seemed on the verge of genuflection.

"I'll let you ride it before the course ends," I promised the instructor.

A wise move.

Now I wouldn't say I was the worst rider in my class at CSM, but I would admit to being the most dangerous. Riding a motorcycle is like anything else you've been doing for a long time; you eventually find your own way of doing it, small eccentricities that give you a personal style. My style featured exclusive reliance on the mirrors—as opposed to the proper method of turning your head at regular intervals to see what is behind you—and rarely using my indicators or even a hand signal before executing a turn.

There were seven students in my class—four men and three women—and our first ride as a group not only highlighted my weaknesses as a rider but also caused me acute embarrassment.

Parking the Harley outside the CSM training quarters, picking up a Kawasaki 125, and heading down on to the training course—in a private parking lot—for some figures of eight and emergency stops was one thing, donning a yellow vest with LEARNER spelt out on the back and packing off down the public highway with my new club was something else again. I felt like the ultimate asshole. All I needed was a sticker below the L-plate that read MY OTHER BIKE'S A HARLEY-DAVIDSON.

We took turns leading the group while the instructor noted our strengths and weaknesses.

"Richard, I want you to take the lead now, up to the third traffic light, turn left, and follow the road to the cafe, we'll stop there for tea," he ordered.

My moment had come. I took off ahead of the pack, accelerating as if to demonstrate my absolute contempt for the uncoolness of what I was being forced to do, forgetting all the little pointers that the instructor had tried to drill into me back in the parking lot, like looking around and indicating. I turned left one street too soon, accelerated, and didn't realize my mistake until I got held up at a red light. Then I looked around and discovered that I was alone. I was also lost.

If wearing the yellow vest and L-plate was a heavy burden while with the group, it was doubly heavy while wheeling feebly around asking passers-by if they had seen six similarly suited L-platers. Fifteen minutes later I spotted the other 125s, parked outside a corner cafe. My entrance bore little resemblance to Brando's in *The Wild One*. "You certainly have a unique riding style," was my instructor's only comment. Thereby chastised, I rejoined the group for the rest of the afternoon, prowling the

side-streets and back roads of Wimbledon. When I got back on
the Sportster at the end of the five-hour group ride I felt like
I was in command of an ocean liner. I had never truly appreciated how big and powerful the Harley was. I even used my
blinker when turning left off Kingston Hill and into my driveway.
Maybe I was learning something after all.

The only near fatality during the L-plate group runs occurred
the following afternoon. And it was not one of the students who
perpetuated the near accident. It was the instructor.

Always leather clad and mounted astride his Kawasaki 250,
the former courier maintained a position behind and slightly
to the side of the pack, like the professional cowboy at the dude
ranch. This enabled him to keep an eye on us without becoming
entangled in any of our misadventures. He could also ride up
and down the line and issue commands.

We were on a steep hill when he decided that it was time
to take on the intricate maneuver of "stopping and turning
while on an incline." After giving the orders he shot ahead to
demonstrate, neglecting to notice the ten-ton truck barrelling
up from behind. Everyone else had seen the truck, but having
total faith in our instructor we assumed that somehow he was
incorporating the large vehicle into his demo.

He was midway through his turn, side-on to the truck, when
he saw it coming. And panicked. The lorry driver hit his air
brakes, the instructor his throttle; the ten-tonner skidded to a
halt while the 250 mounted the curb and stalled.

"Fucking cunt! You fucking cunt!!" from the window of the
lorry. Silence from the stunned instructor.

I waited for the lorry's door to swing open, wondering how
the seat of the instructor's leathers would handle a slide down
the middle of the sidewalk.

A shrill female voice broke the tension, whining from the
middle of the "L" pack: "We're only beginners."

"Fucking cunts," the driver repeated, but this time without
the sting. He threw his truck into gear and rumbled away.

The instructor, acting as if the entire incident had been prearranged (perhaps part of the "evasive tactics under pressure" section of the course), pulled off the sidewalk, completed his turn, and signalled us to follow him down the opposite side of the hill. He was, however, noticeably subdued in the debriefing session which took place back at CSM headquarters.

A week later, and one day before Part 1 of the riding test (a most opportune time), I made good on my promise to let him ride my Harley. We were in the parking lot following a group ride and I had seen him, for the hundredth time, eyeing the Sportster.

"Go ahead," I urged, handing over the keys.

He approached the bike as if it were a wild horse, checking tires, brakes, and mirror adjustments just as he had been training us to do. Then he mounted, started it up, and sat there a minute, shifting his weight in the saddle, trying to get the feel of the bike. Finally he rode tentatively down the driveway, away from the CSM office. I listened as the rumble of my exhaust pipes grew faint in the distance.

Fifteen minutes later, just when I was recalling the lorry incident and getting nervous, I heard the familiar echo of the slash-cuts. The one-time courier reappeared. His entire demeanor had changed: now he looked like Clint Eastwood, riding high in the saddle. The Harley has that effect on people; they get on as Woody Allen and get off as Clint.

The following afternoon, overcast but dry, I passed Part 1 of the test, thanks to the latest fan of the Sportster: after watching me complete an entire circuit of cones and stop signs without once looking over my shoulder or giving a hand signal, he convinced the examiner to let me try again.

I made it on my second attempt.

A week later I was on to Part 2.

This was a bit of an anticlimax. At the time of my examination the rider being tested was required to ride around a designated block of city streets, over and over again, the examiner popping out of bushes and stepping off the sidewalk to see if you were using your indicators and keeping in the proper lane. The high point of this on the road charade came when the examiner pulled the examinee over and informed them that it was time to test their ability to perform an emergency stop.

In order to do this the examiner would risk life and limb by hiding behind a telephone pole, bush, or lamppost before surprising the examinee by leaping in the path of the motorcycle.

He caught me on my second circuit, stepping from the pavement in the path of the bike. I slammed on the brakes, locked the wheels, and slid to a stop five feet in front of him. A few Highway Code questions later and I was a qualified rider.

The license gave me a whole new sense of security; I was finally legal. No more anxiety with regard to insurance claims and no more "American abroad" fabrications. Even my riding style relaxed; I was throwing the bike into curves and often found myself singing at the top of my lungs—"Knockin' on Heaven's Door" was always a road favorite—as I turned the ton out on the A3.

And I began to display very serious symptoms of Hog Fever.

I can tell now when it's coming on, but then it was a relatively new psychosis.

For me, the fever usually began in the garage, and often after a particularly exhilarating ride, just as I finished wiping the bike down and stood back to take a look at it. It was subtle at first, like a gentle gnawing in the pit of my gut. Something wouldn't look quite right. I'd usually break out the Mer and throw a light coat of wax on the parts that were cool enough to touch, then wait, viewing the Harley as if it were a piece of art under wraps.

Twenty minutes later I'd wipe off the Mer and view the bike again. Most of the time, the new shine was enough to settle the situation. But when the gnawing in my gut persisted I was in trouble. Sometimes I could halt the symptoms with a new set of pipes, gas caps with Harley eagles, a change of saddle, even a sissy bar—the bit of steel frame, sometimes padded, that supports the passenger's back. At other times it was more serious, invading most of my waking life, sometimes continuing into various dream states. That's when my inventory of bike mags really soared. *Easyriders, In The Wind, Iron Horse, Back Street Heroes*: I pored over them, searching for that missing piece, often with a magnifying glass, so as not to miss even the subtlest of custom modifications. And my trips to bike shops increased dramatically. At this stage in my biking career the shop was Fred Warr's.

This was one of the most serious cases of Hog Fever that I had ever had; the only one that had even approached it had culminated in the purchase of the 1200. Fred, Dave, and John have had a lot of experience with Hog Fever; they've grown to recognize it in all its forms. Having witnessed it myself, at various times, in several of my friends, I would say it begins with a certain glint in the eye, a look that says, "I'm gonna have it no matter what it costs," and soon extends to the entire body, causing a stiffening of the limbs and a craning of the neck whenever anything remotely resembling the sound of a V-Twin approaches. . . . Which brings me to the real turning point in this episode of the fever.

It came several days after the initial symptoms manifested.

I was lying in bed, my wife snoring in broken rhythm beside me. It must have been about eleven o'clock at night, and I had just completed a three-hour biker-mag marathon. If my wife had known that at least half my recent office time had been devoted to viewing *Easyriders* through a magnifying glass I'm sure she would have been more worried about my mental health than she usually was. Instead she commented, innocently,

"You're spending a lot of time in your office, your new book must be going really well."

Anyway, I was lying in bed, wondering if a new set of drag pipes would change the look of the Sportster enough to ease the fever, when I heard the sound.

It began as a low rumble, kind of a *bub-bub-bub-bub-bub-bub*, coming from the A3 side of Kingston Hill. My ears pricked up. Another few seconds and I was certain it was the sound of a Big Twin. I lay back and listened, allowing it to build in my head, sort of a vibrating brain massage, a biker's lullaby. I heard the engine back off as the Harley came almost parallel with my bedroom (my house sits about fifty yards back from the main road, behind a brick wall). Then the sound changed direction and entered the courtyard.

Derek?! It had to be, I didn't know anyone else with a Big Twin. But I hadn't seen him in months, I'd assumed he was still in LA. I jumped out of bed and rushed to the window.

Sure enough, in the half-light of the moon, the man cruised the driveway—I would recognize that Springer anywhere. He rode up, then down, attired in a tight black leather jacket, matching pants, and the tight, contoured helmet.

He cut a mean silhouette, like a ghost rider astride his metal horse, legs out and shoulders slumped forward and relaxed. He stared upward at the window as he cruised below. Sort of a vision in black leather. He was there, but he wasn't there.

"Derek!" I shouted through the leaded glass.

"What, what?!!" my wife answered from a semi-coma.

"Derek!" I yelled again, sprinting from the bedroom, down the stairs, and to the front door.

By the time I'd opened it he was gone. I stood still and listened. Silence, I couldn't even hear the echoes of that two-into-one.

Had he even been there at all, or was I finally hallucinating? Had the famous *Easyriders* "ghost rider" poster—a skeletal bike and rider silhouetted against the full moon—become so engrained in my subconscious that I was projecting it into my own courtyard? I remained at the door a few minutes, remembering the low gurgling sound of the exhaust pipes, that low-slung silhouette. . . . That Harley-Davidson Springer Softail . . . I had the fever bad, and I had to have that bike.

I walked back upstairs, into the bedroom, and crawled into bed. My wife's snoring had changed rhythm, sort of a *bub-bub-buuuuu.* . . . Even her snores reminded me of a Harley two-into-one. I glanced over at her. She remained totally unaware of the menace beside her. A man willing to beg, borrow, and use any available facility to satisfy his lust.

"Thank You, Nat. West., But I'll Put This One on Gold...."

I must own up. I was stone broke at this point in my life. Not that that condition is new to me; I can't actually remember being in credit at the bank (thank you, Nat. West.) since first discovering the great British tradition of the overdraft. I have always lived beyond my means. I'm not particularly proud of the fact, that's just the way it's been.

In this case, however, I was going to have to come up with a new source of finance. I'd already had a call from my bank manager about the 1200. It was a concerned call cloaked in politeness, like, "Richard, I'm looking at a check for two thousand pounds to Fred Warr's, did your new motorcycle need repairs?"

He meant the 883. I had to tell him the truth. "No . . . I bought a newer motorcycle." Silence. "But I've just signed another book deal, so don't worry."

I knew I couldn't get away with that one again.

I spent the next few hours mulling over a way to get my hands on the money to buy the Springer. By four in the morning I'd worked it out. Then I slept.

* * *

The American Express gold card has a £10,000 overdraft facility attached to it, one of the few perks of membership. The interest rate on the money is a couple of points above base rate and the client is billed every month. In other words, it's expensive money. More like an emergency backup than an actual cash source.

My wife had a gold card, and this was an emergency.

The gold card thing has always pissed me off. I had owned a green card before my wife ever thought of plastic, but then she got successful and went straight for gold. I got the supplementary card. In other words, I had my own card but it was her number. Very humiliating.

The bills, however, arrived in joint names—Mr. and Mrs. Richard La Plante. I usually opened them, then the pair of us would sit down and figure out who owed what.

Ten thousand pounds; the figure had lulled me to sleep.

A new Springer came in at under eight and a half, and if I sold the Sportster I wouldn't need anywhere near all of the facility.

I could cover up the purchase by telling her that I got an amazing trade-in on the Sportster and then pile on the old routine of how wise it is to trade a vehicle in every year to save on depreciation. Added to that, I would insist that the Springer was Harley's classic and that it was guaranteed to go up in value. The old "wise investment" or "like having money in the bank" routine.

She had a fair idea that I was broke but not precisely how broke. We had never shared a bank account, so I was in the clear in that respect. I just had to make certain that she didn't get to the mail before I did.

Yeah, I had the fever. And Fred Warr could see it coming. . . .

He was alone in the shop when I arrived. I had just finished a major polish on the 1200 and I parked it right outside his wall-sized front window. The sun was shining and the bike looked a million dollars—although £5,000 from Fred was what I had in mind. There were no Springers in the shop.

"Remember what you told me when I bought the 883," I said.

Fred was sitting behind a big walnut desk, located in back of the service counter. He was going over some paperwork and wearing a pair of reading glasses, the kind that are like half-glasses. When he looked up his eyeballs cleared the frame.

"Not exactly," he answered, but there was a fatherly curiosity in his tone. Papa Fred.

"You said I'd be back for a Big Twin."

He smiled. Not a salesman's "I got ya" smile (there are never enough new Harleys to meet demand, a smart marketing device), but a friendly, "welcome to the club," type of smile.

"I want a Springer." I announced it like a confession.

Fred laughed. "A Springer," he repeated, "a Springer. As soon as I saw that bike I thought of you."

"You're kidding me?" I was flattered.

"No, I'm not kidding. They're a little flash but a great ride," he answered.

A little flash; Fred hadn't said it like an insult, more of a compliment. I thought of Derek. A little flash?

"When are you getting one in?" I asked.

"I've got three due late in May."

"What can you get me for the 1200?"

"About four," Fred answered.

My heart sank.

"But I've got nearly six into it. Look at it."

Fred stood up and studied my motorcycle through the windowpane. "It's beautiful," he said.

"Custom paint, custom saddle, slash-cuts, chrome oil tank, sissy bar." Suddenly I was selling England's most established Harley dealer a motorcycle.

"Richard, you've got to understand that everybody wants to personalize their own bike," Fred explained.

Personalize. I mulled the word over. It was more accurate

than customize; I'd even had my initials engraved into the chrome oil tank.

"We can't get any more for your Sportster than we could a stock bike with the same mileage. They cost just over five thousand new, you're going to lose a thousand pounds just on depreciation value."

He was right, but the way I was looking at it—five grand on the motorcycle with a thousand pounds in additional parts—I needed a return of five thousand, not four. Besides, even with Hog Fever, I was worried about paying off the gold card account.

"I can't afford to let it go for four," I answered.

"Why don't you sell it privately?" Fred suggested.

I thought about it a moment. I really didn't fancy advertising in a newspaper or bike mag and then playing host to a load of curiosity-seekers and time-wasters. I'd done it with a couple of cars and I knew the Harley would be worse.

"You must know somebody who wants that bike," Fred continued, "the problem I'd have is the cost of the new season's bikes that I've got coming in. For a few hundred pounds more, my customers are going to want a new machine. You need to find someone who appreciates the money you've spent on yours. There has always been a market for these bikes here in England, but, until now, it's been fairly specialized. Things are changing, I've got orders for almost every bike I can import."

"How about the three Springers that are coming in?" I asked.

"One of them is going to a customer in the south of France and one of them is going up north," he answered.

"And one of them is going to me," I said.

Fred smiled.

"I'll give you a deposit for five hundred," I continued, reaching into the pocket of my jacket for the American Express Bank checkbook.

"I don't need your deposit, Richard," Fred said.

"And you won't go selling it to somebody else?"

"Not unless you tell me to," he promised.

We shook hands and I departed.

On the crest of the A3, just as I began my downhill run towards the Robin Hood roundabout, it came to me. That resonant voice, that ever youthful smile, those figure-eights in the GLR parking lot.

I sprinted up the stairs to my office, grabbed the phone, and called Johnnie Walker's number at GLR.

"How's that Harley-Davidson?" Walker's voice.

"That's why I called you. I just placed an order on another bike, a 1340, and I've got to sell the Sportster. I don't want to, but I can't afford to keep them both."

Hog Fever is probably the only virus that is transmittable down a telephone line. I felt it incubating in Johnnie Walker's silence.

"The bike's got twelve hundred pounds of custom parts and only twenty-two hundred miles on it," I pitched.

Finally he responded, his voice down an octave.

"Yeah, it's a really beautiful machine, I can't believe you could let it go."

I could already hear the cogs turning in Walker's brain and wondered if he had a gold card account.

"You caught me at a bad time, but I'm definitely interested," he answered. The Fever had obviously bit pretty deep; he hadn't even asked the price. Or maybe he was just too sophisticated to bring money into a discussion regarding a priceless work of art. "How long have I got?" he asked. His voice sounded like he was asking about a terminal illness.

I relaxed. "Plenty of time, man, plenty of time. The other bike doesn't even come in for two months and I'm not going to advertise the Sportster."

"Give me a couple of weeks to sort my finances out and I'll get back to you." He sounded deadly serious.

Two weeks and a new copy of *Easyriders* later Johnnie Walker called. His voice sounded positive as he asked to come out to my place and have another ride on the Sportster, and we agreed on the upcoming Saturday. Time for a very major polish, including toothbrushed spokes. He arrived dressed to ride, boots, jeans, leather jacket, and a brass Harley-Davidson belt buckle. This guy was not messing around.

I rolled the gleaming beast out of the garage, we looked at it for a few seconds, mounted up, and took off, with me delivering a steady monologue as we poked down the hill. I covered everything from the one-down, three-up gear changes to braking techniques particular to a Harley, like push down hard and pray.

By the time we turned into the Park a fine mist had begun to fall, creating the familiar ice rink effect on the inner park roads; I took the curve leading up the rise like a granny on a skateboard and began to wonder if I was developing Celebrity Freeze Out, a post-traumatic stress disorder brought on by the Terence Stamp pillion ride. The last thing I needed was an accident resulting in a foot peg through Johnnie Walker's voicebox. In the parking lot I was just having some serious doubts about this trial ride when the DJ revved the engine and pulled out on to the main road. I watched him disappear over the rise, heading towards Richmond Gate.

Fifteen minutes later and I was pacing the gravel like an expectant father. Just as my spirits were taking a plunge I heard the *putt-putt-putt* of the Sportster's engine. I looked up to see Johnnie Walker at the top of the hill, riding towards me like a cavalier. He had obviously been born to ride.

"I've got to have it!" he said, sliding to a stop. The megawatt eyeballs and wide grin made him look about eighteen years old. No need for cosmetic surgery here.

'I think you're right,' I agreed, almost climbing on the back of the bike to let him pillion me home. The 1200 had psychologically changed ownership during his spin around the ice rink, no money down.

Thus began one of the longest negotiations in the history of motorcycling.

*   *   *

Around this time—late '88—the Harley scene had begun to
trickle into England. Neither as big or as flashy as it was in LA,
where Mickey Rourke and Billy Idol could be seen cruising
Sunset Boulevard on chopped bikes, with lowered frames and
extended forks, bored-out engines increasing the cubic-centi-
meter capacity and ape-hanger handlebars so that the arms go
up crucifix fashion, but then, you know what they say, "When
it's three thirty in the afternoon in Los Angeles it's 1945 in
London." Part of the spread of Hog Fever into England was
instigated by the Harley-Davidson Motorcycle Company. They
have always been strict, and clever, with their allocation of new
bikes, cautious not to flood any particular market, including
America, but manufacturing just enough machines to remain
in demand. During the late '80s, Harley handled the spill of
new production without flooding their domestic market by
increasing its supply to England, but even then to select dealers
only, based on the dealer's longevity, showroom space, and
advertising budget. It never was, and never has been, a situation
in which a Harley dealer, either domestic or foreign, could pick
up a phone, dial Milwaukee, and order thirty bikes; it has always
been the other way around, and each season Milwaukee informs
each dealership of their allocation. That's why when I went
shopping for a Springer Fred was able to tell me exactly how
many he had coming in. When they were sold, that was it, never
a matter of "Hold on a second, if you miss that lot, I'll call up
and get another one delivered." The cost of the new bikes—
the 1200 Sportster, on the road, was £5,456.52, and the Springer
Softail £8,720—made Hog Fever an expensive illness, made
more so by the need to add custom accessories to the stock
machine. The fever was an affliction of the well heeled. Not
too many rebels without an income could afford to be infected.

But at that time most of the new bikers were content to own
a stock Harley; they hadn't been exposed to LA and Sunset
Boulevard, or *Easyriders.* I wanted to be different; I didn't want
to ride a bike that looked like anyone else's. So, assured of a

private sale, I spent a lot of time at Fred Warr's, determined to create a custom ride.

I discussed my ideas with Fred and Dave, borrowing a few tricks from *In The Wind* and *Easyriders*, and a few from Derek. I wanted black-lacquered paint work with a very simple Harley logo, nothing flamboyant. This time I wasn't going for the gold trim around the tank, just basic black. Dave bent down behind his desk and came up with a box of decals. We sifted through and located a printed version of HARLEY-DAVIDSON MOTORCYCLE CO. in gold letters about three inches high.

"These are nice, came from an '83 Sportster," Dave said. The decals were perfect, simple and clean.

I decided on the two-into-one fish-tail exhaust system—hanging directly above us on the wall—and a solo saddle, courtesy of Derek, plus the eagled Derby cover. That would do it, for the time being.

"How about performance parts?" Dave asked.

He was referring to Screamin' Eagle, a subsidiary of Harley-Davidson that made accessories which would make the bike go faster: a high-performance carburetor or an upgraded camshaft that would allow the intake of more oxygen for combustion.

"How much does it cost to get into all that stuff?" I asked.

"It'll add another five hundred or so to the price of the bike," Dave figured.

I was already over my budget by a couple of hundred due to the two-into-one exhaust, so even with the fever—actually more restrained once inside the confines of Warr's—I knew I couldn't afford the extras. (I actually couldn't afford the bike. . . .) "Maybe later," I replied.

A few weeks went by without hearing from Johnnie Walker. Which was fine by me; I'd made it clear that I didn't want to part with the 1200 till the new bike arrived. The idea of not being able to slip out to the garage for either a polish or purely for the sake of viewing the motorcycle was intolerable.

I know that I am not alone when I talk about my obsession with just plain looking at the motorcycle.

In psychological terms, the motorcycle has been associated with everything from a power complex to a penis substitute. "Hey, you guys, look at mine; I've had it chopped, extended, bored out, and painted black."

The fact is, whether or not the Hog has deep-seated penis implications, and I suppose that makes a major polish tantamount to a very heavy session of self-abuse (God forbid my wife catch me mid-stroke on the tail pipe), the bikes are truly beautiful to behold. An actual pleasure to the eye. Like a vintage car, a Jensen or an old Mercedes or Bristol. Before the never-ending search for something new caused the car manufacturers to fuck up the classic designs with squared bodies and predator grills.

Harley never fucked up their designs; they only improved the engines. In my opinion the simplicity of leaving a good thing alone was Harley's genius. If it ain't broke, don't fix it.

Sometimes, after a few solid hours banging it out on my word processor, the experience of going down to the garage and just looking at the bike is like a brain massage. It's probably similar to the collector who enjoys sitting alone and "breathing in" a favorite painting in his gallery. I escape within the atmosphere created by the bike.

In terms of psychotherapy, I reckon the purchase of a Harley is real value for money. There is nothing like a good ride to throw fresh perspective on your problems. It has something to do with the concentration it requires to handle the motorcycle; again, I'm referring to zanshin, or heightened awareness. Everything else is temporarily placed in the background while the physical and mental action of riding the motorcycle takes first position. Then, when the ride is over, the mind resettles, pieces of the mental jigsaw often finding better alignment.

I'd rather be in the saddle than on the couch.

* * *

Johnnie Walker called a month later. He'd been on a motorcycle course and had passed his test. Everything was set, just a small hitch regarding the money. A few unexpected expenses had cropped up and he was light on cash.

No problem, I thought. There was still over a month to go. And Johnnie had the fever, I knew he'd find the money somewhere.

Two weeks from then I got the call from Dave, at Fred Warr's. The Springer had arrived.

I tried to keep the panic out of my voice.

"They're early, aren't they?"

"Sometimes it works this way, the container comes in and customs clear them without any hassle, straight on through, other times we wait weeks," he explained.

"Ah, how long will it take to do the paint and get the accessories on it?" I asked.

"The paint will take ten days and John will probably get to the other bits this week," Dave replied.

"Dave"—I thought it was time to own up—"I'm not ready with my money."

"No problem." His answer was too easy.

"I've got a buyer for the 1200 and I'm waiting on him," I explained.

"Richard, even if you can't come up with it, we've got a waiting list of customers for these bikes." There was absolutely no malice in Dave's tone, simply a statement of fact. It confirmed my suspicions that Hog Fever was spreading across England and Europe. "You could get one out of the next shipment," he suggested.

"When's that?"

"We've got two more Springers coming in at Christmas."

Christmas! I wasn't waiting till Christmas for the Big Twin. I'd use up the whole gold card overdraft before I'd wait till Christmas. Christmas! I'd miss the entire summer. No way.

"No, Dave, that's all right, but I'm going to need a couple of weeks."

"Ten-four." And Dave was over and out.

I contemplated advertising the Sportster, just in case Johnnie Walker was in the same position as I was. I just couldn't do it. Neither to Walker or the bike. I knew exactly how he felt and I wasn't about to betray his trust. Also I wanted my pride and joy to go to a good home. But I was in trouble.

I phoned GLR and left a message. He got back to me and sounded hopeful. But not hopeful enough to come up with five grand in two weeks.

Fuck it! I decided to go for gold. . . . I'd just have to intercept the mail until I could shift the 1200.

The Big Day came on the last Thursday in May. I remember this well because my good friend Dave Hazard, one of the finest karate instructors in the country, volunteered to drive me down to collect the Springer and video the entire experience with my camcorder.

At this point, just before the collection of a new bike, the fever runs hot enough to completely incinerate any thought of money, overdrafts, or wives discovering bank statements. The mood is full speed ahead.

Upon arrival I cued up the video recorder, handed it to Dave, and asked him to wait on the outside of the wooden doors to the workshop while I made my entrance through the showroom side of the shop. I wanted to get the money business over and done with before I entered the workshop and laid eyes on my new bike.

I filled out the check with a devil-may-care abandon that implied there was plenty more where this came from, whipping my signature off like an autograph, successfully ignoring the £8,500 that I had scrawled above the line, and finally Fred opened the door separating the showroom from the workshop.

And there it was, the most beautiful motorcycle I had ever seen, the black Springer Softail.

John Warr was kneeling beside it, checking the tire pressure. When he looked up, he was smiling.

"Looks pretty damn good, doesn't it?" he said.

Pretty damn good, I thought. Oh, yeah.

There is a strange optical illusion that occurs, at least to me, when a Harley-Davidson motorcycle has been put together right: it appears compact. There is a new economy to the bike, as if it has been tightened up and hardened in perspective.

There were half a dozen other bikes in John's shop that afternoon, but, by comparison to the Springer, they looked large and cumbersome. The Springer stood out like a diamond among rhinestones, cool and hard. Maybe it was the three coats of lacquer on top of the perfect black paint and the simplicity of the single gold decal, or the way that the solo saddle seemed to lower the bike and the two-into-one fish-tail exhaust augmented its clean line. I was transfixed.

I walked to the Springer, climbed into the saddle, and John pushed me towards the doors. Fred opened them and I rolled into the light of day.

Dave hit the record button and the show began. Handshakes from Fred and John, a last-minute check to make sure the gas valve was in the "on" position this time, a push of the starter button, and the Springer roared to life. The tape rolled as the Warrs waved me goodbye. Off I rode, turning left on Waterstone, right on to the King's Road, and sailing towards Kingston. The captain and his new ship, on their maiden voyage.

People did stop and stare at the Harley as I passed them. This time I wasn't self-conscious; I felt completely at home. I parked the Big Twin beside the 1200 in the garage, waited for Dave to catch up, and then the two of us studied them both together. The fleet. £15,000 worth of American iron.

Living the Dream (On Credit)

The fever continued at full pitch into the next week.
I was rarely in my office or even in the house. When I wasn't
riding I was polishing, when I wasn't polishing I was viewing.
"Live the dream" was an old Harley sales slogan, but the reality
of having borrowed the money to do it didn't truly sink in till
Johnnie Walker's next phone call. His voice was somewhere on
the far side of Doomsday as he explained that he was getting
hit from all angles—taxman, ex-wife—and that he was uncertain
as to how long it was going to take to come up with the £5,000.
If at all.

I felt like I was betraying an unwritten code of honor. I
asked if I should try to sell the bike to someone else.

He didn't want me to do it but he couldn't tell me no.

Meanwhile I was scheduled for a business trip to Los Angeles;
I figured that the statement from the American Express Bank
would arrive while I was away. The last thing I needed was for
my wife to open the envelope and discover the truth.

So far she had been very supportive about the Fleet, decree-
ing the new Springer "King of the Road." Even as she said it
I thought of another line in Roger Miller's song: "Room to let,

fifty cents," which is approximately what I'd be looking for if she got to the mail before I did.

Then straight out of the blue came a phone call from Charles Negus-Fancey, who had once looked after my musical career. "George's cousin Andros is in love with Harleys, and we told him about yours," he announced.

"George who?" I asked.

"George *Michael*." As if there was only one "George" in the world.

"The Harley-Davidson, it's still for sale, isn't it?"

I hesitated before I answered, remembering Johnnie Walker's last call. "Yes, I suppose it is. . . ."

"Andros would love to come and take a look at it," Charles said.

He arrived a few days later. He had just returned from LA, where he had been filming a promotional video to accompany his new album which featured several Harleys and several heavy bikers. Andros had picked up the fever. We headed for the garage and the Sportster.

"I love it man, I've got to have it, got to, got to—"

"It's promised to somebody else," I answered. Andros stopped rapping. "But I'm not sure the guy can come up with the money," I explained.

Two calls to GLR and one to Johnnie's home number went unanswered. I was beginning to feel like I was hustling him. The week went by; still nothing. It was Monday and I was booked on a Virgin flight to LA on the upcoming Thursday. On Tuesday I rang Andros. He had the money but he didn't have a driving license, could I deliver the bike? No problem. So I took the 1200 on its last ride with me in the saddle.

It's a strange feeling to surrender something that has been such a big part of your life. I had become attached to the Sportster as if it were a pet dog or some other animate object. When I was away from the motorcycle for more than a few days I truly missed it, and after a few thousand miles of riding my body was as familiar with the bike as if it were a wife or lover. Corny but true.

I had actually wanted Johnnie Walker to have the 1200; I knew he'd look after it. I wasn't at all sure about Andros.

Maybe it was because Johnnie was my own age or maybe because I had seen that look in his eye. . . . I felt like a criminal as I taxied back to Kingston. I was happy not to get a return call from GLR; I didn't know what I was going to say. I ran into Andros about nine months later. He was sitting with his cousin George at a restaurant and I asked after the Sportster; he told me he'd sold it and bought a bigger one.

Celebrity Spotting

West Hollywood is less than two miles square and sits between Beverly Hills in the west and old Hollywood in the east. It is a center for nightlife and entertainment.

Sunset Plaza is like an oasis in the midst of the action. It is a district of expensive shops and outdoor restaurants, all within an area of about two hundred yards, covering both sides of the four-lane boulevard. For some reason the Plaza seems to be a favorite gathering spot for Europeans, commonly called Euro-trash by the West Hollywood residents. The restaurants extend right on to the sidewalks, and their long tables are shaded by canopies or umbrellas, affording their clientele a non-stop view of passing traffic mixed with the aroma of vintage fumes.

When I wasn't having a business lunch, or "power lunch" as they were known in those days, I often went up to Sunset Plaza, ordered a bird-bath sized cup of cappuccino, and got into some serious Harley spotting.

White guys, black guys, Oriental guys, and the occasional female on a Sportster. Nobody wore a helmet, and they were all into cut-off denim jackets, T-shirts, or light leathers. Suddenly everybody in LA, from theatrical agents to rock stars and their attorneys, rode a Harley—although I still estimated the proportion of Harleys to assholes to be about two to one. Owning a Harley had become a prerequisite to star and social status. Many Hogs were purchased, but few were ridden (beyond the mile-long zone between Gazzarri's rock and roll club and the Comedy Store on Sunset Strip). It was an elite club—the "Yeah, I've got a Harley" set—that guaranteed an instant starting point for business deals and cocktail ("Cranberry juice, please") conversations. Harleys had become equivalent to the Armani jacket as executive equipment—and they were less expensive than a Porsche Carera. Harleys mattered.

I was sitting there one afternoon in mid-June, already on my second bird-bath when a Godalmighty roar came up from the dip in Sunset adjacent to the Tower Records parking lot; it sounded like Concorde taking off. I looked in the direction of the disturbance and saw against the sun a classic sixteen-inch ape-hanger silhouette. It was the archetypal heavy biker, cut-off denims and wraparound shades. His hands were in the crucifix position above his head, his feet were forward, and his ass was about a foot and a half above the ground. This guy was seriously in the wind.

The closer he rode the more detail I picked up, from the tattooed biceps to the high cheekbones and bleached white hair. It only dawned on me as he roared past—and I'm talking no mufflers—that I was watching one of the great Hollywood bikers, Billy Idol, formerly of the English punk band Generation X and now a major rock star in the US. Billy was several steps ahead of the Harley-riding execs; he was "inked" and "chopped." An hour later, back in my hotel room, I picked up a magazine called *LA Style* and saw an article about celebrity bikers: Billy Idol, Sylvester Stallone, Arnold Schwarzenegger, Mickey Rourke (the original anti-Hollywood biker); all Harley men. There was also a brief profile on Bill Bartel, founder and owner of Bartels', the celebrity bike shop. I grabbed the yellow pages. Bartels'; the address was given as 8910 Washington Boulevard, Culver City; I phoned up to make sure they were open. "We sure are, partner," a deep voice assured me. My new partner gave me some directions and I was on my way. It felt like a trip to the Hollywood Holy Land, sort of a pilgrimage; I was half expecting to see Arnie, Sly, and Mickey kneeling in prayer beside a gilded chopper.

After a long drive in my rented Honda Civic I made it to the promised land, a glass-fronted building with BARTELS' HARLEY-DAVIDSON above the door. The actual store front and showroom were a bit of a let-down; maybe twice the size of Fred Warr's place on Waterstone. I'd expected the Taj Mahal.

Once inside, however, there was a distinct difference. First of all, out of the twenty or so bikes on display at least half were customized. And I'm not talking about gold eagles and slash-cut pipes; I mean truly modified. Lowered, forks extended, mudguards and fenders specially molded, carburetors that looked like cappuccino machines, all detailed right down to the hand-made saddles and gold-leafed paint; nothing home-made about any of the modifications, the work was better than factory perfect, even the wheel nuts were chromed.

I walked over to a customized Evolution Softail. The bike could have come right off the cover of *Easyriders*; it had upswept fish-tail pipes (*à la* Peter Fonda in *Easy Rider*), a black-lacquered gas tank inlaid with deep-red flames, and high, pulled-back handlebars. The carburetor resembled a wind funnel, and the tiny leather saddle was hand-tooled and stitched. The bike sat low to the floor and looked deceptively small. I could feel the power of the engine just looking at it.

I reached down and flipped over the price tag. $19,000.

I was amazed. $19,000 was the equivalent then of about £10,000, and this was a show bike.

"Can I help ya, partner?"

I recognized the voice from the telephone. Looked up to see a youngish, tanned face with medium-length dark hair and a Hollywood smile; in other words, lots of big, white celebrity-chomping teeth; my partner wore a Bartels' T-shirt, faded jeans, and lizardskin cowboy boots.

"Ya like that little sled?" he asked.

"It's beautiful," I answered.

"I could cut ya' a deal on that one," the voice continued.

"I'm from England," I said, as if that was the single reason I wasn't buying the sled.

"That's fine, we ship there all the time."

"I really just came in to take a look," I confessed.

By now he was studying me in a peculiar way, as if he was just on the verge of remembering something.

"Rick Bartels," he announced, extending a beefy hand.

"Richard La Plante," I replied." Do you own this place?"

His eyes seemed to focus for the first time as he gripped my hand and he nodded his head slowly. "No, no, not me, that's my dad you're thinking of. C'mon, I'll show you around."

I was surprised by his offer; there were other customers in the shop and they weren't getting shown around. I followed him to his desk, where he stopped and lifted a small picture of twin snake heads, set in gold and laid out on a jeweller's work bench. "Had these made up for Sly, right after he did the film, *Cobra*, side mounts for his gas tank," he explained.

"Beautiful," I answered. They were.

From the showroom we walked to the parts and accessories section of Bartels', a room filled with racks of leather jackets, riding chaps, T-shirts, kiddies' leathers, handlebars and exhaust pipes, plus glass-fronted showcases loaded with everything from carburetors to engine heads.

"Follow me, Robert, I'll show you where it all happens," Rick continued.

Robert, did he just call me Robert? I wondered.

We went through a hallway of signed photographs: Sylvester Stallone, Mickey Rourke, Gary Busey, Arnold, and a gallery more, out the back door and into a workshop the size of an aircraft hangar.

A couple of hundred Harley-Davidsons, each in its own state of repair or rebirth, lined either side of the walkway leading to the open double doors at the far end of the building. A dozen men were attending the bikes.

Rick guided me through the sea of chrome straight to a stripped-down Softail with drag bars and pipes, temporarily minus its gas tank. A big, broad-shouldered man was squatting beside the bike, working on the carburetor.

"This is one of Mickey's, it's gotta have a hundred and forty horsepower," Rick said as we approached one of Mickey Rourke's sleds.

"And this is my father, Bill Bartels," Rick continued.

The big man stood up; he bore a resemblance to his son but had more character etched into his wide face and clear eyes. He wore a plaid shirt and had a working man's calloused handshake.

"This is Robert Plant from England," Rick went on.

It hit me then, right between the eyes, Richard La Plante, Robert Plant; it wasn't the first time someone had misheard my name. I did have long blond hair, but I usually got mistaken for the tennis player, Vitas Gerulaitis.

"Lead singer with Led Zeppelin," Rick ploughed on.

"Pleased to meet you," Bill Bartels said, his voice dry, definitely not star-struck. Thank God he wasn't a fan.

I smiled and nodded, not wanting to speak and give away my American accent. Rick hadn't noticed but his dad might; it was all very embarrassing.

We stood another moment then Bill went back to Mickey's hundred and forty horses and Rick ushered me out through the front of the shop. I was praying he wouldn't ask for a signed photo for his wall.

"Listen, if you're ever in town again, we'd love to build something special for you. . . . We just finished one for Eric Clapton." Another celebrity bro.

I nodded, grunted, and shook Rick Bartels' hand once again, then exited via the front door, walking very slowly toward the rented Honda Civic and hoping I wasn't being watched from the window. Surely Robert Plant would have had a limo, or, at least, a Mustang convertible.

I ducked my head as I drove past.

*   *   *

Back in London I performed my general ritual of greeting my wife, greeting the dogs, then slipping out to the garage to re-establish myself with the motorcycle. Usually this requires a solid coat of Mer and a quick rub with some very soft steel wool over areas of the bike—wheel rims and brake discs—that have picked up a little rust because of the condensation. Then off comes the Mer and on to a polish. Following that, if I'm still stable after the ten hours in the air, I start her up and take a quick ride.

It was over dinner that my wife told me that Johnnie Walker had called, a week after I'd left London. He had raised the money. She'd told him that I'd sold the bike and he replied that that was a hell of a way to end a friendship.

I felt about an inch tall.

I mulled it over during the next day and rationalized my side of the situation. Then I phoned GLR. Johnnie was no longer angry, in fact he claimed to understand my predicament with the bank; he'd had his own problems. He'd bought a new red Sportster from Fred Warr, and loved it.

We agreed to meet up and do some riding and that was that, crisis resolved.

A week later Walker's forgiveness was confirmed; he called me for a "live on the air" conversation with an Australian rock star. We talked about music and Harleys. Johnnie Walker was officially in the saddle.

The Springer

I rode the Springer all through July and half of August, in and out of Soho and back and forth to the video shop, not a very impressive schedule for a 1340 cc machine. Here I was with my Big Twin and my bookshelves full of bike mags, and I wasn't exactly living the life.

It was time for a change; I decided to take the bike on a proper run. It was just a question of where. I had in-laws in Southport, a good friend, Terry O'Neill, in Liverpool, and Dave Hazard in Brighton. Brighton was too close and the ride up north was too boring. Wales kept coming to mind: legendary for great scenery and clear roads, unless it rained. But if I worried about getting two clear days strung together, I was never going to venture out of Soho, besides I had the wax-coated jacket and riding pants. And I did know someone in Wales, the author, Patrick Tilley. I had once done a joint book signing with him, got on very well, and, if I remembered correctly, he had invited me to visit him in Snowdonia. In my latest incarnation as a biker. I decided to take him up on his offer.

First I broke out my *Motorist's Atlas of Britain* and checked to see where Snowdonia was. It looked a long way away. Then I phoned Patrick.

"On a bike?! Great stuff! . . . Shouldn't take you any time at all, two and a half, maybe three hours."

"But, Patrick, according to the map it's about two hundred and twenty-five miles from here."

He must have read the hesitation in my voice. I should have heard the cabin fever in his. A long time back Patrick and his wife Janine had opted out of the rat race for their quiet sheep farm in Wales. But Patrick still enjoyed the buzz of city folk and tales of Hollywood showbiz.

"Is it that far? No, no. Anyway, you're on a bike! What kind of man are you?"

"Right! I'll be there by noon Saturday," I promised.

Once committed I did have a moment of doubt. As legendary as those rolling hills and grassy plains were reputed to be, my sense of direction, or lack of it, was—among family and friends—equally well known. What happened if I got lost, if it rained, if the bike broke down in the middle of nowhere?

But Tilley's challenge prevailed.

Still, I was cautious. I studied the *Motorist's Atlas*, plotted a course, and figured if it was a four-hour ride for an average bro I would give myself six and a half. If I left Kingston at five thirty in the morning I would be lunching with the Tilleys at noon.

I prepared for it as if for some sort of clandestine military operation, like a drop behind enemy lines. I laid everything out on the bedroom floor. I had a backpack—the Springer had no panniers or any other place to store belongings: never let it be said I sacrificed style for practicality. I had a map, waxed rain suit, long underwear, engineer boots, socks, jeans, toothbrush, razor—"How many weeks are you planning to be on the road?" my wife inquired. She had tolerated my frequent absences in the garage and the disappearance of several toothbrushes for spoke cleaning, and now seemed prepared to accept my new identity as a long-distance biker with a degree of amusement. Tough to take when I was treating it as a matter of life or death.

I hardly slept the night before; I kept getting up to make weather checks. It was one of those windy nights when the moon and stars were out one minute then hidden behind clouds the next. As long as it didn't rain. . . . I didn't need the alarm to tell me it was five thirty. The *bleep bleep* did wake up my wife; she mumbled something about "phone me when you get there" then went back to sleep.

Pack on back, I headed through Richmond Park, heading towards Ealing and the M40, the only stretch of motorway I planned to use. After Oxford it would be on to the smaller, less-trafficked A-roads, all the way to Snowdonia.

The roads were dry and traffic sparse. By the time I hit Kew Bridge the sky had turned a beautiful burnt orange and the sun was rising. Everything felt right; the Big Twin was purring like a pussy cat and rolling with the road.

I picked up the M40 on the other side of Ealing, stretched my legs out on the foot pegs, and took the bike right up to sixty. It felt fine. So fine that I let it slide to seventy, then seventy-five miles an hour. There were lorries to my left and lorries to my right and I wanted to get to Oxford, away from them, and on to the scenic A-roads.

I was in the outside passing lane when the wind started blowing at gale force. That was fine; the Harley was so heavy that it would take a hurricane to disturb it. What wasn't so fine was my backpack. For the sake of comfort I had not hitched up the waist-belt and now it was bouncing around like a weather balloon, tugging at the straps that wrapped beneath my armpits. I felt like I was being drawn and quartered. Every time the pack whipped back and forth, from shoulder to shoulder, the bike wobbled. And I couldn't pull over or slow down because of the lorries behind and to either side. So I continued to roar ahead, in extreme discomfort and some degree of danger. It took another ten minutes—eternity if you're being drawn and quartered—to switch lanes and pull to the side of the road, slow down, and stop. At last I battened down the hatches, repacked my jeans, which had been flying like a flag from the side of the pack, and continued on my journey.

After Oxford, everything changed, the sun came out, the

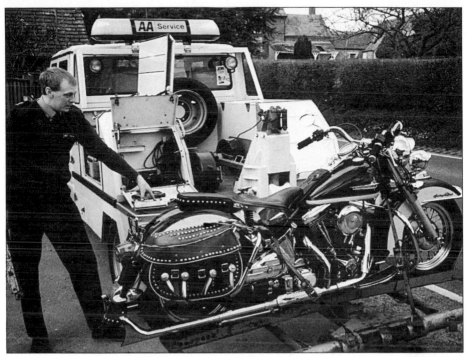
The Digas' ride is rescued in Dorset following three days in Highway Heaven

Chopped in Dorset

HEAVY DUTY

FEB/MAR 92
No 4
£1·95

9 770963 260001

MMP

Four Play

Snob's incarnation: the Hog's first time in *Heavy Duty* magazine

The Digas' ride, locked and loaded

The Warr incarnation, packed light for Spain

Me and Bro Si high and dry in the Sierra Nevada, on route to Marbella

Fiona, Daniel and the mighty Snob

The Digas: bike night at the Rock Garden

Terence Stamp as a biker

The Battistini incarnation as photographed by top UK
biker/photographer Gary Stuart

The Hog in all its glory, worth its weight in borrowed bullion.

roads were dry and clear, and the Springer was officially run in; it had over five hundred miles on the clock.

I got on the A40 and rode towards Gloucester.

As I entered the Cotswolds, the roads narrowed and gently curved. In front of me was a clear dry winding ribbon and to either side green fields, rolling hills, and wide-open space. The ride became a kaleidoscope of physical sensation: colors and smells, everything fresh and bright, with the scent of wild flowers on the breeze. Highway heaven came on like a hallucinogen, as if I'd taken the mildest possible dose of the purest LSD, just the perfect amount to heighten my awareness without affecting any of my physical functions. I was breathing full, deep breaths and my mind was a jukebox of fragmented melodies, songs I hadn't thought of in years, all rolling in synchronized rhythm with the unfurling highway. If I closed my eyes or removed my hands from the handlebars the Springer rolled along on automatic pilot. Compared to the stop and go of city driving, the gagging exhaust fumes and the noise of horns, this was a state of moving meditation, Zen in its proper sense, beyond the awareness of self-consciousness or self-image. I was alone on the highway, merged with the bike, no one to ask me how much it cost, or how fast it went, not even "me," polishing or viewing—separating myself from the machine. I was at one with the bike, simply riding, absorbed by the wind and the scenery. "I" had dissolved. Free. Absolutely free.

I wanted the ride to go on forever. . . .

I got my wish. Two hours later my ass was sore and I had definitely come down from my state of transcendence. My trip-meter was reading one hundred and twenty miles, which meant it was time to take a break and refuel. Unfortunately I seemed to be in the middle of the country, probably somewhere over the Welsh border without a town or petrol pump in sight.

I'm all right, I thought, I've still got my reserve.

Another ten minutes and the Springer was stuttering and coughing; I leaned over and moved the toggle on the gas valve, finding the halfway reserve position between off and on. The bike came back to life and I continued my magical mystery tour, this time on the paranoid side of my highway acid.

Unpleasant thoughts flooded my mind, of having to abandon the Springer while I hitched—wishful thinking since I hadn't seen a car in half an hour—or walked in search of a petrol station, which produced images of Welsh bike bandits in pickup trucks lifting the Springer and whisking it away like a prize Hereford bull.

I checked my wristwatch. 8:45. I'd been on the road over three hours and had managed a feeble hundred and thirty miles. Roughly estimated that put my average speed at 44 MPH When I subtracted the sixty or seventy miles of M40 I came to the realization that I had been winging across the A-roads at about 18 MPH. In the wind, or what? Then I had a flash of anger directed at my upcoming host, Patrick Tilley. *You're on a bike. What kind of man are you?*

At about this time a very light sprinkle of rain began, descending like a silk shroud and coating the road with a silvery sheen. So I did the right thing and slowed to 9 MPH. Ten minutes later and the bike was coughing again. This time I was in sight of something which resembled the general store from one of those old Hollywood movies set in the depression of the American 1930s.

I literally coasted the last twenty yards, sliding to a halt beside one of the general store's two petrol pumps. I thanked the Lord, filled her up, then went inside to pay. The man behind the counter was thin, bearded, and wore farmer's overalls and bifocals. He might as well have been speaking Greek. I was dumbfounded, finally just handing over my ten-pound note and trusting him to find the change.

One thing I did manage to ascertain was that I was in Wales—and he was speaking Welsh. Somewhere in my euphoria I had managed to drift off my intended flight path and leave the A40.

I held the shred of paper containing Tilley's address beneath the magnification section of his glasses, hoping he was going to tell me I was already in Snowdonia. Instead he pulled a map out from behind the cash register and pointed to a place called Fan Foel, communicating to me that it was the nearest town. Then he pointed to a distant region, high-lighted in green. That was Snowdonia. . . . I was about halfway.

Back on the road and the sun was shining once again, but this time I was less involved with the Zen of motorcycling and more concerned with the highway signs, which were in Welsh as well as English. The ride went on, minutes of euphoria broken by panicked seconds of "Where the hell am I?" During the panic I tended to listen closely for telltale rattles, wobbles, and any indication of mechanical problems, gauging my gas supply by keeping one eye glued on the tripmeter. I fueled up at sixty miles.

Patrick had mentioned—in a set of directions that I had only half listened to, preferring, instead, my road atlas—that Betws-y-Coed was the major town before his own, approximately twenty miles south. A couple of hours later I saw a sign marked Betws-y-Coed and felt like Christopher Columbus in sight of land. The old highway jukebox belted another golden oldie from my memory bank—Jim Morrison's "Roadhouse Blues," which I bellowed at the top of my lungs to the back beat of the Big Twin—and every anxious moment was obliterated in song.

Patrick had warned me that his farm was a few miles off the beaten path, not to mention the surfaced road. In fact, the turning for P. Tilley's sheep farm was a single-lane dirt and gravel thoroughfare which inclined at about seventy degrees.

"Let it roll, baby, roll," dwindled to a cautious lament as I dropped both feet for balance and twisted the throttle. The back wheel spun, threw some grit, and dug in. And suddenly I was in motion, riding a 650 lb. dirt bike, pushing off with one leg then the other, and gripping the handlebars like a rodeo rider on a bucking bronco. Up I went, trying to avoid the grooves that had been left by the farmers in their four-wheel-drive vehicles and praying that I didn't run head on into one of them. There were enough twists and gullys to ensure no visibility beyond my front forks and the small rocks and pebbles were winging off my gas tank like rifle shots. Then the road forked and I turned right. If I had raised my arms in crucifix position I could have touched the dense bramble and bushes to either side. By now I was doing little more than pushing the bike along with the aid of the engine. Until the crest of the hill. If it had gone up at seventy degrees it appeared to drop almost vertically.

I just sat there, on the crest, on top of my mud-covered monster, and cursed. Planning to greet my "What kind of man are you?" host with a solid kick in the ass.

Then I started down, leaving the bike in first gear, as I balanced with both feet and pumped the front hand brake until my forearm ached, trying for all I was worth not to drop the bike. By the time I came in sight of Tilley's farm I was a mud-splattered, nervous wreck. I hadn't gone above four miles an hour for the last two thousand yards. And there was Patrick Tilley, waiting at his gate, bearded, overalled, Wellington-booted, and laughing. "You took the wrong turn, that was the walking path! How did you get that bike down the walking path?"

Cancel the ass kick, I thought.

After I'd met Janine, Patrick's French wife, had a cup of coffee, and called home, "Yeah, I know it's three thirty in the afternoon and I left at five. . . . I got lost, what did you expect?" we rolled my bike towards the barn. I'd never seen it look so rough.

"Have you got any polish?" I asked. Obviously polishing had become a built-in reflex. No matter where, no matter how tired, how impolite, if the bike didn't shine, I polished.

Patrick seemed to understand. "I've even got some T-Cut," he replied. "It's a fine abrasive, a paste, it'll take the nicks from the gravel right out from the bottom paint of your tank." He set me up with a hose pipe, a bucket, a couple of cloths, the T-Cut, and a bottle of wax. I went to work and found a new dimension in polishing, the intimate polish after a long ride.

An hour later I summoned Patrick and Janine to come and view my motorcycle. New American iron set against the old wood of the Welsh barn, a dead cert for the "Readers' Riders" section of *Easyriders*.

After the viewing, I bathed, dressed, and joined the Tilleys
for dinner, so tired that my hands were trembling and my back
and shoulder muscles felt permanently frozen as if I had a
clothes hanger hidden under my shirt. Janine offered me a
glass of white wine. Thinking it might revive me I drank half
of it in one gulp. We sat down to eat.

"Patreeek saays you have wreetten a nowvel? . . . What is eeet
called?"

Another swallow of wine, and, for the life of me, I couldn't
remember the title of my own book. I sat staring at her.

"Theee boook?" Janine repeated in her sparkling accent.

Another swallow, still stalling for time, and I was one step
away from a coma.

"Ahhh?" I groaned.

Patrick filled in with the title and I guffawed like a half-wit.
By the end of the glass I was asleep at their table, the consum-
mate house guest.

The next day was better. It had rained during the night and
then cleared. The sun was shining and the air was fresh and
clean. It just plain felt good to breathe. I finally understood
why London was referred to as "the Smoke." Patrick and I
walked in the hills, tended his sheep, and devised a couple of
film plots. I only visited the Springer once, which was indicative
of my mental health: relaxed. That night at dinner I was the
life of the party.

Now that I was rested I couldn't wait to get back on the
road. There is something addictive about long-distance riding:
I planned to leave at six the next morning.

At five thirty there was a gentle knock on my door.

"Richard, I think you had better look out the window." It
was Patrick's voice, somewhat concerned.

I rolled back the quilt, slipped out of bed, and creaked
across the old floorboards to the curtained window. Outside
the visibility was about three feet; the rain was coming down in
sheets and we were almost submerged.

I walked to the door and confronted Patrick; he was wearing a long flannel nightshirt and a stocking cap like Rip van Winkle. "How long is this gonna last?"

"Could go on like this for days," he replied. Visions of spending an ice-locked winter in Snowdonia flooded my mind; I'd be waiting for the spring thaw to finally roll the sled out of the barn. "Or it could clear up by midday," Rip van Tilley pronounced.

On that note I returned to my bed, pulled the quilt over my head, and listened to the downpour. By breakfast time the rain had subsided to a steady trickle and I decided it was time to depart. Patrick walked beside the bike, herder's staff in hand, as far as the proper access road and waved me off.

By the time I'd made it to the highway the bike was once again covered in mud and the Red Barons needed windscreen wipers. So with one hand on the handlebars and one wiping the water from my goggles I headed for home. Gradually, somewhere past Betws-y-Coed, the rain let up.

A half-hour later the sun had appeared and the highway jukebox was belting them out. I was motoring. And continued to motor all the way back to the Smoke.

By now more and more Harleys were appearing on the English roads. There was also an upsurge in biker magazines—*American Iron, Outlaw Biker*—geared specifically for the Harley man. Warr's had increased their accessory range to include clothing: official Harley biker boots, T-shirts, and jackets, even a version of the Red Baron riding goggles, all marketed through Milwaukee; and, as in LA, although several years behind, there was a definite non-bike-owning clientele shopping for accessories only. Fashion magazines and television advertising featured Harley-Davidson motorcycles as backdrops for their products. The biker look had come to town.

On the road the look of the bikes was still relatively stock, and the majority of Harleys around were still the most affordable, the 883 Sportster. Most of the new generation of Harley riders were first-timers—at least first time on a Harley—and the Sportster was the most realistic tryout bike. Any time a Big Twin made an appearance heads inevitably turned and since there was (is) this obsession by Harley people to check over each other's bikes for even the slightest variation from the stock norm and I was more obsessive (call me "anal retentive") than most, any time I was down at Warr's and there was anything "special" parked out front I would examine it with all the care of a collector of vintage stamps.

It was during one of these examinations that I met my first riding buddy.

I was down beside a Heritage Softail, going over everything from its standard black and cream paint to its custom oil-pressure gauge and bank of rear brake lights. I had just spotted the five-thousand five hundred miles on the clock—giving instant credibility to the relatively new bike—when the owner strolled over, extended his hand, and said, "Hi, I'm Mark," then, pointing to my bike, which was parked beside his, "Is that your Springer?"

Mark was a bit shorter than me, a bit stockier, with a squarish face, short black hair and matching wraparound Raybans; he wore a red plaid scarf and proper motorcycle jacket (see Brando as the Wild One) over his T-shirt and jeans. I told him that yes, it was my Springer, and that my name was Richard. . . . There was a moment of silence which I bridged with, "You've done some miles," delivered in my best "bro on the road" voice.

"I just came back from Marbella," Mark answered.

"Spain?"

"Yes. The bike ran like a baby, all the way there and back then died at the car wash. . . . Jet spray, I soaked the ignition coil."

"You rode down there on your own?"

"Yes," Mark confirmed, throwing my solo journey to Snowdonia into the micro-league of "in the wind" adventures. "How do you find the Springer?"

"I love it," I answered.

"I'm thinking of ordering one," he went on.

"Instead of this?" I asked, looking down at the gleaming Heritage.

"As a second bike," he explained.

I was still getting used to the idea of "a second bike"—I suppose it was like having a second car, you know, just a little runabout—when Mark asked, "How does it handle with that front end?" The Heritage Softail has the hydraulic shock absorber system developed for the Hydra-Glide, rather than the Springer's original forks.

"Here," I said, handing him the keys, "take it around the block."

As I watched him slide into the saddle I realized I'd done it again. Every time someone I respected admired the bike— in this case it was Mark's mileage that humbled me—my reaction was to hand them the keys. I sensed that this brotherly reflex was inevitably going to lead to trouble and as I watched Mark (minus his helmet—very "in the wind") lean low into the corner at Waterstone I hoped this wouldn't be the time I heard squealing rubber and broken glass. Five minutes later I had begun my standard highway prayer (Please, God, let me hear the sound of my bike, soon. . . .). A minute from then I did as Mark glided in like he owned the Springer.

"Nice, very nice," he said, dismounting and handing me back my keys. "Do you fancy a bit of riding?"

Riding, riding, what did he mean . . . Marbella? "Yeah, sure," I answered, when, in fact, after Tilley's, I wasn't at all certain I was up to a cross-continental run.

"Here's my card, have you got a phone number?" Mark went on.

I took his card as I recited my home phone number. Another handshake and Mark saddled up and started his Heritage. Although it had the same two-into-one exhaust system as my Springer, it sounded much deeper and more impressive. (Could this have been a classic Freudian example of penis envy?) Then he strapped on his helmet—obviously he did wear one for rides over the distance of five miles—and slipped away. I use "slip" because he appeared incredibly at home on his bike and just seemed to slip out from the lineup of bikes, slide around the corner, and then slip in and out of the backup of cars on the King's Road.

I checked his business card once he was out of sight. He was the director of a fashion house; that made sense of the red scarf and authentic motorcycle jacket, sort of the Ralph Lauren of British biking.

Mark rang midweek. "Are you up for a little run to Southern Cycle on Saturday?"

I was on the spot; I mean, was I a biker or not?

"Sounds good to me," I answered, not knowing what "Southern Cycle" was or on which side of Marbella it was located.

"Where are you?" he asked.

"Kingston, right off the A3." I gave him directions to my house.

"Good, we'll come by at about noon. See you."

We'll? Who was "we"? I pondered. Did Mark lead a gang of fashion execs? Was this all part of a sales program for "authentic leathers," or was the business card merely a front for the Marbella Connection, a band of two-wheeled drug barons in need of a new mule?

I disappeared from the house to perform a major polish.

Saturday at quarter past twelve and my courtyard echoed with the sound of unmuffled Harley-Davidsons. Two to be exact.

I broke out the coffee mugs, and a quart of caffeine later Mark, Simon, and I headed for the back garden.

Age is a relative thing; I had assumed that because Mark was so assertive regarding the motorcycles and because of his position as director of a company that he was about my age, but in the late summer sun I could see that, in fact, both Mark and Simon, who had known each other since childhood, were a lot younger than me, at least ten years.

Simon, it turned out, had been a fashion photographer and was currently shopping for premises in which to open a restaurant.

I remembered that John Warr had told me that his average Harley buyer was between thirty and thirty-five years old; I figured that thirty was about it for Mark and Simon. They did, however, seem pretty sophisticated, particularly when it came to motorcycles. It turned out that like me both had started in their teens on motor scooters and the Softails were their first Harleys. They were as obsessed as I was. And where Mark's obsession was with the nuts, bolts, and performance of the bike, Simon, like me, had spent more than a few hours reading *Easyriders* and *In The Wind*. He was into biking style, the real bikers.

As soon as we found we had that in common the laughs started and by the end of our conversation I had begun to refer to Simon as Bro Si.

Finally it was time for that moment of truth: the ride.

Well, almost.

There was still the bike assessment. I rolled my squeaky-clean Springer out of the garage and lined it up beside the twin Heritages. It did appear to have the highest gloss, due to my late-night work in the garage, and, to me, it won hands down in the aesthetics category.

It was with a shade of arrogance that I asked, "Is there anything else you think it needs?"

"Well, for one, you should take all the eagles off it," Bro Si began. By now I had added a smaller eagle to the ignition cover, matching the big one on the Derby cover, and a couple more on the gas caps—I was "eagled up." "They're incredibly corny," he added.

I kept my grin in position as I deflated behind it.

"It would look great with a smaller saddle, really accentuate the size of the engine," Mark added, more tactful in tone than Bro Si.

"And replace those indicators with bullets," Si commanded, walking around the Springer and eyeing it from different angles.

Bullets? What the fuck were bullets? Suddenly I was very defensive. Nobody had ever done anything but fawn over my bike before, and now these young dudes were shredding it.

I turned toward their bikes and saw things for the first time, like the small bullet-shaped tail-lights and front indicators that replaced the larger, more cumbersome stock ones, the thicker handgrips and smaller round mirrors.

"And, Mark, you really ought to lose those landing lights, your bike is beginning to look like an aircraft-carrier," Bro Si continued, pointing at Mark's bank of tail-lights, six on each side.

"Where did you get that stuff?" I asked. At least my breach in biker taste was no longer the focus of attention.

"Southern Cycle," Mark answered, his eyes still directed at his landing lights—Bro Si's remark had obviously hit home— "they sell all the aftermarket parts." Aftermarket? I pondered the phrase. "That's where we're going. It's a custom shop in Great Bookham," Mark continued, mounting up, "about twenty miles from here, a nice little run."

Except for my brief encounter with Derek, this was the first time I'd ridden in a group. Admittedly, when compared to tales of sixty Harleys at sunset in the California desert, or the gathering of three thousand Hogs during Bike Week in Daytona, riding with two other Harleys was a pretty minimal group run, but for me it was the beginning. Even with three bikes together there was a terrific feeling of power. It probably had a lot to do with the combined roar of the engines and the fact that I could not only feel my own bike but see similar bikes ahead or to my side. There was also a physical linkup, like a team sport. I had to be aware of a group movement, a different type of timing and distance. The old zanshin or mental alertness principle, except with a group mind.

We formed a natural unit, like a wedge, Mark and Bro Si side by side and me behind, and as we headed down the A3 I noticed one big difference between riding solo and riding with

Mark and Simon: the pace. Whoever was out front, usually Mark, set the speed. When he went out and around to overtake a car or truck, Bro Si followed, and then me. There was no choice, either that or drop back and get lost. They both rode a lot faster than I was used to, so by the time we turned off on to the smaller, slower A243, I was relieved. Until the first roundabout. Then I was just plain humiliated. We all arrived at approximately the same time, doing about 40 MPH, and neither of them slowed down. I could hear the grating noise of metal against pavement and see the sparks fly from beneath Mark's bike as he leaned the Heritage so low into the curve that the edge of his foot rest made contact with the road.

Twenty years ago, during a period of oneness with the Norton, I had swung into a corner with one hand on the bars and the other adjusting my shades. I fell off. Badly enough to need a knee operation. Maybe I was permanently traumatized.

Any way you cut it, I obviously cornered like an old lady. And, unfortunately, there were about ten roundabouts between Kingston and Great Bookham.

For me the little run became a series of drag races, with my bike always starting a hundred yards behind. On top of that Mark and Bro Si were so relaxed and obviously having such a good time that each of them, at various times, rode with one arm while dangling the other to the side, stretched their backs, shifted in their saddles, or dragged their boot heels along the road (Mark's were cleated and sparks flew from beneath his feet), creating, to me, the distinct impression that they were completely at home on their bikes. I, on the other hand, former Zen master, was anything but at one with my motorcycle. Talk about self-conscious; I was having panic attacks every time we approached a roundabout, then suffering red-faced embarrassment as I caned the Springer in an effort to catch up on the straights. At one point I actually considered turning around and slinking off back to Kingston. But the idea of running into Mark and Bro Si again at Warr's or some future biker event made retreat too humiliating to undertake. So I continued, having one of the most uncomfortable rides of my biking career.

By the time we turned the last corner on to Eastwick Road and coasted into the narrow parking lot in front of Southern Cycles I was breathing so hard that it looked as if I had sprinted on foot from Kingston. It sure as hell felt as if I had.

"That was pleasant," Mark said. I lowered my kickstand and prayed my bike wouldn't let me down further by falling over.

Southern Cycles was a long, thin shop with £250,000 worth of parts and accessories filling its store rooms and hanging from its walls: racks of leathers in the corner, a chopped Harley in the middle of the floor, and everything from buck knives to biker's jewelry on display inside the glass-topped and -fronted show case. Plus a half-empty bottle of tequila sitting on the customer side of the cash register.

After-market parts: I remembered Mark's phrase. Now I saw what they were. S&S carburetors, drag pipes, modified engine heads, ape-hanger handlebars: they were the performance parts and custom accessories that had been created after the stock Harleys were manufactured and marketed, and supplied by companies other than Harley, companies that specialized in making the stock Hog look lower or move quicker. They often refined their performance parts on the racetrack, in direct competition with Milwaukee's attempts to do the same thing with their Screamin' Eagle product line. The difference between Southern Cycles and Warr's was that Warr's, like any authorized Harley dealer at that time, would have been "discouraged" by Milwaukee from dealing in any parts not made by Harley-Davidson. In other words, it would have severely jeopardized their situation with the factory if they had sold a competitor's products. Southern Cycles was not a Harley dealership and consequently catered to a different type of rider. Their clientele were more apt to arrive on a Shovelhead chopper than a new Springer. It was a proper custom shop, devoted to Harley-Davidson motorcycles. Not that a Kawasaki rider couldn't fit a set of drag pipes (short, straight, and without baffles) to his bike, or wear a pair of the leather trousers that were racked in the corner; it was just that the pipes, as well as the trousers, were styled for Harleys and Harley riders.

The staff, Mick, Nik, and Simon, made us feel right at home. Before long I was pulling saddles off the wall and taking them outside to hold up against my bike.

"Yeah, yeah, that looks excellent," Bro Si said as I placed a small seat on top of the stock Harley model. To me it looked like a bicycle saddle.

"Leave it there and come take a look at it," Mark suggested.

When I stepped away from the bike I saw exactly what they were talking about. The smaller saddle gave the Harley an entirely different look, accentuating the size of the engine and lowering the profile of the motorcycle. "Very in the wind," Bro Si commented.

That did it. I had to have the small saddle. The only problem was that it was not made of leather and I didn't like the idea of putting a vinyl-covered piece on the bike. Nik, the youngest of the three behind the counter, said he thought they could get it covered in leather.

They were terrific guys, long-haired, well inked and obviously in the wind for many seasons. Simon even stepped outside to have a look at our bikes and wave us off. It was a tricky moment for me, due to the awkward angle of their parking lot in relation to the adjoining road. I think I managed to stall only once while navigating the turn before taking off like the Lone Ranger.

The ride back was a repeat of the ride down. Two single-handed cruisers followed by a demon drag racer who seemed to be developing a technique for the vertical corner.

Once back at my place it was a quick cup of coffee before Mark and Bro Si took off. I watched them ride out of the courtyard and wondered if I'd be hearing from either of them about any runs in the future. I could imagine them passing comments to each other on their ride home: "Did you see the old guy try to take that last corner, I think he had both feet down for balance!"

* * *

Riding a motorcycle is a physical skill; it requires balance, coordination, timing, and practice. I've always been a better than average athlete so my weakness on the corners really bothered me. It was an ego thing. I decided to apply a bit of the martial attitude to the art of riding a motorcycle. Practice and perseverance.

Fifteen years before I had been a newcomer at the Japanese Karate Association's dojo in Philadelphia. Now I was a third-degree black belt at Sensei Enoeda's dojo in London. Practice and perseverance had formed a big part of my learning a martial art. If I had a weak technique, I practised it until it was at least functional. If I ignored it, it inevitably caught up with me, and sooner or later I would be standing in front of someone during kumite, or sparring practice, who would attack my weak side. All the talk about Zen and the non-ego status of the martial arts is, with the exception of a very few masters, just talk. There is always plenty of ego involved. Humility, yes, but also a lot of pride.

In other words, when I arrived at Tibbet's Corner, the big roundabout which linked Putney to Wimbledon and the A3 on my way to or from Soho, I would take the extra minutes and go around it twice, maybe three times, relaxing and allowing the bike to roll into the curve of the road.

Three weeks later my leather saddle was finished and Mark and I rode down to collect it. He slowed down a bit without Bro Si, and that, combined with my practice of the martial motorcycle arts, narrowed the gap between us to about thirty yards. I celebrated my first after-market purchase with a few slugs from the customers' tequila bottle, stowed the saddle and its attachment bracket in Mark's saddle-bags, narrowed the gap to twenty yards on the way home due to alcohol-induced relaxation, and took off for Warr's. John Warr groaned about installing parts that were not Harley, promised that the new saddle would induce hemorrhoids, and managed to weld the attachment bracket into position and bolt the saddle on.

Young John smirked and said, "Wait till you try and ride

it," but I thought the bike with its new saddle looked great, a potential centerfold for *Easyriders,* and Mark confirmed that it looked the business.

Before we left John asked if we were on for the Littlecote Bike Rally at Peter de Savary's place.

The only Peter de Savary I had ever heard of was a property tycoon, one of the richest men in Britain. I asked John if that was the same de Savary he was talking about.

"Yep. He loves Harleys, owns a few of them. . . . We're going to meet here at eight o'clock Saturday morning and ride up to Littlecote"—the name of his estate—"in Berkshire. Should be about twenty of us here and another few hundred bikes there. It lasts the weekend so either book a hotel in Hungerford or bring a sleeping bag."

I was already aware of a few bike shows and rallies. In England there were the Kent Custom show and the Bulldog Bash, and, of course, I had read about Daytona in Florida, and Sturgis, the annual bike meet in South Dakota with an attendance of three hundred thousand people. Thousands of Harleys, thousands of people, rock and roll bands, and every variation of the custom Harley that you are ever likely to see. But I had never been to one. This was mainly because in my first year on the road I didn't have anybody to go with and I had always envisioned these events as group events. But now I had Mark and Bro Si, and both of them were on for the Littlecote Run. Mark had organized a couple of rooms at the local hotel and we agreed to meet outside Warr's, Saturday morning at seven forty-five. Rain or shine. I was excited all week, checking long-range weather forecasts and popping in and out of the garage for detailed touch-ups to my last polish.

I was so excited that for the first time in my Harley-riding incarnation I began to think of leisure drugs, employing the old philosophy that if it's fun straight it's got to be twice as much fun high.

My own career in substance abuse dated way back to the '60s, when LSD was a sacrament and marijuana more common than Marlboro. As a psychology student I had taken Timothy

Leary's "turn on, tune in, and drop out" philosophy seriously enough to spend that winter living alone in Mexico, ingesting any plant life that the local natives felt kind enough to bring me. Add on my Mexican import business and the six years I'd fronted a rock 'n' roll band and I knew my way around a pipe, a joint, a cactus leaf, a mushroom, or a line.

But I'd been out of the drugs game for a long time, had no contacts, and things in general had changed. In America, I had read about Harley-mounted chapters of Alcoholics Anonymous, with mottos like "Ride clean, ride free." With so many people into health foods and substance-abuse clinics my nostalgic desires were out of date and out of fashion. So I racked my memory and came up with a herbal alternative.

Once, during a lean period in my rock 'n' roll days, I had read of an Amazonian plant named guarana that had the same basic chemical breakdown as cocaine; it was legal and available at the local health-food shop. I had hustled out of my hotel room, located a shop, and bought their entire stock. The instructions suggested one or two capsules of the dark powder every four hours to "sustain energy." The band and I each shovelled down a packet of twelve prior to our performance. By the second set everyone was reporting two distinct sensations: one was a high similar to coke, and the other was a blow-out of the lower gastrointestinal tract. The last set of our late-night gig featured a wind section that had never before been part of our four-piece band.

Guarana. . . . I wondered if they sold it in England. A call to my local Food for Thought and I was in luck. Half a dozen boxes of twelve tabs each, plus a flask of tequila, and I was ready for the Littlecote Rally.

Wet T-shirts and the Celebrity Tooter: Littlecote

*Littlecote took place on the last weekend in Septem-*ber; it was a sunny morning with frost on the ground and a chill in the air.

I dressed in jeans and a heavy cotton pullover but also wore long underwear, then my engineer boots and Irvin flying jacket, cramming my credit cards, toothbrush, and guarana in the pockets. My flask of tequila fitted nicely on the inside of the jacket, snug behind the zipper. I popped four tabs of guarana on my way to the garage then took a quick hit of tequila, for stability.

On the ride down to Warr's I felt nervous. Not the guarana; that, so far, wasn't doing anything; it was the idea of riding with such a large group of people. I hoped Mark and Bro Si were there when I arrived; I hated the idea of not knowing anybody.

When I rounded the corner at Waterstone Road the line-up of Harleys looked like something out of *Easyriders*. All had their back ends to the curb and their front tires aiming towards the King's Road. There seemed a lot more than twenty of them, with more bikes pulling in behind me. Most of the riders were men, with the exception of a few leather-clad women on Sportsters.

Mark and Bro Si were at the far end of the line.

I navigated into position, backing carefully until my rear tire stopped at the curb, then shut off my engine.

As my ears got used to the roar of incoming bikes my eyes scanned the crowd for anyone familiar. I saw John Warr, sitting on his FXR, a Big Twin that featured a rubber-mounted engine, making for a smoother ride than the solid-mounted Softails. John's bike was filthy from his recent trip to France: obviously he was not an advocate of the major polish. Beside him his two younger brothers, the twins William and Robert, were mounted on Sportsters, and there, at the far end of the line-up, was Johnnie Walker. God bless him, he looked the part: he had a Dennis Hopper fringed jacket, a sleeping bag rolled on the back of his bike, and a female companion. I dismounted and strolled over to say hello.

He told me he was totally in love with his Sportster; that was apparent from the considerable number of gold eagles which he had mounted on it. I was quick to note these things, being a former eagle man myself. I also noted that he had more miles on his clock than I did. Walker was doing some serious riding. His female companion turned out to be his daughter and I wondered whether Littlecote was going to be the wild biker rodeo of my in the wind fantasies or a family outing.

A few minutes later John Warr announced that there were coffee and doughnuts inside the shop (another frightening symptom of a civilized event), following which we would be pulling out.

Mark, Bro Si, and I decided to opt out of the doughnuts and fill our tanks up around the corner in preparation for the seventy-mile ride. I revealed my supply of guarana at the service pumps, breaking open a capsule and laying the powder out on my saddle as if it were the real thing. Then I bent down and snorted it up. It burned like battery acid.

I swallowed the next four capsules, then passed another dozen or so to Mark and Bro Si, followed by a liberal shot of tequila. It may have been a family weekend for some, but for me it was party time.

Once back at Warr's we joined at the tail end of the group.

John Warr, shouting above the revving engines, announced the route: straight down through Shepherd's Bush, around the roundabout, up on to the M4, and all the way to the A338; about sixty miles. We would turn off there for Hungerford. The only stop was to be at the Heston Service Station, about twenty miles west along the motorway. "Once we hit the motorway it's sixty miles an hour, keep it at sixty!"

I don't know if it was the guarana or the tequila or just the adrenalin from being in the midst of that much noise and horsepower, but the rush of riding down the road in line with twenty or so big motorcycles was unbelievable. Automobiles stopped to let us pass, people stared from the sidewalks and I had an ear to ear grin that felt permanent. I glanced over at Mark, who was on my left, and then up to Bro Si, who was a bike ahead of us, and they were both in a similar state.

Once we reached the motorway it got even better; the group formed a natural column about ten bikes long, and two wide, John Warr at the front. He held the speed to sixty and we took over the left lane of the M4. It was a tremendously relaxed feeling, as if I was encircled by a net of steel; it felt much less exposed than riding solo. My bike seemed to be drawn along in the slipstream of the bikes in front of it. I just stuck my feet out, resting my boot heels on the foot pegs, and cruised.

We pulled over at Heston, got off, and stretched, while a few of the group fueled up. If I had any doubts about being the least experienced rider of the group they were put to rest by a conversation I overheard at the gas pump. One of the leathered cavaliers was questioning John Warr about the mileage that his new Heritage was getting.

"Sixty-five miles is all I'm getting to a tank of gas, there's got to be something wrong with this bike," he complained.

John Warr stood watching as the guy unscrewed the right side gas cap, stuck the hose in, and filled till gas splashed over his paint work. Then he replaced the gas cap and slammed the petrol hose back into its holder, turning again toward John.

"Maybe when it comes in for the five-hundred-mile service you could check it out, there has got to be a leak in the system."

"Wait a second," John said, "is that the way you always fill the tank?"

The guy looked at John as if he didn't know what he was talking about. "Yes, that's the way I fill it."

John reached over and unscrewed the cap on the left side of the tank. "Well, the reason you've had to stop every sixty-five miles is that you're only filling half of it. . . . You've got to fill both sides."

The fellow turned a couple of shades of red, forced a laugh, mumbled something like, "Oh, luvvie, nobody ever mentioned that," and proceeded to splash gas over the other side of the tank.

Back on the road, our speed increased by about five miles an hour. This time there was a bit of lane shifting as we overtook some of the slower traffic.

The Springer is about seven and a half feet long and there were about ten bikes in line, all approximately the same length; so, leaving say three to five feet between each bike we had formed a line of between forty and fifty yards in length. When the lead bike passed a car or lorry the last riders in line didn't get to make their move for a minute or so. Since I was one of the last, it required a bit of judgment, and a greater degree of control and respect for group safety than I had exercised on previous rides. Obviously a few didn't reckon it was worth it, because at the halfway point several bikes suddenly accelerated, shooting ahead like bullets, not to be seen again until Littlecote. For me, the frustration of staying together was more than compensated for by the clear patches of highway that allowed me to stretch out and roar along with the pack.

Littlecote was two worlds welded into one. It had the baronial manor house and stately grounds right alongside a couple of hundred pitched tents, a string of tented dealers—everything from *Hog* magazine, a new British mag devoted to Harleys, to vintage parts—and a fully carpeted marquee with a drinks bar. Outside, on the grounds, there were barbecue pits with pigs roasting on spits and huge logs positioned in teepee formation waiting to be set alight.

It might have been the natural high of the event, or it might have actually been the guarana (although I have an in-built distrust of anything that legal), but Mark, Bro Si, and I were all sailing once we entered the grounds. Just to make sure we stayed in the wind I doled out another dozen tabs and a couple of slugs from the flask.

The major group event of the day was the ride-out, led by Peter de Savary, with lady companion on the back, wearing matching black-fringed leathers (tops and bottoms) and full-faced helmets astride a new black Electra-Glide Tourer: 765 pounds of panniers, fibreglass saddle-bags, and running lights, featuring cruise control and twenty watt-per-channel stereo system, coming in at just about twice the price of an 883. It was sort of the Honda Gold Wing of Harleys. But to each his own, and this was Mr. D.'s party, so he was entitled to swing a bit.

We lined up along the macadam drive; there must have been between three and five hundred Harleys—some dating right back to the '40s.

Then, on Mr. D.'s wave of the hand, we rode out along a carefully designated course about fifteen miles long, circumnavigating Littlecote. The police had been alerted and had set up barricades to stop the flow of other traffic and to allow the bikes a clear run. If riding with twenty bikes had been an experience, riding with a group that extended as far forward as I could see and as far again behind was unbelievable. Nothing but roaring steel, unstoppable.

Well, at least, for all but one. This particular gentleman, two up from me in line, dressed in the appropriate fringe, had one hand on the handlebars of his bike, the other wrapped round a bottle of Guiness, and managed, while travelling at approximately five miles an hour, to mount a grassy knoll and plough through a wooden fence, continuing into a farmer's field until his wheels became bogged down in the mud and the bike rolled slowly on to its side. I caught enough of his performance as I rode by to know he wasn't injured: in fact, he had managed to keep his bottle of beer in an upright position and was last seen sitting beside his partially buried motorcycle finishing the brew.

Once back at Littlecote, the day's events started, and Mark and I entered our bikes in the Best of Show competition. Bro Si modestly declined. It came down to a line-up of about a dozen motorcycles, most in various stages of eagle-mania, with a couple of proper customs thrown in to remind us of what it was actually about.

Ballots were cast with winners to be announced later in the evening, just before the wet T-shirt competition. Yes, that's right, Peter de Savary was in the wind, at least enough to know what the bros had come for—although a serious scan of the crowd, heavily male, led me to wonder just where the participants for the much-heralded event would be found.

Meantime, on the far hill, there was what resembled a biker's rodeo in progress. It started with a slow race, in which the riders "raced" over a distance of about one hundred yards and the last one to cross the line without dropping his feet for balance (or his bike) was the winner. Tough going to ride a Harley at three miles an hour for a hundred yards: I remembered my own experience down Patrick Tilley's walking path. . . . Then came the "tire dragging" event: huge truck tires tied behind the motorcycles as they navigated through an obstacle course of plastic cones. Also tough going, as I recalled my own figure-eights on a 125 cc Kawasaki in the CSM parking lot. And, finally, the jousting, two guys riding at each other with the idea that one knocks the other to the ground, like on horseback but with padded poles and on bikes. From where I was standing I couldn't tell whether they were actually stunt riders hired for the afternoon or fellow party-goers. We watched for a while then settled back behind one of the wooden teepees and whacked down some more guarana—by now I was trumpeting like the exhaust system of my Hog—and finished the flask of tequila. At this point a wandering biker shared a joint of Colombian the size of my forearm, and suddenly I was transported to levels formerly attained only in the Sonora Desert.

Darkness fell and a team of fire lighters lit the great log teepees. The flames soared into the starry sky, and the smell of old wood burning was everywhere; it was just one of those perfect nights. Sometime later the music began, a bluesy rock and roll that drifted up from the marquee and completed the psyche-delic sixties feel of the evening. Mark and Bro Si would have been about ten years old at the time. People started to drift toward the music and we decided to follow. God forbid we miss the wet T-shirt competition, let alone the winners in the Best in Show event. Inside, the marquee was full of people (ratio of men to women, ten to one), and a constant stream of bros in various forms of inebriation flowed along the red-carpeted floor to the drinks bar. I started on whiskey and water. Then back to the dancing area where a few couples were delivering varied renditions of dance steps big at the Filmore West during Janis Joplin's era.

My kind of music, my kind of steps; unfortunately no available partner. After a couple of covers from the Rolling Stones—"Satisfaction," "Heart of Stone"—I followed Bro Si and Mark back to our secluded spot behind a wooden teepee. However, the teepee was now burning, so we stood with a dozen or so of the others and stared at the flames.

I thought I recognized one of the circle of flame-starers; not someone I knew directly but a TV personality, an actor in a popular cop drama. It's funny with celebrity faces; they become so familiar that you assume you know them, when in fact you only know the character they play. I became fixated by this guy, dressed head to toe in new black leathers, with a pair of spurred cowboy boots on for added effect. He was apparently on his own and had a strange glint in his eyes, or more a glaze. After a few minutes of not too subtle observation I decided that however stoned I was, the celebrity bro was that times five.

He stayed another couple of minutes then weaved his way

over towards the tent section of the field, stopping by a small gnarled leafless oak tree. Propping himself up, he reached into the pocket of his leathers and came out with something that I couldn't identify—until he lifted his hand to his nose and had a snort. Then another. The celebrity bro was two steps ahead of my guarana when it came to being in the wind. After he tooted he wandered to the other side of the tree and appeared to urinate. Then he made his way back towards us and the flames.

I was still studying the celebrity bro, a.k.a. the celebrity tooter, when I was grabbed from behind in a two-armed bear hug. . . . Powered by the magic of the Amazon and made loose by a combination of tequila and whiskey I slipped the grip and spun round to face my opponent. None other than Fred Warr, wife by his side, up to Littlecote for the entertainment.

Fred, John, the twins, Johnnie Walker, me, Bro Si, Mark, the celebrity tooter; the evening was heating up. Confirming it came a roar from our side of the marquee and we stared in the direction of the applause. Lo and behold, there was a stark naked bro, skidding figure-eights in the dirt outside the marquee, handling his Hog with incredible grace and dexterity. In another second he was heading for the red carpet, disappearing inside the marquee. The next sound we heard was a round of applause from the bar section, then a revving engine as the naked bro skidded out of the marquee, a single security guard chasing him on foot, back on to the grounds and away down the macadam drive, leaving the security guard panting on the pavement.

It must have all been an inspiration for the celebrity tooter because within moments he was *en route* back to the gnarled oak. Silhouetted against the full moon he banged back a couple more toots then stood, gazing majestically at the far-away flames. He was still in toot position when the announcement came that it was wet T-shirt time.

Mark, Bro Si, and I wobbled towards him, *en route* to the marquee. The celebrity tooter sort of motioned with his hand as we walked by, a subtle gesture that neither Mark nor Bro Si saw. But by now, being obsessed with who he was and what he was doing, I stopped. He motioned again, this time with a crooked yellow smile—sometimes capped teeth look luminescent beneath a full moon.

I joined him at the gnarled oak.

No words were spoken, just the silent offer of a tiny silver spoon containing the real thing.

I felt honored and performed in a fashion developed through many years in recording studios. Then, leaving him leaning against the tree, I proceeded to the marquee.

And there they were. I don't know where they came from, but they were there. The babes. About six of them, blue-jeaned and T-shirted.

And also there, in the middle of them, was Peter de Savary, still leathered but without the full-face, which left a trimmed beard and a pair of glasses. He tried to announce the winners of the Best of Show competition but was having a spot of microphone trouble. A couple of crashes and a lot of ear-shattering feedback later, I realized that neither Mark nor I had won. The guys that actually jumped up on to the stage to get their trophies had obviously done more to modify their bikes than complete a "major polish" the night before the rally. . . .

That out of the way, Mr. D. called our attention to the six busty beauties on stage. Amidst catcalls and drum rolls they strutted around like potential champs. And I've got to hand it to them for courage; in front of a few hundred intoxicated cowboys they looked right at home. With the exception of one, a reticent brunette who had possibly been propelled into the spotlight by her old man; he was cheering from the footlights.

Peter the D. left the stage marginally ahead of the buckets of water which were then thrown at the babes, soaking their T-shirts and revealing the goods, in various stages of uplift and sag. Then the band kicked into overdrive and they danced while the front man held his hand over each of their heads, signalling for applause. It was a tough call. So the competition escalated, one particularly sassy redhead whipping off her T-shirt to reveal milky-white orbs. Another followed, and then they were all taking it off as the crowd went wild. All except for the reticent brunette; she was still in her T-shirt. So the redhead tried to help her disrobe, catching a nice left hook in the process. A moment later the redhead and the reticent brunette were rolling around the stage in mortal combat. The band played on.

The front man, at least a head shorter than any of the contestants, finally separated them, and after a last right cross the reticent brunette retired in tears from the competition, leaving the redhead shouting abuse and, to cement her position as the champ, stripping out of her jeans and knickers. Not to be outdone the remaining four did the same, until they were all stark naked. . . .

At this point I slipped outside for a breath of air and noticed that a small queue had formed at the gnarled oak, and not for autographs. The celebrity tooter was dispensing his stash with devil-may-care abandon. Suddenly the celluloid cop was the hero of Littlecote.

Back inside the marquee, the winner of the wet T-shirt competition—not the redhead—was receiving her trophy. A glorious moment. . . . Applause followed by a further announcement: would all contestants for the wet underpants competition please report to the back of the stage. . . .

At this point I received a strong nudge from Bro Si. "I don't think I can handle this." Mark was already out the door. We followed. By now the queue at the gnarled oak was down to just a few die-hards so I suggested we round the evening off with a visit. By the time we got there the celebrity tooter was clean out of toot. I slipped him a few tabs of guarana (he downed them without even asking what they were) then asked if he could make it home.

"Got a tent, man, a tent," he mumbled as he sank down into a squatting position, catching the seat of his pants on his spurs.

His eyes remained open, and he continued to breathe, but there was no apparent consciousness. I bent down and looked into his eyes. They were like mirrors, reflecting the dying flames of the teepee on the hill.

"Are you going to be all right?" I asked, a little shaky myself.

"Got a tent, man, got a tent," he repeated, reminding me that I didn't have a tent and still had to make the ride back to the hotel.

I think one of the most depressing places in the world is a campsite at a biker's rally in the cold and rain the morning after the party ends. Littlecote resembled a battlefield, although most of the corpses were walking. Even Johnnie Walker, though miraculously freshly shaved, looked somehow decrepit, rolling his sleeping bag and scowling at the sky. And then there was the celebrity tooter, literally in boot hill. Only the spurs of his pointed Tony Lama's were stretched out beyond the flap of his single-man tent. And the tent itself was no more than a stone's throw from the gnarled oak, a testimonial to his amazing foresight. We cruised the grounds once—never finding out who won the wet underpants competition—and hit the road.

The ride home had only a small percentage of highway heaven, like about two hundred yards when the sun peeped out and the road dried up, quickly replaced by a chilled drizzle and some slick macadam, and I felt like I was dying for the next three days, as a gastrointestinal flurry accompanied a general depression. It took till Thursday to limp back into the garage and begin the post-rally polish. And by then I had the urge to do it all again.

I did try to do it all again, a few months later, when it was time for the Pied Bull Boxing Day Run.

Americans have great trouble with the concept of Boxing Day—I think it's the name—and the fact that England seems to close for three weeks between the 20th of December and the 7th of January. My parents had come over for a visit, and the added knowledge that her forty-two-year-old was headed out of town on his motorcycle caused my mother great consternation. She couldn't quite believe that I was serious about getting up at seven, rain, snow, or shine, to be part of the Boxing Day Run. She kept asking me, "Are you in some sort of motorcycle gang or something?"

"No, Mom, not at all. Just a bunch of us who like to ride together," I answered. At this point my father winked at me, indicating that he was aware there would be loose women involved. It was the same knowing look that he used to give me when I had returned in the family car, after an evening with my girlfriend, at the drive-in movies. Except then I was seventeen.

The run to the Pied Bull was an annual affair, hosted by the Harley Club of Great Britain, and riders from all over the south would be there. It was the first I'd heard of either.

Boxing Day was a particularly dull morning, overcast and cold. By this time I had made a trip to Lewis Leathers and had picked up a pair of riding pants: it was like walking around in tubes of corrugated iron. Just to be certain I was warm enough, I pulled on a pair of long johns before getting into the corrugated tubes, then slipped into a thermal T-shirt covered by two sweatshirts, and over all this my Irvin flying jacket. By then I looked like the Michelin man, and my walk, always a touch bandy-legged and enhanced by the bulk and stiffness of the various fabrics, now took on arthritic overtones.

Maybe there were a few mothers in town, or a few fewer free-thinking wives than my own, or maybe it was just because it was the day after Christmas and just plain cold as hell but the turnout at Warr's was minimal: six or eight of us. Coffee and mince pies and a couple of whams from my flask, this time Glenfiddich, and we set off.

Whether it was the cold, or the heavy gray sky, or the fact that a large part of the ride was through built-up areas of city, I don't know, but it never quite felt right. By the time we hit the motorway the group was split, my hands were freezing, my corrugated legs felt locked to my tank, and Mark and I were exchanging "What the fuck are we doing here?" glances.

At times like these I tend to get furious with whoever is ahead of me, so I was blaming my discomfort on John "You've got to keep up" Warr. In fact it wasn't John's fault. There had

been so many traffic lights on our ten-mile cross-town journey
to the motorway that it was inevitable that somebody was going
to get caught as the line of bikes moved forward. The correct
procedure to follow in this circumstance is for the lead riders
to pull over and allow the riders who are stuck at the light
to catch up. By the thirtieth light the correct procedure was
impossible if anyone wanted to get to the Pied Bull before New
Year's Eve: by the fiftieth light it was every man for himself.
Fortunately, the back four (Mark and I included) could just
about see the front four when they hit the motorway, so at least
we knew which direction to take. After that the route to Brand's
Hatch, then to Farningham, was signposted.

There was a substantial turnout at the Pied Bull, maybe a
hundred motorcycles, and the lager flowed. Now I haven't got
anything against standing around in a parking lot on a freezing
day discussing the nature of camshafts and single-spark igni-
tions—and there were some good people at the Pied Bull and
a few laughs—but after a couple more gulps of my Glenfiddich
I began to wonder what was happening at home. Like was dinner
ready . . . ? I gave Mark the nod and we silently slithered out of
the crowd and on to our bikes.

As we split up back at Warr's, with me waxing on philosophi-
cally about really only enjoying the riding part of the runs, "Just
give me a good long ride, so I can get my feet up and relax,"
Mark popped the million-dollar question. "Marbella's a good
long ride. Are you up for that?"

"When, now, in the middle of winter?"

"No, no. Late spring, early summer. You want a ride, that's
a ride; the only thing you think about when you wake up in the
morning is your bike and the road."

"Yeah, I'm up for that, sure," I answered, figuring by spring
I'd have a thousand excuses for not going, just in case.

"Five-star hotels all the way," Mark added.

We wished each other a Happy New Year and took off for
our respective mince pies. I couldn't get Mark's Marbella pitch
out of my mind. "Five star all the way."

Five star all the way. . . . It provoked images of French châteaux and Spanish castles, not to mention the jet-setting stringed-bikini brigade (nubile and female), all paying homage to the (well-preserved) gentleman on his chromed horse.

Yes, five star all the way, that could be my kind of ride. . . .

Hog Fever, Level II: The Next Incarnation

Winter rolled in, and the bike was pretty well restricted to rolling to and from Soho. As a result of this restriction I experienced an over-activity in the fantasy section of my brain, and magazine intake increased. By now I was a subscriber to *Hog*, although my tastes still ran to *Easyriders* and *In The Wind*, and a new mag, *Outlaw Biker*, which had appeared on the shelf of my local newsagent. *Outlaw Biker* had the same basic format as *In The Wind* but, coming from New York City instead of originating in California, it covered the East Coast bike scene: parties in Boston and runs to Daytona, Florida.

Since the weather on the east coast of America is not dissimilar to the weather in England—a bit colder but less wet—it featured a lot of articles about winter rebuilds, when bikers took their rides off the road between November and April and rebuilt the engines or customized the entire motorcycle, giving it a complete reincarnation for the next riding season.

By now I had seen enough Harley-Davidsons, both in the flesh and in the magazines, to know that an after-market saddle and bullet tail-lights (John Warr, under duress, had put them on for me) did not make a custom motorcycle. Mine was still, basically, stock.

So, gradually, level II of the Fever kicked in.

Level II is a serious condition: it involves an absolute hatred for the look of your motorcycle and a general dismissal of anyone riding a stock bike. Anyone riding a stock Harley "doesn't know." Doesn't know that the whole idea of buying a Harley is to take it apart and change things. To personalize it, to give it some identity, make it unique. Stock bikes are boring. And I sure as hell was bored with mine. I wanted something different, something sleeker and faster. A dangerous Hog.

The magnifying glass came back out as I studied the most minute details of "Readers' Rides." After several hours of this and a few more talking to Dave, Fred, and John Warr, I decided that simply replacing my stock carburetor and camshaft with Screamin' Eagle performance parts wasn't going to make it.

"If you want that motorcycle to really fly, you could fit on a set of Branch heads," John finally said.

"Yeah, that sounds good," I agreed. "What are they?"

"Heads are the top of the engine, the place where the flow of gas meets the flow of air; the gas and air get fed by the carburetor through the intake valve of the head, where they combust and drive the pistons then the carbon dioxide exits via the outlet valve and through the exhaust pipes."

"Ten-four," I answered, borrowing one of Dave's lines. "So how come I need Branch heads?"

"Well, you said you wanted the bike to shift. Jerry Branch is a genius; he's been porting and polishing heads for the Harley racing team for years."

At this point John grabbed a set of heads off his work bench. Now at least I could see what he was talking about.

"You see these chambers?"

I looked inside the metal blocks and saw a couple of tunnel-like gullies.

"That's the intake valve and the outlet valve; you see how rough they are?"

I looked inside; they appeared to be no more and no less than cut grooves of unpolished metal.

"What he does is smooth them down in some areas then build them up by adding metal in others," John explained.

"Couldn't you do that?" I asked.

"Yeah, I could, but Jerry Branch is a real master; he knows just how much to smooth down and take away and just how much to add in. If you get it wrong they aren't as efficient as stock pieces."

Stock; it came out like a curse.

"I'd better have some Branch heads, then," I said, naturally not asking about the price. A major symptom of all levels of the Fever is that the victim *never* lets money stand in the way of fulfilment.

"It's going to take a couple of months to get them in," John added.

Better still, I thought; in a couple of months I may have even cleared the overdraft on my stock Springer.

"No problem, I'll wait on the carb and cam and you can do all the work at one time," I answered.

Three weeks later I had an unexpected lucky break. I received a telephone call from Los Angeles; an American television company was interested in turning my first two fantasy novels into a miniseries, and I was slated for the lead role.

By the time I put the phone down I was already a multimillionaire and was mentally retracing the route from West Hollywood to Bartels' in Culver City.

There was a problem, however. The character I was to play had long flowing blond hair, the same hair that I had in the stills taken at Pinewood Studios several years back to help sell the idea as a movie for Goldcrest. A close inspection in the bathroom mirror suggested I had been waiting a long time to get discovered. "Nothing a few sun-bed treatments and a bit of stringent dieting couldn't disguise," I told myself. But the hair; I'd just had it cut short. Luckily my hairdresser, the wondrous

Felicity, was also an expert with hair extensions, and I decided to fool 'em in LA—they'd been foolin' me for years—and had her give me a set that looked like the mane of a horse.

Two days before flight time I washed them and ended up resembling an Afghan carpet. A panic call to Felicity, who told me to pick up some silicon spray at Extensions in Kensington. It was a decent day, weatherwise, so I decided to take the bike.

Coincidentally, a friend had come for a visit and brought with him a good-sized lump of hashish. Apart from Littlecote I hadn't smoked anything for about a decade and why, in the midst of a theatrical crisis, I started in on the lump, I'll never know. Fifteen minutes after the embers had died in the pipe I was mounted on the Harley with my three-foot toupee crunched beneath my helmet.

My friend was riding beside me in his bullet-fast BMW. In fact he seemed to be racing me up the A3.

I freaked out at seventy miles an hour.

The BMW was about two feet from my right leg and a white Ford van was equidistant to my left. It began with feeling totally exposed and vulnerable and escalated quickly to the certain knowledge that there was *no way* that my two-wheeled vehicle could balance in an upright position. It defied the laws of nature. The more I concentrated on my own instability the less stable I felt. The bike felt like it was wobbling (I envisioned a loose wheel) and I was convinced the back tire was going flat. I slowed down. By the time I reached thirty I had regressed, psychologically, to the level of a six-year-old the first time he ventures down the family drive on a pedal cycle without the aid of his stabilizers.

I managed to pull on to the shoulder of the road and cut the engine. I sat there and allowed the weight of my extraordinary ego to cave in my mind.

Here I was. A middle-aged man dressed head to toe in black leather, pumped up on barbells and honed down on Joe Weider metabolic boosters, sporting an artificial sun tan and riding a 600 lb. motorcycle that he hadn't fully paid for, with a three-foot mane of fake hair clumped beneath a half-face helmet, preparing to fly off to LA and pretend he was young, virile, and twenty-eight years old. That is, if he could ever get his head straight enough to accept the enormous leap of faith required to believe that a vehicle the size of his soon-to-be-customized Harley-Davidson could actually balance on two wheels.

I was a total fraud. . . .

On top of which I was stuck on the hard shoulder of the A3, suffering something between a nervous breakdown and a midlife crisis.

"Something wrong with the bike?" It was the resonant voice of Sterling Moss in his BMW. He'd circled the roundabout and returned to the scene of the crime. Luckily he couldn't see my eyes through the dark lenses of my Raybans. I don't think I was actually crying but I was definitely close.

"Yeah, the gas shut-off is stuck," I lied without quavering, "it's got enough to get me home."

"Do you want me to follow you?" he asked.

"No, I'm fine."

I waited till he pulled away, then I waited some more, vowing never to touch the deadly smoke again. Ten minutes later I had come down . . . way down. After that I forced myself to continue my journey to town and pick up the silicon spray, wiser through insight.

This time the television company took care of my air fare, and for once I found myself in the first class section of the aircraft.

When I arrived in the Land of Dreams I was met by a limousine and deposited in a hotel that had peaked in the seventies and now was the meeting place for moguls on their third hair weave. Being on my first, I fitted right in, my confidence given an added boost by the fact that I was about twenty years younger than most of the other patrons.

Three days later, we had had fifteen hours of script meetings and decided that my character should begin as an undercover cop who had infiltrated a drug-dealing motorcycle club (the Tegne Fantasy adventure would be worked in as his hallucination after a head injury); the TV company's art department had airbrushed a portrait of me: looming motorcycle, ape-hanger handlebars, chiselled face, piercing eyes, and long hair in the wind. I was ready for a trip to Culver City.

I tied my extensions back, slipped into a pair of black shades—to avoid recognition by "partner" Rick Bartels—and drove to the Mecca of the Hollywood biker.

Bartels' had enlarged their stock; their showroom was crowded with custom bikes and there were twice as many handle-bars, saddles, saddle-bags, and exhaust systems lining their walls. In the accessories department there were hundreds of Harley T-shirts, racks of studded riding chaps, Marlboro-man style, and even a section of leather jackets for the child passenger. Accessories had become a family affair.

This time I was ready to buy.

And I did. I started with drag handlebars (straight, low, and about a foot and a half long from end to end) for $29.99 and extra-thick hand grips for an additional $19.99, then moved into larger purchases. A mini-tachometer (to count the engine revs from those Branch heads) for $110.00 and a crossover exhaust system (ordered from the wall sample but manufactured to order) that set me back $1,200. When I'd added to that a full range of T-shirts to dispense as souvenirs of my travels and a new leather jacket, I had dropped the better part of $2,000, paid for on my Access card and easily covered, I figured, by my writing fee for the synopsis I had already delivered to the television company.

A couple of things had changed, or evolved, in the LA bike scene since my last visit.

The most noticeable was the sheer bulk of Harley-Davidsons on the roads. The asshole to Hog ratio had decreased to one to three and I would see the same guy pull into Sunset Plaza on two consecutive days, once on a Heritage, the next on a Sportster. I even overheard the tail end of a conversation that went, "Yeah, I was thinking of a GT Cobra but it's much cooler to own a vintage Harley. . . . Not that I'd ever have one as my main Harley." In the land of excess the only way to travel was by fleet. And down on Sunset, between Sunset Tattoo and the famous celeb night club, Roxbury's, Thunder Road had opened.

Thunder Road was a boutique-style bike shop with everything from Indians to chopped Shovelheads. It was located for and geared to appeal to the new breed of biker, the person with the kind of money necessary to drop twenty to forty thousand dollars on a Harley-Davidson. The fellow that owned the place was a big Germanic biker named Max; he had the company insignia, the Native American symbol for the thunderbird, tattooed on his right shoulder.

I also noticed people were riding around with a new patch sewn on the back of their jackets. Not an outlaw patch but a gold and white American eagle gripping a gold wheel between its taloned claws. On the left side of the wheel was an H, on the right a G, spelling HOG, and beneath HOG, a banner with the words Harley Owners Group. I saw quite a few of these patches on all types of riders, from the squeaky-clean business executive on his day off to the more seasoned highway vets on their Full-Dressers, but I just couldn't quite figure out what type of club it was and what, if any, criteria there were for membership.

One week later everyone I had been doing business with was fired from the TV company and my project was cancelled.

"Howdy, Partner!"

Three weeks later and no package from Culver City.
Now the misery really began. I was dealing with partner Rick
by long-distance telephone.

"Yeah, we've been having a little trouble with our supplier,
another few days ought to cover it," he said with his usual Wild
West twang.

Another week went by and we had the same exchange.

A month later and there was a ray of hope: "Almost ready;
we're having a little problem with our chromer."

"Are you saying that the pipes have been made?" I asked
cautiously.

"Yeah, they came in a couple of days ago, all they need is
to be chromed and polished."

I let go and waited for the Post Office to deliver. By now I
had even taken to drawing my own renditions of what my new
monster bike would look like, and my main reason for visiting
the garage was to stand there and try to imagine how the new
parts would make the bike look and perform.

A couple more weeks and John Warr phoned to announce
the arrival of the Branch heads, "works of art."

I didn't want to get the bike partly done; I wanted the whole

Hog. I promised John I'd ring in the morning with a delivery date on the exhaust system. I waited till six o'clock English time, which made it ten o'clock in the morning in the Land of Dreams, and made the call.

I could now recognize my partner's voice halfway through the word "Bar-tel's," *Barr* like he was saying *grizzly barr* or something equally authentic. The voice I got was female.

"May I speak to Rick, please." I asked.

"I'm sorry, Rick is no longer with us," the feminine voice replied.

"What . . . ?"

"Rick is no longer with us." She repeated it as if partner Rick had been excommunicated by the Roman Catholic Church.

"Well, he's been taking care of an order for me, a cross-over exhaust system; I've already paid for it and I want to make sure it's been sent. I'm in London, England."

"Uh-huh. Well, I don't remember anything going to London. Hold on I'll transfer you to our parts manager."

A few minutes later and the cost of another set of drag bars in phone time, I got the parts manager.

"No, I haven't shipped anything to London; I can't even remember a crossover system going out on order. Let me go through Rick's desk, his paperwork's in a real mess. Give me a phone number, I'll get back to you."

A day and several resolutions to pay a hit man (gold card overdraft, of course) to fly out to California and track down my former partner later, I received the return call.

"Ah, Richard, to be perfectly honest"—something which may not actually be possible in the Land of Dreams—"I can't find any record of a cross-over system or a check from you to us."

That did it. . . . I went berserk.

"Hold on, hold on, Richard, I'm sure there's been a misunderstanding. I'm sure you gave us a check, let me have a look around the stock room for the exhaust pipes, give me a few minutes and I'll call you back."

A few minutes later . . . "Ah, Richard, we do have a crossover system here, it's actually got somebody else's name on it"—Robert Plant's?—"but I'm going to ship it to you anyway, now what was the rest of that stuff you ordered?"

So I finally got my after-market parts, in a brown cardboard box big enough to hold a Sportster.

I couldn't resist opening it.

Then I couldn't resist pulling everything out and lining it up on the floor. Then I couldn't resist hauling the pipes out to the back garden, where I emptied two cans of heat-resistant black spray paint down them because Simon down at Southern Cycle had told me that the heat spray would keep them from blueing, a condition that occurs when the chrome is discolored by the heat which turns it a metallic blue. Then I polished them before rewrapping them in a newspaper and carting them down to Warr's in the back of my Nissan Patrol like the Crown Jewels.

I knew John would be difficult regarding the non-Harley parts, but I hadn't expected him to go on strike.

"Look at those things, do you really expect me to put those things on your bike?"

"Come on, man, I've gone through hell to get them over here; you've got to put 'em on."

"They're not Harley parts; they're junk." He was heartless.

"John, they're specially made for my bike."

"Where? In Singapore?"

Silence.

He gagged and groaned and actually kicked one of the pipes—I suppose to make sure it was dead—then said to call him in five days. I genuflected and left for home, visions of "Readers' Rides" dancing in my head.

Waiting for the new creation is actually more demanding than waiting for a new bike to arrive. You know what a new bike is going to look like; you've usually seen an identical model to the one you've ordered and, give or take a different color scheme or a strategically placed eagle, yours is going to look more or less the same. But a custom ride, and one that is guaranteed to fly, is something else again.

I made a phone call to make sure that work was in progress. Dave was on form, saying that he had seen my bike only a few minutes ago and that it was looking "mean" but in the background I heard John bellow something about the way the "junk" pipes had not been made to fit a proper Harley, then a metallic crash which I interpreted as another kick to the chrome.

Friday came, the day of collection; I was rip-roaring to get to the bike. My wife was out of town, which suited me fine, since that would allow me the appropriate time in the garage—all day and half of the night—to polish and view.

I arrived at Waterstone Road like an expectant father, craning my neck to get a peek at the bike from the back window of the cab: and there it was. . . . Parked beside a lineup of new stock arrivals right in front of the shop.

It was magnificent. Low and mean by virtue of the flat drag bars, with the twin pipes jutting out of either side like missiles on a fighter plane. John had discarded the slash-cut mufflers that I had supplied and added his own touch, a set of "shorties," short metal cylinders that looked like firecrackers. I loved them.

I was still staring out of the window when the minicab driver asked, "With all the new Japanese technology, what makes you want to ride one of those?" There's a Harley T-shirt with the slogan on it *If you've got to ask* why? *There's no point in explaining,* so I didn't try. Besides I couldn't get to the bike fast enough.

I performed a relatively major viewing right there on the sidewalk: back, front, and sides. I crouched down, looking through the gap between the joined index finger and thumb postures—like looking through the eye of a camera, an LA technique that I had acquired during location scouts for my portfolio of unmade films—for good measure.

Oh yeah, oh yeah, oh yeah, this baby could go right into the "Readers' Rides" section of *Easyriders*, no problem.

I couldn't wait to get on it.

John was behind the counter when I sprinted into the shop. "You're going to have to learn to ride that bike all over again. It really shifts. . . ." Oh yeah, oh yeah, oh yeah . . . "Now, here's the bad news," he said, then handed me the bill.

I stared at the figures, took a deep intake of breath, and reached for the American Express check-book like a holstered .45.

£2,828, plus VAT. My stomach did a few flips before settling like a punctured inner tube.

Oh man, I've done it, I've actually lost it completely this time. What an asshole, I thought.

John noticed my hesitation.

"I warned you that it was going to be a lot of work, the Branch heads alone cost nearly a grand," he explained.

I must have appeared on the verge of a coronary.

"Look, if you want, you can pay by installment," John added.

I wrote out the check for the full amount and followed John out to the motorcycle. It was still magnificent, but now in the sense of a cosmic phenomenon, like a shining black hole that sucks up any money that drifts into its orbit.

It took me as long as it takes to start the motor to forget my financial plight. It sounded great, low and throaty and with a different kind of exhaust beat than a stock engine.

"You can tell it's had work," John confirmed, "I had it going a hundred and ten when I took it for the test ride."

I climbed into the saddle.

"Be careful with it, it's very quick, particularly after three thousand revs," he continued.

The bit about the revs didn't mean much, but the continual warnings about the bike's quickness made me feel like I was riding a thoroughbred. I sat there, afraid that even a slight twist of the throttle would result in a wheel-standing crash through Warr's plate-glass window.

"Well, enjoy it," John said, waving me off.

I held the clutch in and literally rolled away, coasting around the corner, giving it just enough throttle to make it to the King's Road. Once on the straights I was tentative, until, finally, I eased the throttle open. . . . And then couldn't understand what the hell John had been talking about. I'd expected to fly off the saddle. I didn't. In fact, down the King's Road, the Springer felt like it had always felt, maybe just a little more choppy in first gear.

I hit the A3 and opened it up a bit more, watching the rev counter reach three thousand. Now something was definitely happening, the Springer felt like it was just coming to life. Another twist of the throttle and I flew backwards, ending up with my ass on the rear fender. It did fly. It really did. And it roared; I owned a monster.

Back in the garage I performed the polish to end all polishes, took it back out again, charged up and down the A3, came home, repolished, phoned Mark, phoned Bro Si, announced that I had the fastest sled in Britain, and then took off again down the A3.

I spent most of the next twenty-four hours either on the bike, polishing the bike, or simply looking at the bike.

The minute my wife walked through the door of the house I grabbed her by the arm and dragged her out to the garage. "It's beautiful, absolutely beautiful," she said. She's never let me down. If she likes something she says it, if she doesn't she says it. Very simple. And she has impeccable taste. So "beautiful" it was.

Mark arrived Saturday afternoon. I put him in the saddle and forced him to the highway. He returned fifteen minutes later grinning like a kid.

"I blew off a Kawasaki, the guy never expected it, pulled up next to him at a light, revved it and took off. A hundred and ten miles an hour. I could hear him trying to catch up all the way to the roundabout."

My wife's endorsement for aesthetics coupled with Mark's endorsement for speed completely vindicated my use of the secret overdraft. I had a paranoid flash: a headline in the *News of the World*, HUSBAND DIES LEAVING WIFE ONE MILLION POUNDS IN DEBT DUE TO OBSESSION WITH COSMIC HOG; but, basically, I was a free man.

If I had enjoyed my Springer before, I was absolutely crazy about it after John Warr's tuneup. I wasn't a particularly fast rider—especially when it came to cornering—but there was just something about every now and again opening the bike up that made the time, the money, and the potential coronary all worthwhile.

Five Star All the Way

It was over coffee at the Dôme—one-time meeting place for Harley posers—that Mark reminded me of our run to Marbella. I had instant visions of myself being several towns behind by the time he and Bro Si hit the Spanish coast—how many depending on the number of roundabouts or substantial bends in the road there were between here and there—and I figured I should probably get a mobile phone in order to stay in contact with my riding companions. "Hello, Mark; I've just come out of the south side of the Pirineos, it's raining here, what's the weather like in Barcelona?"

"It will be five star all the way," he reminded me.

I swallowed hard and said: "Absolutely."

I told my wife that evening, suggesting that we rent a flat there for a week and make a holiday out of it. She could fly down, meet me there, and then fly home. Finding a place was easy; Mark owned an apartment in a block of luxury condominiums. He set it up, I paid a deposit, and we were committed.

The run was scheduled for the last week in June. Mark had allotted five days for the seventeen hundred miles and he, being a born executive, was busy packing his gear and getting a windscreen installed on his bike—"Cuts down on wind, bugs, and rain, if we're unlucky."

I, on the other hand, a born optimist, was concentrating on how to carry nothing; I didn't want to affect the lean and mean lines of my motorcycle and certainly would never have considered a windscreen. Not even a set of saddlebags. I would wear one shirt, my leather jacket, leather pants, and engineer boots; I'd carry a few pairs of socks stuffed down the left side of my pants, sort of a Mick Jagger type of thing and a couple of sets of underwear jammed with my passport, credit cards, toothbrush, and razor in a small carryall that I could belt around my waist. It was also loaded with everything from Neurofen to Anusol—a sweeter-smelling version of Preparation H—just in case John turned out to be right about my saddle.

Never let it be said that when the chips were down I was prepared to sacrifice style for plain common sense.

After a last-minute check over tires, oil, brakes, nuts, and bolts, I was set. All that remained was dry roads, hot sunny days, and that smell in the air when the desert meets the ocean.

We agreed to meet halfway across Waterloo Bridge at five thirty on the morning of the run. The night before I was as high as a kite with anticipation, so high that I dropped two Valium in order to get to sleep. But in spite of the drug-induced stupor I dragged myself to the window at hourly intervals to check on the sky. Clouds, no clouds, slight drizzle, stars, moon, overcast; it changed every visit. Then, certain that my alarm clock was going to malfunction, I wound it back round and set it off by accident, bleeping like a time bomb, waking my wife who wished me goodbye and rolled back over. I reset the alarm and staggered back to bed. By now the Valium had full control of my body and I was about as stable as a drunken sailor. Finally the starting gun sounded. My wife rolled back over, announced that she had dreamed I had already taken off, and got up to watch me leave.

It took me all of three minutes to use the bathroom and dress, then another ten seconds to clip my carryall over the Joe Weider weightlifting belt I figured would prevent kidney vibration over the long haul.

I kissed my wife and exited.

Downstairs, an affectionate word plus half a Mars bar each to the family hounds, something to remember me by in case this was big Daddy's last big run, then out the back door to the garage. I viewed my bike as if it was the Space Shuttle, about to take me to the moon, realizing just how much I was going to be relying on it over the next few weeks. I started it up and rode out, waving manfully to my wife, who was looking out the bedroom window as I cruised below.

The sky was overcast, but I remembered my grandmother's old saying, "clouds at seven, clear by eleven." It was still only five. I thundered down Kingston Hill and up the A3, through Wandsworth and Battersea, hugging the river all the way to Waterloo Bridge, a great time to ride, while the city is still asleep and the vacant streets are like long concrete corridors echoing with the rumble of the bike's exhaust.

I took a left at the traffic circle and there they were: saddle-bags, windscreens, maps, toolkits, cameras, plus major polishes all around. Mark and Simon had come prepared to travel.

I, on the other hand, was about as kitted out as I would have normally been for a run to Southern Cycle, with the exception of the Weider weightlifting belt and the tube of Anusol.

I pulled over, said hello. Bro Si, picking up on my in the wind look, remarked, "Travelling light, hey, bro?" We surveyed the sky; it looked promising, just a thin layer of gray cloud, light above.

Mark had our route planned, down through Greenwich, Dartford, along the A2, all the way to Dover, about seventy-five miles, in time to catch the eight thirty ferry to Boulogne. Then another four hundred miles into France before nightfall. Initially it sounded like a long day in the saddle, but after we'd cleared town, linked into the A2, and started down towards Dover the sun appeared, the feet went up on the pegs, and a collective highway heaven took hold like a mild hallucinogen. The idea of five hundred miles seemed like a trip to paradise.

Halfway to Dover and we pulled over to the side of the road, checked to make sure everything was battened down tight—I was ahead on this one, nothing to batten down—and grabbed a cup of coffee from a roadside vendor.

Back in the saddle and the bikes were humming, Mark ahead, Si in the middle, and me to the rear, our natural order, established through a dozen runs to Great Bookham. At this point I was actually looking at my riding companions and feeling mildly superior; I was sure as shit glad I wasn't packing an extra hundred pounds of rolled-up jackets and stuffed saddlebags, let alone a windscreen. Very Honda Gold Wing, I thought, but then, they're just young guys. It dawned on me that I had been dreading this trip, as if it was going to be some type of physical and mental test of my strength and endurance: miles of strenuous riding, hairpin curves and ten ton lorries. The reality was pure pleasure. I'd only been gone a few hours, and already I was beginning to unwind, putting business, secret overdrafts, and writing deadlines to the back of my mind.

Just me, the bike, and the road ahead. I stretched my boots out over the highway pegs, leaned as far back as my drag bars would allow, and turned on the highway jukebox. *You can't always get what you want, but if you try sometimes, you just might find, you get what you need. . . .*

We pulled into Dover right on schedule. Mark had already booked us on the eight thirty boat to Boulogne and we rode to the front of the queue of cars and into the cargo hold of the ferry; it was like a warehouse, full of canvas-covered crates and vacant automobiles.

"Don't worry, these guys do this six times every day," Mark assured me as one of the deck hands began to lash my two-wheeled overdraft to a rubber-padded railing.

"Do they ever fall over?" I asked the man.

"No, mate, they're very secure, nothing to worry about. Won't even get scratched."

Having supervised the lashing down we went up to the top deck.

I noticed Mark putting a layer of suntan lotion on his face with a UV protection factor of 25.

"Al bon Digas is already brown, so he must be anticipating some heavy road work," Bro Si said, under his breath.

I asked about the word "digas," pronouncing it "deegas."

"It's Spanish for meatball," Si explained.

Very flattering, I thought, glancing over at Mark, who was now shimmering beneath the protective oil. He had removed his jacket and boots, rolled up the sleeves of his Harley T-shirt, lathered up his arms with the lotion, and was stretched out on a wooden bench, basking in the early morning rays. He looked very brown and very oily. The Digas, in all his glory.

The ferry arrived in Boulogne right on time; it took another forty-five minutes to get the bikes unshackled (not even a scratch) and clear customs. Then we were on the road in France, winding our way along tiny cobblestone roads and through storybook villages.

Mark, a.k.a. the Digas, had mapped the route out in fine detail, retracing part of his last trip and even alerting a couple of five-starrers to expect us. I had to hand it to him, as always he was Mr. Organization. We stuck to the small roads and villages for another hour, bringing us up to about noon, then stopped at a roadside cafe for sandwiches and some espresso that definitely rivalled guarana for liftoff.

"We should get on the motorway and make some distance," Mark announced. "We can stay on these secondary roads for another hour or so, and then link into the A26 and ride for another couple of hundred miles." I nodded. "We'll stop every hundred miles for petrol and to take a break."

By then I now couldn't look at him without thinking of the word so I just had to use it. "Anything you say, Digas," I replied. Mark smiled generously.

After that, as I watched him ride ahead of me, leathered legs straddling his heavily laden craft, shoulders squared and one arm dangling casually, I realized the dignity of his title; the Digas was a championship road man.

By two o'clock in the afternoon the sky had taken a turn for the worse. It was so dark we had to turn on the headlamps of our motorcycles. I could hardly see through the tinted lenses of my aviators—the Digas had already switched to a clear plastic set of riding glasses, designed for just such an occasion—and Bro Si was trooping onwards in his '50s Rayban wraparounds.

We were still about half an hour from the motorway and moving at about thirty miles an hour due to the potholes and gravel which covered the country roads. Highway heaven gradually gave way to highway purgatory as I noticed the black clouds moving in from the direction we were headed. Fifteen minutes later the sky opened.

It started in fine, sharp pellets blown on the chilled breeze and hitting my face like buckshot, and rapidly escalated to a torrential downpour. I'm talking about buckets of the stuff, filling the potholes in the road within minutes, making them impossible to see.

We slowed to about twenty and carried on; there was really nothing else to do. We were in the middle of nowhere and out in the open. The road was not exactly heavily trafficked, but there was the odd French sheep farmer driving his stock to market. Ramshackle trucks and blasting horns, coming up from behind to ensure a few buckets of dirty water caught the side of the bike as they passed.

Bro Si and the Digas were a lot better off than Mr. In the Wind by virtue of their windscreens; I was taking the entire brunt of the gale-force flood on the aviators. In fact they were completely misted over and dripping wet and by then it was so dark that I couldn't see at all. I employed the old one hand on the handlebars, the other wiping the sunglasses routine perfected on my ride back from Patrick Tilley's, gritted my teeth, and followed the Digas. Right into a pond in the middle of the road. The concrete dipped and the muddy water filled in, about two feet deep. The three of us were up to our knees in water, halfway covering the engine cylinders, but they kept on firing. Sputtering but firing. The pond was about six feet across and once on the other side the Digas signalled a halt. "We've got to get some shelter."

We ploughed on into the dark and dirty rain, until we saw a sign that advertised a camping site.

The Digas led the way, off the concrete and on to a dirt trail slipping and sliding beneath a canopy of trees to the caravan site. Several busloads of German tourists had beaten us to the trees with the most foliage and we were reduced to a young sapling with new leaves. We parked and got off the bikes, as soggy as water-rats (right down to my multiple-sock crotch-implant), black leather hanging like wet chamois cloth on cold quivering flesh. Bro Si surveyed the Germans, sharing flasks of hot coffee while staring at the Harleys as if they had just landed from outer space, looked at me, and then at the Digas.

"Five star all the way," he said with a straight face.

"Naturally," the Digas replied.

We huddled under the tree for a good hour, hoping for a change in the weather.

It changed all right.

The rain got heavier, the sky got darker, and the chill factor increased by fifty percent. The German tourists were pulling out, waving from the windows of their bed—and bar—equipped coaches as if we were all having a ball.

"We'd better make a move." The voice of the Digas, alone in the dark, taking a pee on the far side of the tree.

"To where?" Bro Si. Another voice in the dark.

I was shivering too much to chip in.

"We'll get to the A26 then find a town." Followed by the sound of a lonely zipper in the night.

We sloshed back to the country road and proceeded at ten miles an hour for about half an hour, lorries and coaches—probably Germans—barrelling around us, splashing mud and water broadside. By then, the added moisture added little to the already terminally soaked leathers.

Another few miles and the rain let up; the Digas made his move, accelerating to forty, Bro Si hot on his tail and me beginning to curse the day I'd given Mark my phone number. We hit the motorway in a gust of wind and a new downpour, and the Digas kept his foot to the floor, or, more accurately, his hand on the crank.

There was some overhead lighting and the road was wide, which meant that the lorry traffic could cruise at seventy and motorcyclists with windscreens at sixty. For the poor elderly asshole who would *never* sacrifice style for common sense, this was a major health hazard. I was trying to keep up and I was virtually blind. Leaning forward over the tank, one hand controlling the bike the other wiping the lenses of the aviators, while wheeling along at a mile a minute. If I had thought about it I would have probably fallen off, but the never ending flow of truck sidedraughts and backdraughts was pushing and pulling my motorcycle and forcing a state of zanshin that excluded thought of any kind; and the knowledge that if Bro Si and the Digas got away from me I was destined for a solo ride to Marbella, and with my sense of direction that could mean months on the road meant I hung in.

Every now and again I caught a glimpse of Bro Si's taillight, like a beacon to a sailor lost at sea. On top of this my Weider weightlifting belt was squeezing my kidneys like a vice and I needed to urinate, and although I did consider letting it rip inside my leathers—they were so wet a little added urine wasn't going to matter—I was held back by consideration for my socks.

So on we went into the night. And on, and fucking on.

I now hated the Digas; he was not only my torturer but my executioner. I envisioned beating him to a pulp, trashing his motorcycle, verbally abusing him. And then I started laughing, cackling like a banshee, the forerunner of a complete breakdown. No problem there, either, since I was a good twenty yards back from Bro Si, and maybe fifty from General Five Star, and the wind was gusting in my face at about eighty miles an hour; my deranged cries were swallowed along with a couple of gallons of rain water.

I laughed and cackled until the futility of my emotions evolved into a state without feeling, numb, mentally and physically. No more anger, no more fear, no more pounding bladder, as if it had all just evaporated, discarded like unnecessary baggage, leaving me riding by faith alone, in great doubt as to whether I would survive another mile yet determined to keep going. "Faith, doubt, and determination," the three essential requirements of Zen. And there I was: the Harley Buddha.

We pulled off the highway sometime after that metaphysical high point. The Digas had spotted a road sign for some obscure town; we cruised its desolate streets until we found a small stone building with a VACANCY sign in its front window. We pulled the bikes into its courtyard and checked in. It was eight o'clock by English time; we'd been on the road for nearly thirteen hours. We trudged to our rooms (one star all the way) and met again twenty minutes later to try and find something to eat. Both Bro Si and the Digas looked as fresh as choirboys; they had both changed into dry T-shirts, jeans, and shoes. I sloshed behind them in search of a restaurant.

There is fatigue and there is just being downright tired to the bone, when your muscles take seconds to respond to brain stimulus and your flesh quivers with nerve endings that fire like after burners. I think I had nodded off by the time the *Boeuf à la Bourguignonne* arrived; in any case I wasn't talking and neither was Bro Si or the Digas.

Later, back in the one-star, I hung my leathers on the radiator, tossed the pair of socks I had been wearing in the wastebin, and entered a sleep beyond deep.

I awakened to a beautiful blue sky and the overwhelming desire to jump on the Harley and get on the road. My leathers were so stiff they had slipped from the radiator and were literally standing, unassisted, in the corner of the room, and from the window our three motorcycles looked like mud-covered mules.

We met in the hallway, agreed to make some time before breakfast, and got going.

The road was wide and dry and the first thing I did was take off like a bat out of hell, running the bike up to a hundred and fifteen miles an hour, the fastest I'd ever been on a motorcycle, before settling back between the Digas and Bro Si.

All the work I'd had done to the engine really started to

make sense. The Springer was a great highway bike, sitting nice and steady at seventy then kicking in like a turbo when I wanted to overtake a car or lorry. The responsive power of the combination of cam, carb, and Branch heads was pure joy, plus the sound of the double pipes. . . . I fell in love all over again.

The French motorway was littered with motorcycles of varied origins, including one fellow, red scarf blowing in the wind, careening along on a camouflage-colored Second World War Harley, his English sheepdog, wearing a pair of wraparound shades, belted in the side-car next to him. BMWs, Hondas, mopeds, they were all out there, and unlike London, where there is a certain elitism about what type of bike you ride, and Kawasaki ZXs stick with ZXs while Harleys hang with Harleys, everybody exchanged a wave or quick nod of the head.

We stopped for breakfast and fuel. The Digas, after performing some navigational calculations, informed us that we could make Montpelier by dusk. He knew a nice little five star there and had told them to expect us.

The day ran like clockwork; we stopped every hundred miles for fuel, sometimes food, and then back to the highway. My bike had really come into its own; it was like a yacht formerly deprived of its rightful heritage and confined to putting around the harbors of Picadilly and Soho finally let loose on the high seas. A cruiser.

Unfortunately we had made a relatively late start and by dusk we were still eighty miles from Montpelier. I'd been having such a good time I really hadn't paid any attention to the darkening sky until the rain began, coming down harder than it had the day before, turning highway heaven to highway hell. My body tensed and in minutes I was riding with one hand on the bars, window cleaning with the other. I tried taking my shades off, only to end up squinting so hard that I was virtually blind.

No need for the Digas to adjust speed, his windscreen was keeping him dry. In fact, he didn't acknowledge the rain at all. He carried on with the attitude of a man who was going to make it to Montpelier, come hell or high water—or both as it seemed. Bro Si was taking up the rear. The previous three hundred miles had flown by. I had loved everything, the roads, the countryside, my bike, Bro Si, the Digas. Now I hated everything, particularly the Digas.

The more I studied his silhouette against the wind and rain, shoulders squared, legs slightly splayed, and both hands draped casually over his handgrips as if to signify his total control over the situation, the more I hated him. It was added to by a residual fury from the torture he had administered the night before.

He was going to do it again; I knew it.

The miles hazed by. I was soaked, shivering, and out of my mind. It may have been only an optical illusion but the Digas looked dry, composed, and very together.

"You fucking bastard!!!" I started. "You asshole, you fucking asshole, I'm gonna get you, oh yeah, I'm gonna make you pay for this!!!" My voice boomed into the night, aiming words like arrows at the Digas's back. And he rode onwards. "Motherfucker!! Do you hear me??!!" I continued, for several miles.

The wind and rain were blowing against us so my words were blowing backwards, to Bro Si. Bearing in mind that neither Mark nor Simon knew me particularly well and that I was about fifteen years older than either of them and, at my worst, a bandy-legged, somewhat muscle-bound paranoid, with deepset homicidal eyes, they could have been forgiven for leaving me howling my threats to the wind, particularly since my travelling hardships were, for the most part, self-inflicted.

At the height of my vocal violence, I did manage a backward glimpse of Bro Si. He was laughing. Which got me laughing. Right up to the turnoff for Montpelier.

The hotel that greeted us from the hillside was an old converted manor house, four and a half stars, and the owner, who remembered Mark, had a special space right below our bedroom windows reserved for the motorcycles. I discarded my jacket, removed my waterlogged boots and positioned them beneath the radiator, pulled on some dry socks, and made my way, shoeless, to the dining-room, trying not to look down at my feet as the *maître d'* seated me. I had an inch of water in my underwear and my leathers squished as I sat down. Other more appropriately dressed guests of the hotel cast discreet, if disapproving, glances in my direction. With my hair flattened by ten hours in a helmet and my face dirty and covered in stubble, it must have appeared that Cro-Magnon Man had dropped by for dinner. I compounded the image by ordering a couple of bottles of red wine and starting in. Eventually, Mark and Bro Si showed: both looked like they had just stepped out of the fashion section of *Esquire,* Bro Si in fresh black jeans and matching polo-necked pullover, and Mark in new jeans, Docksider deck shoes, and a green Chevignon sweater. I wondered if they'd ask for a separate table. As they were led in my direction I spotted a glint in Mark's eyes.

"Are you still going to make me pay for it?" he said as they sat down.

I cringed. "You couldn't *really* hear me out there, could you?"

"Every word," he confirmed.

I flushed with embarrassment. Then there was silence as Mark and Bro Si surveyed the chastened Cro-Magnon. Finally Si eyed me carefully and stated, "Every inch the heavy bro. . . ." And the good times rolled, lasting through several bottles of the regional red and extending to comments regarding Mark's designer-label travelling apparel and Bro Si's Simon Le Bon style leather riding pants (flared at the thigh, Duran Duran, *c.* '87)—in the breeze. The long days in the saddle and my temper tantrum had begun to break down the walls between acquaintance and friendship.

I woke at six. Another fresh blue morning, birds singing, I was glad to be alive and looking forward to getting on the road. I lay there thinking of my Harley-Davidson Springer as if it was the main love interest in my life. No fantasies of nubile French girls in stringed bikinis or señoritas in long black stockings, absolutely none; just a set of drag bars, a solo saddle, a crossover exhaust system, Branch heads, and a twenty-one-inch front tire.

I got out of bed and went to the window to behold my dream in all her glory. There she stood, between two equally beat Heritage Softails, covered in dust with lumps of mud hanging like brown icicles from her frame. Hardly erotic.

Immediate action was required. I jumped into the standing leathers, pulled on T-shirt, boots, and another pair of socks (I was tossing the worn pairs out after each day's ride, thereby decreasing the size of my crotch), and moved silently along the hallway, down the stairs, and through the kitchen. I borrowed a pail, some washing-up liquid, and a sponge and headed for the Hog.

By eight o'clock I had completed a modified polish.

The chef, arriving to cook breakfast, pitched in with some soft cloths for the final assault on the chrome and the hotel's owner appeared with some leather soap for the saddle. After the polish I stealthily rolled my bike into its original position between the other two and went back to my bedroom.

Bro Si and the Digas woke half an hour later and were greeted by the sight of my gleaming sled. I heard the garbled words. "I don't believe that guy."

I was actually embarrassed, as if I had defiled some unwritten highway code by washing my bike, so when questioned I denied it. It took till breakfast to make a full confession.

Mark and Simon managed a minor hose down before we hit the road.

Spain has a closeness to life and death that brings instant clarity. Its arid deserts and beaches, its hot sun and wide skies can be either merciful or merciless depending on its mood, nurturing its green valleys and hills or depriving its wastelands of the water of life. It is not an in-between place; there is no compromise. In this way Spain reminds me of Mexico and Mexico was the single place in my life where I felt completely free.

We crossed the Spanish border at La Junquera, in the north-eastern section of the country, and the feeling of freedom came over me right away. Something in the air, drier, clearer; the roads were flat and wide and the turquoise sky stretched forever. The texture of the place made me feel connected, as if it possessed a vitality that could be breathed inwards. We were in the south-eastern section of the Pirineos mountains, less than a hundred miles from the Mediterranean; and the highway climbed and rolled with a gentle rhythm, becoming flatter as we rode down towards the coast. Green trees and valley vistas replaced the parched shrubbery that thrives in sandy soil. We left the main highway and continued on a narrow winding road through small gray-stone villages. Brown-skinned children and mothers hanging washing on the line, pointing at the motorcycles, waving. Another fifty miles, and we could just smell the salt in the air. The bikes worked in a synchronicity, as if their sound had merged into the sound of a single engine, not loud, more a low-throated echo, fanning outwards across the road. Another town, another stretch of gravelled asphalt, another gentle hill; we rode to its crest and looked down. There it was: the Mediterranean, set like an emerald in the flickering gold sunlight. We rode towards it along the coastal road, the sea on our left, the mountains to our right, finally pulling into a small roadside cafe, leaving the bikes like chrome horses in the parking lot. The first *cervezas* of the trip, and the Spanish beer cut the last edges off time and miles.

"This has got to be what it's all about," Bro Si stated.

The weather was no longer a concern and we were able to ride in T-shirts or with no shirts at all, the road climbing back into the foothills, the valley vistas of the afternoon replaced by the green-blue sea, and the inland stillness by an ocean breeze. Bro Si was at the head of the group, riding without hands, singing the old James Brown number, "I Feel Good," and dancing, from the waist up. When it became too dark to ride comfortably we pulled into a tiny seafront town.

And then we couldn't find a place to stay, five star, one star, or no star at all. So we trucked on, one village to the next, until we came to the predominantly Spanish resort town of Tarragona. There we got lucky, or comparatively lucky, and managed to secure a couple of rooms in a hostel. About one quarter star, cots and a communal toilet, no screens on the windows and hundred-degree heat, but at least the bikes were safe, locked up in a tiny courtyard below our rooms.

The first battalion of mosquitoes struck at midnight. I employed the "it's harder to hit a moving target" technique and leapt off my cot and began ducking and swatting. By three in the morning I was hot-footing around the stone roof of the hostel in my underwear, hoping the damn things wouldn't know where I'd gone. Bro Si captured me: he popped his head out of his bunker and accused me of being an old poof, exhibiting myself to the resident holiday-makers (mostly male).

After that I retired to my three-by four-foot cell and continued to slap and scratch till daybreak.

Getting on the road never felt so good.

We continued south, hugging the coast right down through Valencia, then inland, west through Granada, before dropping into the Sierra Nevada desert.

The ride through the Sierra Nevada, location for many famous Spaghetti westerns, including *The Good, the Bad and the Ugly*, was surreal. Beneath the white-hot sun the dunes and craters looked like the dark side of the moon—lit by an overhead spot. The sky was electric blue, and the vacant highway, alive with heat mirages that appeared like small puddles of shimmering water, wound and stretched through valleys and hills formed by hard baked sand. Tumbleweed, like skeletal globes of sticks and grass, rolled lazily in front of us, and desolate cactus reached out with spiked arms.

We pulled to the side of the road at a vista overlooking one of the old wooden movie sets; there was an abandoned stagecoach, the front façade of a mock-Texas saloon, and a fully constructed hotel. There was barely any traffic on the road, and the only sound we heard was the peculiar sound of the desert itself; at first it seemed still, hollow and empty, then as my ears acclimatized to the stillness I could hear the humming of bees, the far-away cry of scavenging birds, and the rustling of the faint breeze through the shrubs.

The bikes roared back into life and although the roads were wide and flat, and extended for as far as the eye could see, the beauty and mystery of the place dictated a respectful speed, one that allowed us to blend into the sounds and sights without intruding upon them. In fact the forward momentum of the motorcycles enhanced the sensual texture of the heated air.

Bro Si was dancing again and we all felt good.

We rode out of the desert at dusk. Mark checked the map and said we were making excellent time, averaging four hundred miles a day, and that we should be arriving in Marbella late the next afternoon. We rumbled through Spanish towns and villages that looked like extensions of the movie sets we had seen in the desert: low, flat buildings made of stone, wood, and mud. Horses and donkeys were tied to posts beside them, and families were seated on front porches enjoying the tail end of the afternoon siesta. Daylight turned to dusk and we switched on our headlamps and kept on going, through the lower, flatter regions of the western Sierra Nevada and south down the secondary roads towards the A340, which runs along the coast all the way to Marbella.

It was sometime after nine o'clock at night, and we were quite a few miles from anywhere, when we had the first of any trouble with the bikes. Mark suddenly pulled to the side of the road, shut off his engine, climbed out of the saddle, and squatted down beside his engine. We followed with Bro Si aiming his headlamps at Mark's carburetor.

"My throttle cable's going," he declared.

I had a moment of "Fuck, what are we going to do now" before Mark said, "It'll last till the next town then I'm going to have to repair it."

Bro Si shot a sly look at me and whispered, "the Digas loves these on the road emergencies."

I got off my bike and stared at the cable; it was badly frayed. If it had been me, alone, I would have been in deep trouble;

no matter how many times I have studied the owner's manual, I just don't seem to have the talent to actually work on the bike—which is probably one of the reasons I have become an expert at sublimating it by polishing. And no matter how many people tell me that anyone can work on a motorcycle, I'm convinced that being a good mechanic is an art, some people have it and others don't. I don't. Maybe it's the manual dexterity, perhaps the patience, but I have always had to remind myself of the simplest facts, like turning a screw clockwise to tighten it.

So we ambled on, covering another twenty miles of lonely road before spotting a building lit up like a Christmas tree. Live *mariachi* music and people dancing. In the center of the festivities, a young woman cloaked in a frilly white gown danced with a man dressed like a matador's version of Fred Astaire, tight shiny trousers and wide padded shoulders. It was a Spanish wedding party.

We rode on to the sand and gravel parking lot of the building, which turned out to be a hotel, accepted a few glasses of the tequila-laced punch, encouraged the party guests to ogle the motorcycles, and booked three rooms for the night.

When I came out to polish my bike the next morning, Mark had nearly completed his repair. He had removed the frayed pull cable of the throttle, then replaced it with the push cable. It was going to alter the way he used the throttle—it would no longer snap back on its own—but it was solid enough to last till Marbella.

En route to the coast, I took the lead, then managed to lose both Mark and Bro Si by taking the wrong turn on the outskirts of Granada and winding up in an intricate maze of one way streets. Within minutes I was surrounded by a thousand smoke-spitting automobiles and no Harley-Davidsons. A moment of panic was quelled by the realization that I was close enough to find my way alone, at least to Marbella, if not to Mark's condominium, but I still felt like a horse's ass. Plus I wasn't sure how to get out of the one-way system and back on the main road. I was rescued by the Digas, Bro Si on his tail, riding the wrong way up a one-way street in order to find me.

I followed them out of Granada like a lame dog.

Back to the coastal highway. Mountains on one side, the Mediterranean on the other, the road climbing up then winding down, wide and dry. The sun just dipping enough to cool things off, and the air as fine as silk. Coasting along, letting the bike flow into the curves. No tension, no strain, just the rumble of the engine and the hum of the tires against the road.

We pulled into Marbella at five o'clock that evening, four and a half days and eighteen hundred miles from London. By then, a type of inertia had developed; I could have ridden that Springer on those roads forever.

Mark's and Simon's ladies were already in residence and my wife arrived by cab from the airport in Malaga a couple of hours later. She laughed her head off when she took in my total transformation from man to chipmunk—the Raybans had left two white circles around my eyes and the rest of my face was dark brown, a combination of sun and dirt—and the family half of the vacation began: a week of pools and beaches, and a bit of body reconditioning. Bro Si threw his back out while performing gymnastics on the ladies' tennis circuit and had to enlist the aid of a mysterious Spanish physician—christened Dr. Injecto because of his supreme skill with the extra-long syringe, full of mysterious fluid which Injecto claimed would cure anything from piles to tennis elbow. . . .

Mark had Warr's send him a new throttle cable, Fedexed from Waterstone Road to poolside Marbella, then did the installation himself. I polished daily.

A Sulphuric Monster

One week later we were on the road back to Lon-
don. This time we rode inland, right across Spain, through
Madrid and up through the northern Basque region to connect
with an overnight ferry at Santander. It was a faster route and
would give us a different taste of Spain, trading the sea for the
big mountains.

Rain is one thing, heat is another. We found heat like I
hadn't experienced since my days driving a van through the
inland villages of southern Mexico. Heat that starts by making
you sweat, and then, after every drop of water has drained from
your body, grills you like a sirloin.

We had taken the coastal highway to Malaga, then turned inland
towards Cordoba, leaving the Spanish superhighway there in
favor of a more rural route through the farming valleys and up
towards Madrid.

It was when the road got rougher and we were forced to
slow down that we noticed the intensity of the sun. At first it
seemed a handy way to keep the Marbella sun-tans at maximum
level, so we pulled off our shirts, coating up with Mark's UV25.

An hour later, my shoulders—even beneath the UV25—had begun to feel distinctly parched, and I noticed Mark drifting from left to right across the road. I assumed he was on some sort of technical maneuver, checking tire pressure, or the balance of his pack, until he swerved sharply to avoid riding into a dry irrigation ditch. After that he pulled to the side of the road, turned off his bike, and removed his helmet. His eyes were glazed.

"Isn't this heat bothering anybody else?" he asked.

"I could use some water and some shade," Simon replied.

I touched my forehead; beneath the Marbella bronze, it was raw. A couple more miles and we came to a sign that indicated a rest stop and lavatories. We rode in and parked beside what looked like a gypsy caravan.

To the side of the caravan a family of Muslims sat picnicking on a wide woollen blanket. There were six of them, apparently a mother, father, three sons, and a grandmother in full black dress and veil. They were listening to a portable radio and paid little attention to us as we staked out our own shade tree then opened a bottle of water.

Simon got out his camera, handed it to me, and asked for a couple of *In The Wind*-type shots.

I really don't know why I did what I did next; maybe it was the heat playing games with my brain, or maybe just a moment of irresponsibility, but I stood up with the camera, turned it on the group of picnicking Muslims, and took a snap of the older woman in the veil. I was on my second shot when the father noticed, shouted, and pointed at me. A few seconds later we were surrounded by the three young men, one of whom was carrying a long serrated knife.

I heard Bro Si grumble, "Well, you've really done it this time," and from somewhere remembered that Muslims believe the camera robs a woman of her soul.

The Muslims motioned for me to surrender the Nikon. Internally I was midway between fight and flight, adrenalin kicking in like a turbocharge. The fact was I didn't fancy the knife and there was nowhere to run. So I lied.

"Empty, the camera is empty," I intoned, pointing towards the back of the box, where the film went.

They stared at me and I stared at them, a stalemate. Then their father shouted something in Arabic, and the dangerous moment passed.

"You American?" one of the boys asked.

"Yes."

"You know Arnold Schwarzenegger?"

And I knew we were going to be all right.

"Let's just hope the fact that Arnie rides a Harley keeps them from trailing us into the sunset and running us off the road," Bro Si whispered as we waved goodbye to the sheik and his family.

Not many miles later, when I was reasonably certain that we weren't going to be part of a re-enactment of *Deliverance* (this time on wheels), I relaxed, leaned back, and inhaled the dry air. And nearly passed out from the fumes. Pure sulphuric acid. I was directly behind the Digas and could only conclude that the near-fatal encounter had left him with an impaired bowel. I rode alongside him. "Do you smell that?" he asked.

"Yeah, do you need the Anusol?"

The Digas did not look amused. "It's my battery. It's fried."

"From the heat?" I asked, mechanical genius to the end.

"It'll be my voltage regulator."

I wasn't exactly sure what that implied until we stopped for gas and Mark couldn't restart his bike. Then I knew; it meant a lot of pushing by Bro Si and me to jumpstart Mark's Softail.

We made it to Madrid, debated whether or not to go into the sprawling town to try and find a Harley shop, and decided against it. Bro Si and I would just keep pushing.

On the far side of Madrid I came close to a bad fall. I was at a main intersection in the middle of a hundred horn-blasting cars and trucks. Mark and Simon had squeezed through a traffic light; I attempted to follow when the light turned red. I braked. Nothing happened, the bike just kept going forward, heading straight for a fast line of moving traffic. At first I thought the rear tire was flat, or maybe it had come off entirely, like there was nothing beneath me. I dropped both feet, trying to stop the motorcycle by the friction of my boots against the road; they slid like they were touching ice. I looked down into a river of grease. Completely helpless. It crossed my mind that I was going to run side-on into the line of cars and trucks, end up sprawled in the road, and neither Mark or Simon would know what had happened to me. I could almost see it: the crash, my body beside the road, and no one there to help me. Then I got lucky; the line of traffic separated, giving me a window of about twenty yards on either side. I slid right past the red light, through the window, and kept going.

Mark and Simon had pulled off the road about a mile ahead. We degreased the wheels with a rag and a little petrol from my tank. Then Bro Si and I shoved the Digas's bike to life and we got back to riding.

It was near dark and between heat strokes, mad Arabs, greased tires, and the sulphuric monster, we were on our last legs, looking for shelter of any star. What we found was, perhaps, the nearest to a "five star all the way" that we'd come across since leaving Dover: an old Spanish castle, in several acres of green fields, trees, and lawn, somewhere outside of Sepulveda, about two hundred miles north of Madrid. We pulled in, climbed off, locked up, and limped inside.

The former castle had been converted by the government into a *parador* (a state-owned hotel), with the idea of maintaining the integrity of its traditional structure, including great exposed beams, a spacious dining hall, and several log fires. It was very expensive, but at this point we would all have written bad checks just to get a bed.

The man behind the desk noticed our clothes and the fact that we were carrying helmets and, for a moment, I thought it was a "no room at the inn" situation. Instead he smiled—I believe Mark had just flashed his platinum Amex card—and asked if we would care to leave our motorcycles in the lockup garage.

Anyone with fantasies of sweet young nymphets at the end of a day's hard ride ought to spend twelve hours in the saddle. By this point in the journey the only things capable of achieving a vertical position were my leather trousers, so stiff with dirt and grease by now that they were standing guard duty at my door.

Morning came sweet and bright—after a few weeks in Spain you naturally expect sun. We ate breakfast, settled our bill, and went to the garage to roll out the sleds.

In Spain, as in Mexico, the chief mechanic in any village is known as the *maestro,* or expert. And one hour after Mark had removed his saddle—to check battery leads and water—we were awaiting the maestro's arrival. He drove an ancient Ford pickup truck, wore a Yankees baseball cap, and carried a toolbox. Mark communicated in sign language, the maestro grimaced, grunted, nodded his head emphatically, and connected a battery charger to the Softail. Several pesetas later we were on the road, travelling north, along unsurfaced highways, towards Santander and the ferry.

By dusk we had entered the mountains of the northern Basque, the road winding up gently and then dropping down to farming valleys and villages. The deeper we went into the mountains the more the road curved and forked, until we were forced to forget the view and concentrate on the riding and keep an eye on the shoulder for gravel or loose stones, anything that could cause a skid and a fall. The moon was just coming out, full and bright, and the road wound on and on. Beautiful. Like a cobra.

We were travelling with Mark in the lead, me behind him, and Bro Si taking up the rear, keeping about twenty feet between us. We had gone on like this for a couple of hours, at between ten and forty miles an hour, hoping that the next small town or village would feature a hotel, and it was getting darker and darker. Mark's bike had begun to backfire, stink, and sputter.

"It's the lights, too much drain on the battery, I'm going to have to find a place to get a new one or recharge it again."

Fat chance. In the heart of the Basque the only conveyance that looked likely was a horse and buggy.

We rolled on for twenty more miles, then the road dipped down into a tiny village. Very tiny, like three buildings, one of which was a hostel. It was the same cot and communal toilet affair that we had occupied in southern Spain but this time we greeted it like the promised land. We parked, locked, and alarmed the bikes (Bro Si and Digas, mine of course was alarm free), leaving them beneath an improvised lean-to by the side of the hostel, and slipped a local Harley fan a handful of pesetas to keep an eye on them for the evening. It was no problem since he couldn't keep his eyes off them anyway.

It turned out the hostel was also the town's, and several neighboring villages', social center, and by ten o'clock the joint was jumpin', with the jukebox blasting out Beatles' hits and pompadoured dark-skinned James Deans cruising the strip and staring at the bikes. Which did not make for blissful sleeping, added to by the fact that my bedsprings had been new in 1935 and at this point in time were incapable of supporting anything beyond the weight of a pea. I tossed the mattress on the floor, covered myself with a blanket that had more holes than cloth, and dozed off to the chorus of "Daytripper."

Some time later I was awakened by the sound of a bleeping horn. Repeating. The bike alarm. *I knew it!* A team of Mediterranean James Deans was heading for Porta Banus on our sleds. Struggling to my feet while unkinking the lower lumbar region of my back I ripped open my cardboard door, and charged down the hall in my underpants, ranting, raving, and disturbing several other similarly attired *hombres*, who peered out the doors of their torture chambers. Meanwhile the horn was blaring and I was certain they were getting away with the bikes. Then silence. Was I too late?!

I would never have found the staircase if it hadn't been for Bro Si, coming up. Shaving kit in hand.

"I left this on the bike then forgot I'd set the alarm," he mumbled, heading back to his orthopaedic haven.

At the crack of dawn Mark headed north in a farmer's truck, melted battery in tow, returning about two hours later with a semi-charged melted battery. "This ought to get us to the boat," he said.

We only had a hundred and twenty miles to ride and the ship didn't sail till late afternoon, so we took a leisurely pace along the winding valley roads—a lot friendlier in the daylight—then continued upwards into the last of the mountains between us and the sea. Mark's bike was moving along, dispensing sulphur but minus the pops and backfires of the night before, and Bro Si had made a complaint about my cornering technique so I had been relegated to rear position.

In spite of the fact that our sleep had been irregular and our bathing facilities not always five star—the hostel's "shower room" comprised a pipe dribbling cold water and a plastic sheet hung by a nail in the wall between the door and the drain—I felt as clean as a peach, fresh and clear. Whatever was happening was good for the mind and body. The sheer concentration of riding the motorcycle was forcing me into a present-tense reality, making every moment new. Even when I was listening to the highway jukebox, the rhythm of the road dictated the beat and tone of the music. Whatever other mental processes took place—thinking, listening, or creating—were directly related to the concentration of riding, as if the secondary process radiated like an aura from the main stream of consciousness, which was the forward momentum of the motorcycle.

We were by now at the top of the mountain range and beginning our descent. The weather was fine; clear and cool compared to the microwave flatlands in the south. The view was breathtaking, miles of green fields and stone villages and beyond them our first glimpse of the Bay of Biscay, just a pale blue haze, maybe fifty miles north. Fifty miles down.

The road had begun to wind and it seemed our ride down

was nearly vertical. There was an insane Basque pig-farmer hanging on my tail like a lingering fart, his ten-tonner full of squealing bacon, pushing us to ever greater degrees of roadmanship as we rode downhill towards Santander.

A few more miles of our enforced sprint and the Digas suffered the rider's equivalent of the surprise left hook, the one you never see coming. He rounded a tight bend, only to be confronted by a tighter one, but to add to the need for quick reflexes the guard-rail had been battered down and the view from the ridge was a sheer drop. That plus a bit of gravel and rock in the center of the road, compounded by twin blasts from the pig-farmer's air horn, and the Digas hit the brakes. His rear tire skidded, that scream of rubber against cement that sounds like the shrieking victim of a violent crime, and his bike zigzagged across the road. It took him a few perilous seconds of two-fisted bronco-busting to get the Hog back in a straight line. Luckily nobody was coming in the opposite direction.

After that we pulled over, letting the bacon by. By now, every roadside stop and every cup of coffee took on overtones of "the last supper"; we all knew the trip was coming to a close and, after three thousand miles of riding, the bikes felt like a way of life. The danger, the discomfort, the near misses, all had added to the intensity of the ride. We completed the journey to Santander at twenty miles an hour, savoring the last of the mountain air and riding in procession like mourners to a funeral. We pulled in about two hours before the ship sailed, stowed the bikes below decks, and checked into our single cabin. Three bunks for three *amigos*; it was a night of five-star dining, two feature films in the ship's cinema, and some monumental snoring.

We disembarked at Plymouth, pushed Mark's bike to life, and began the final two hundred miles to London.

England was the downer we had all dreaded: crowded roads and weaving caravans. The whole place was just a different color from Spain, grayer even though it was sunny, land, time took on a new perspective, every mile feeling like ten. We trudged along between Plymouth and Bournemouth, stopping at a Happy Eater for a high-octane load of sausage, eggs, and chips, and parted company on the M3, where the road forked and the sign read Kingston.

It was the first time I had ridden on my own in over three thousand miles and it felt strange not to have Bro Si and the Digas around. As if I knew them better than anyone else in the world and they had just vanished. It was a lonely six miles home.

Edward, my neighbor, formerly of Baghdad, is a non-riding Harley man who pops out of garages, bushes, bedroom windows, and from beneath the hoods of cars at the sound of my bike. Now he had had my imminent arrival confirmed by my wife and was hovering in his doorway, wearing his Harley T-shirt and clutching a bottle of champagne.

"I could hear the 'Haarleey' from a mile away," he said, and looked over my shoulder to check the mileage. "You reeally did go all the way to Spain!"

Harley Owners Group, the Chelsea and Fulham Chapter

Warr's was expanding, taking care of the influx of new customers by enlarging its premises and hiring more staff. Fred had semi-retired and John, by now, seemed more a supervisor than a mechanic. When I rode the Springer in for my next oil change and tune-up there were lots of fresh faces around, some so fresh that I wondered if they were old enough to ride a motorcycle, let alone repair one. A fellow who looked about sixteen years old attended my bike.

"Kid's name is Martin," John said, "he's going to be real good. He'll be running this workshop before long."

It dawned on me then that Johnnie Walker, Bro Si, the Digas, not to mention myself (old enough to be Martin's dad) were destined to become the "old order" of the new urban bikers.

While Martin, teenage tuning ace, did the honors, John Warr did the talking. After asking me about the Marbella ride, he invited me to a meeting the following Thursday at the Hand and Flower, on the King's Road. He had a proposal that Mark and I might be interested in.

* * *

"I don't know if you guys have ever heard of HOG," he began. "The letters stand for 'Harley Owners Group.'" I remembered the HOG patches from Los Angeles. 'Well, we're starting a chapter here, the first one in the south of England, and I thought you and Mark would make good road captains."

I have never been a "group" type of person; I've never been into college fraternities or team sports. But I was flattered that John had thought of me.

"You won't have to do much, organize a couple of meetings, lead a few runs; we can handle all the paper work from the office."

"And who gets to be a member?" I asked.

"Anyone who buys a bike will have the opportunity to join," John answered. "Look, we'll make sure your bikes are looked after, no waiting for oil changes or services, we'll keep you guys on the road. You'll be a priority."

"Sounds good to me," Mark replied, always with an ear for business. I had my doubts as to my own commitment but went along with the Digas; after all he would naturally lead the club runs, due to the fact that I couldn't find my way to Soho without an *A to Z.*

Besides, Bro Si had just opened the Arizona, a Tex-Mex restaurant in Camden with plenty of street parking. I reckoned we could have our monthly meetings there. So I said yes and walked out of the Hand and Flower as the first road co-captain of the Harley Owners Group, Chelsea and Fulham Chapter.

Two weeks after our meeting I received, by post, two touring handbooks—one for Europe and one for America—along with a HOG membership card, HOG lapel pin, and HOG emblem for my jacket. The touring handbooks were excellent, details of factory tours of the Harley company's plant in York, Pennsylvania, climate charts, fly and ride schedules—in which the HOG member could fly to his US destination and pick up a rental Harley, at $50 per day, or $250 per week, and tour America— and detailed maps of countries, states, and cities.

I still use the handbooks today, although the lapel pin and jacket emblem remain buried somewhere in my closet.

* * *

Several days before our first meeting Mark let me in on his little secret; he'd been picked up for driving under the influence and was shortly to lose his license.

"So how the hell are you going to make the meeting?" I asked. "Or lead the club runs?" That was my real panic.

"Don't worry, I'll get a chauffeur," he answered.

"What?!"

And so he did. He arrived at the Arizona clad in his customary leathers and pillioned on the back of his Heritage, his old school friend Jonky the video director doing the steering.

John Warr was there on his Buell, a Harley-powered racing bike designed by racing engineer Erik Buell that looked, to me, like a Kawasaki and was capable of doing wheel-stands— as demonstrated by John himself, right up and down the quarter-mile strip in front of Si's restaurant. There were also about a dozen other Harley dignitaries, including Johnnie Walker, his music biz pal Adrian, a fellow guarana advocate and owner of a Full-Dresser, "Proops" the bearded scrap-metal merchant on his souped-up Sportster, Piers the smooth private detective, Richard the famous paparazzo and long-time Harley man, "Huggie," tattooed and stylishly tattered—the king of street credibility—on what appeared to be the first Harley ever imported into England, and, of course, Bro Si, refusing to join HOG, but none the less hosting its monthly extravaganza. Then there was Kathy, the roving slammer girl, sporting a fine floral tattoo that ran the length of her upper arm, with a mix of tequila and champagne which she threw together in a shot glass from her gunbelt and slammed down on the table in front of you.

And we all did what comes naturally at biker events. We got pissed and stood around staring at each others' Harleys. "Did you get that eagle at Warr's?" "No, no, that's an after-market eagle; I got it down at Southern. . . ." Or, "How do you find starting in the winter with that Screamin' Eagle carb?" "I don't know. I never ride in the winter. . . ."

And the slammers flowed. Bro Si and I grilled Kathy as to where she picked up her inked flowers.

"George Bone," she replied, "in Ealing. He's world famous. In *The Guinness Book of Records.* He's the most tattooed man in England."

And the drunker I got the better that tat looked. . . .

Having a tattoo had always been one of my intentions, as far back as the '60s. In fact I had once driven from Boston, where tattooing was illegal, up into New Hampshire carrying my hand-drawn design (a religious cross with a yin-yang symbol in its center) into the first shop with TATTOO flashing in neon above its door. I was greeted by a fellow best described as an ancient mariner, if the crude anchors, sailing ships, and naked ladies embellishing his arms were any indication. He greeted me with trembling hands, whiskey breath, and a gruff "How fuckin' old are ya?" I wasn't carrying any identification. "Nobody's gonna tattoo ya without ya provin' you're twenty-one, now get the fuck outta here," the captain croaked, shoving me towards the door.

And that was it. Twenty-some years later my flesh was still virgin.

Not so with Bro Si. Fifteen years ago he had a MUM and DAD tattooed on a scroll with a swallow in flight dividing them, faded, but still visible, on his left forearm. When I had first spotted it, I'd studied it as if it were the Holy Grail.

Tattoos seemed as essential to bike-riding apparel as boots and leathers. Almost everyone, male and female, in the bike magazines was flashing a bit of "ink." And as far as I was concerned a good tattoo was a piece of art.

"Wouldn't mind paying a visit to Mr. Bone," Si said, glancing again at Kathy's bouquet.

"I'm on for that one," I agreed, and we went back to drinking.

The first HOG meeting ended with me, the co-captain, wheeling off towards Regent's Park, sans helmet, with visions of a tapestry of tattoos running up both arms and down my back.

HOG was a success.

The second meeting was a repeat of the first, except with twice as many people.

Definitely a success.

Nitrous

John Warr had already told me that I had gone as
far with Harley parts as I could, that the Springer just couldn't
be made to go any faster and still be a reliable motorcycle. And
why did I want it to go faster anyway?

The answer was I had become addicted to change, to the
thrill of seeing each reincarnation of the bike as a new and
fresh entity, and to the kick I got when I twisted the throttle,
listened to the engine growl and rev, then took off like a bat
out of hell. And no matter how many times I had recreated the
Springer, after a certain amount of riding and viewing hours I
was yearning to do it all again (or, more accurately, to pay
somebody else to do it). Maybe if I'd had the money I would
have started a fleet of Harleys, but because a modification was
less expensive than a new motorcycle, I began creating my fleet
out of a single bike.

The speed angle was fired by Harley's reputation as "the
slowest motorcycle on two wheels." I thought it would be nice
to have one that not only looked the business but actually
performed. So I began researching beyond Harley parts and
came up with the idea of nitrous oxide. Nitrous oxide is a more
refined gas than pure oxygen and when injected into the fuel

mix of a twin-cylinder engine sends the whole thing into super-drive. Sort of like Methedrine for the motorcycle. I'd seen pictures of small silver canisters of the stuff mounted on the sides of American drag bikes, not to mention the nitrous-powered cars in the second *Mad Max* film. A can of nitrous would certainly take care of those Kawasaki ZXs at the traffic light on the A3. Not to mention the damaging psychological effect it would have on Bro Si and the Digas.

I investigated and found a fellow in Reading, a performance engineer by the name of John Williamson; he had a business called R.M.D. Motors—devoted to making Harleys go faster—and a Low Rider with a nitrous hook-up. He was going to be drag-racing his bike at the Bulldog Bash, the Hell's Angels' annual party in Stratford-upon-Avon, on the old airstrip. Since my plans to go nitrous were clandestine I decided to attend the Bulldog Bash on my own.

The weather was fantastic, hot and sunny, and the ride up, about a hundred miles north-west, was highway heaven all the way. About five miles out of Stratford I started seeing signs for the Bulldog Bash, along with groups of bikers obviously headed for the event. It was equally obvious—many were riding beat-up "rat" bikes, while others were nailed to the sky-high apes of their radical choppers—that these were not charter members of the HOG's Chelsea and Fulham chapter. In fact I doubted if any of them had spent time at the Dôme on the King's Road. I decided not to use my credentials as road captain unless absolutely necessary.

The closer I got to the old Stratford air strip, home of the Bulldog, the more I realized that this was a big event. There were hundreds of bikes heading in, almost all of them in groups, and I had a few doubts as to my own attendance. How the hell was I supposed to find John Williamson and, when I did, was he supposed to drop everything and welcome me with open arms?

Another mile and I spotted the line of demarcation, the

police on one side the Angels on the other, all friendly but still very businesslike. In the middle, a group of club members was collecting money and tickets. Beyond this line of demarcation the Angels were running the show. I rode on and paid, then continued into the encampment. Followed the waving arms—substantial ink on display—to a guest parking bay, locked the bike, and took a stroll. I have never seen so many Hell's Angels in one place in my life. There appeared to be thousands of club members, on foot, in open-topped Jeeps, carrying walkie-talkies, policing the grounds, making their presence felt, and ensuring that their party ran smoothly. It was like a military compound, everything had a precise order and the staff were all in uniform. The Angels certainly commanded respect, like a proud tribe.

It took me a while to loosen up, first because I was on my own and secondly because I have rarely felt so outnumbered. Then, gradually, I began to get over the "me and them" routine that plagues most self-confessed paranoids. I started talking to a group of club members, asking them about the drag racing, even about John Williamson, who turned out to be "John of Reading," a club member himself. And they were just fine, friendly and helpful, telling me that if I couldn't find John down at the drag strip that I could try the temporary club house (the control building) and they would page him for me. After that I relaxed and started seeing what the Bulldog was actually about.

Because I often use my years in karate as a frame of reference, for me it was like walking on to the floor of a new dojo. Everything has to do with respect and attitude. If you project a challenge then a member, or members, of the new dojo will be obliged to respond. If you obey their rules and etiquette—i.e. show some respect—chances are, you'll enjoy your time there, and probably learn something.

I walked down to the drag strip, grabbed a seat in the bleachers, and watched the bikes run. The first part of the day was a "run what you brung." There was everything from 50 cc mopeds to Jap superbikes to 1941 Indians lined up against each other, two at a time, for a blast down the quarter-mile strip.

A commentator, twenty stone, polished head, and man-eating smile, was a man by the name of Horace. Horace announced the bikes and their riders. Then, at the end of the straight quarter-mile, he announced their time and top speed. There were a few stock Harleys on the strip and I was curious to see how they performed. Compared to the stock Japanese bikes, the answer was not too well. This did not come as any major surprise or shock, it was just disappointing to witness. I can't remember any of them touching a hundred miles an hour at top speed and their times were all between fourteen and eighteen seconds, more towards eighteen.

I remembered John Warr telling me that with the motor work I'd had done he reckoned I should pull under thirteen seconds (which would have meant I'd be going over a hundred) in the quarter, although he did condemn drag racing as an "old man's" event. Well, I was an old man and I had spent the money. I thought about it, but I was just too self-conscious to get my Springer and roll it on to the strip. So I continued to watch. The Indian took twenty-four seconds to make the quarter with a top speed of fifty-seven miles an hour and I don't think the moped finished at all, just kind of cruised off to the side of the runway. I had a couple more urges to go get my bike and wheel on out to the track, but I suppressed them by promises to myself of "I'll come and race it next year."

After that I got up and walked around the grounds, checked out the concessions—after-market parts, T-shirts, etc.—and asked a few more people if they knew of John Williamson. I ended up in the temporary club house. It took about thirty seconds to locate John of Reading. I relayed, via an Angel using a walkie-talkie, that I had come to talk about hooking a nitrous canister to my motorcycle, and John agreed to meet me in front of the club house. He pulled in a few minutes later on a three-wheeled tractor cart and drove me the short ride to his caravan.

John's Harley, an FXRS Low Rider, was painted red, and the canister of nitrous was mounted on the carburetor side and fed into the engine via a network of hoses, all controlled by an on-off switch on the clutch side of his handlebars. Once the bike was "armed," i.e. the switch turned to the "on" position, the gas would cut in automatically at a certain number of revs. Then, if everything was working correctly, the Harley would blast off like a rocket.

"What can you get out of this bike in the quarter?" I asked.

'Should go just under eleven, maybe a hundred and thirty miles an hour,' he replied.

I thought about it. One hundred and thirty miles an hour, all within a space of four hundred and forty yards. Incredible acceleration. I looked again at the red motorcycle; this was definitely wheel-stand territory.

"And you could hook one of these things up to my bike?"

"Setting the nitrous up is no problem but you've got to make certain the rest of the engine is strong enough to take the power surge."

I told him what had been done to my engine.

"The nitrous isn't really compatible with the Branch heads, the valves are too large. . . . Are you thinking of running the bike in the quarter?"

"No, not really, I want to use it in the street."

"I could suggest a lot of things you could do performance wise to a street bike, but nitrous isn't one of them."

He went on to talk about switching carburetors, camshafts, even enlarging the cubic-inch displacement of the engine. But the bottom line was I wasn't going to get a cylinder of explosives. The idea of having the engine taken apart again and the amount of time it would keep the bike off the road didn't appeal to me. I never thought about the money; at times like these, when the fever was coming on, I never did.

It was beginning to dawn on me that I could go on and on modifying and changing the Springer, that I hadn't really even scratched the surface of what performance or custom was all about. For me it was not just an obsession with looks; it was more about maximizing the potential of what I had, taking the product that the factory had provided and making it more beautiful, stronger, and more efficient. I had that urge, even in the beginning, when I was sticking on the gold eagles, but as my experience deepened, I began to realize what thousands had realized before me: that the stock Harley is only the basis for a very personal form of expression. And I wanted not only beauty but power.

Again, like martial arts or bodybuilding, I could never get into building a body that was not functional; I needed the muscles to work, the old "looks like Arnold Schwarzenegger, moves like Bruce Lee" approach, but with my own style.

I was beginning to see myself in the motorcycle, or maybe the way I wanted to be. When I was in college a psychology professor had once asked me what animal I would most like to be. . . . "A cat: a tiger or a lion," I'd answered.

"Why?"

"Because they're beautiful and dangerous. A lethal beauty, and the way they move, powerful and graceful." A bit of romantic fantasy, but the motorcycle allows that fantasy to take shape, develop.

You can turn a motorcycle into a tiger or lion, make it look low and sleek, and make it roar.

Essential Ink

Pass through my door, it's up to you,
But just remember this,
I have the power to hold you there,
With what is in my fist.
For when inside, that's where you'll stay,
Like moths around a light,
And I'll keep you with my patterned walls,
Of pictures colored bright.
Once there, you'll have no choice,
But to give to me your skin,
And with skills as old as man himself,
My work I shall begin.
Don't try to run, there's no escape,
For I have cast my spell,
With wand of steel once energized,
That's cold, but burns like hell.
And I'll leave my work upon your skin,
For all the world to see,
'Tis the only thing you can obtain in life,
And take it to Eternity?

Brian John Nye
(inspired by George Bone)

After my trip to the Bulldog, I decided to get inked. My first tattoo. I saw it as sort of my permanent commitment to the universal tribe of bikers. I was old enough and set enough in my ways not to worry about a tattoo affecting my job possibilities; I really didn't care if I was banned from the golf club . . . plus I intended to ride a metal horse for as long as my legs would wrap round a tank. It was time for the tat.

I called Bro Si and asked if he would get George Bone's address from Kathy. He'd beaten me to it. No only did Si have the address, he also had a design of his own that he wanted committed to his right arm for posterity: the classic dagger and heart motif, resurrected by the David Lynch film, *Wild at Heart.*

We phoned Mr. Bone, found that no appointments were necessary, and decided that the following Friday was a good day for the ink. It was eight days before the annual Littlecote Rally, and that would give the Bro and me time to adjust to our new tats in preparation for a public display. After all, I was the road captain; the least I could have was a flash of color.

In the meantime, I didn't have the slightest idea what I wanted. I scoured *In The Wind*, particularly the "Ink" section, even bought a couple of *Tattoo*, an ink-only subsidiary of *Easyriders*. Still nothing struck me. I wanted an original.

It just so happened that Terence Stamp was coming to Sunday lunch, along with George Sharp, then the art director of Pan Books. As men of impeccable taste, I mentioned my quandary to them. George came through with a book of Japanese Samurai crests and the day revolved around a careful study of the various insignias, until Stamp pointed to a swirling figure at the top of a page that was labelled "the crane, symbol of health and long life."

"That has a bit of class," he said, studying the rather abstract rendition of the bird.

"Yes, very tasteful," George added. Five minutes later he had ballpointed it on my right shoulder, and I spent the rest of the afternoon sneaking off to the bathroom to look at it in the mirror. Oh, yeah, that's definitely me, the crane. . . . I'll have it done in blue, the blue crane. An original!

Friday came, and Bro Si and I Harleyed down to Bone's, parked the bikes in a lot across the street, and walked to the front door. George Bone's "Den of Skulls," as his front was called, featured human skulls in the window. "Jesus, I think the guy's a Satanist," I whispered as the lights went on behind the blinds.

A pretty woman opened the door and led us through a narrow corridor and into the waiting room. It was decorated with more skulls, some for sale, and a wall full of flash—patterns for tattoos, everything from Bro Si's heart and dagger to classic Japanese designs, huge prints of Samurai warriors and dragons —and beautiful photographs of George's work.

His studio was adjacent to the waiting-room, separated by a chest-high partition, so those waiting to be tattooed could watch those in the process of being tattooed. There were twin chairs in the studio and shelves containing tiny bottles of ink and equipment, plus an autoclave (a sterilizing unit) and more pictures of his art and flash. There was also, a large spider, either a tarantula or a black widow on steroids, crushed flat and mounted like a butterfly in a glass-fronted wall frame.

George arrived a minute later, descending a flight of stairs and entering via a back door. He was fully inked, from his fingers to the visible part of his neck, which appeared from the top of his high-collared shirt. He wore a suit, dark and Gothic, perhaps once used by Christopher Lee in a rendition of Dracula. Slipping out of his jacket, he smiled at us and snapped on a set of latex gloves. I had my first moment of nerves. It was as if I was about to have open-heart surgery without anaesthetic, performed by a potential devil worshipper.

"Who's first?" His voice was very soft.

"I'll go," I said gallantly, wanting to get it over with. I walked past Bro Si and through the entrance to George Bone's operating room.

"What are you having done?" his assistant (his wife) asked.

I produced a small copy of the crane and handed it over. She took it to George's photostat machine and made a transfer.

"Sit down here," George instructed, guiding me to a black padded chair equipped with an armrest. I moved like a robot.

"Relax," George whispered, seating me and positioning my arm on the rest, "now where do you want it to go?"

I pointed to my right shoulder and he pressed the wet transfer into position, leaving an imprint of the crane.

"In blue, I want it all in blue," I said.

Fuck, what was I doing? After forty years, defiling my body. What would my mother say?

"Relax," George repeated, stepping down with his foot and starting the motor of his electric needle. It sounded like a high-pitched dentist's drill. He dipped the needle into a small pot of bright blue pigment then touched it to my shoulder.

At first it was hot. Then it felt like a thousand bee stings, but quick, their pain over as fast as I felt them. Then nothing, a kind of numbness. I looked over and saw a tiny trickle of blood which George wiped with one gloved hand as he tattooed with his other.

Five minutes later and the outline of the crane was in place. After that George traded for a flatter needle and did the shading. I looked across at Bro Si and winked.

It's a funny feeling, being tattooed. Psychologically. You have the undivided attention of the person working on you, and there is a kind of telepathic link between the tattooer and the tattooed arising from the shared knowledge that what he is doing is indelible and, in some way, will define you forever.

"Do you want to take a look at it?" George said, turning off his tattoo machine and wiping the last of the blood from the crane.

I stood up and looked into the wall mirror, positioned for just these occasions. The crane looked fantastic, a beautiful turquoise swirl of color. Unique.

"Thanks, it's perfect." My voice was as reverent as if I'd just unveiled the *Mona Lisa.*

George smiled and gently placed a nonstick bandage over the fresh tattoo. "Keep it on for a couple of hours, then give it a good wash with soap and warm water."

Whatever his obsession with skulls (he called them his "friends"), George Bone was a gentleman.

"How much will it be?" I asked.

If he had said two hundred pounds I would have paid without quibbling. You can't put a price on art.

"Twenty quid."

It felt like he'd done it for free.

I handed over the money then took my place in the waiting room and watched Bro Si get his heart and dagger.

Littlecote: Tattoo Review

Ten days later, just enough time for the tats to scab
up then peel and heal, we were getting ready for our second
Littlecote Rally. Jonky intended to make a video of the entire
event, including the ride down, and it was Mark's job to operate
the video camera from the back of his bike while Jonky did the
steering. It was the first rally since HOG had been organized.
I had been too occupied with studying my blue crane in every
available mirror to pay any attention to routes or road maps,
and I hadn't really given my own position as road captain much
thought, but we expected a good attendance from the Chelsea
and Fulham contingent.

By now we had had several HOG meetings at the Arizona,
and our group at least knew each other, which was a step ahead
of the previous year, and, potentially, made the whole thing a
lot more fun. Even Bro Si, non-member to the last, would be
on hand for Littlecote.

We arranged to meet at eight o'clock Saturday morning for
an eight thirty ride-out.

* * *

The morning of the run was overcast, and by the time I had turned the corner on to Waterstone there was a hint of drizzle. The rain started, stopped, started, then stopped again.

A lot of the faces there I knew: Mark, Si, Proops, Walker, Adrian, Richard the Paparazzo, Piers the Detective, John, William and Robert, Martin, a few black-leathered female riders from previous runs; and there were more that I didn't. In all, at least thirty bikes, which seemed a strong presence in that twenty-yard space in front of the shop. Some of the participants had sewn their HOG patches on the backs of their jackets and many were wearing the HOG lapel pins that came with their membership.

I was tatted. And I was the only road captain with a license. Which meant what?

"You'll lead from here to the M4, keeping everybody together, try to stay at sixty on the motorway. We'll turn off at Heston for gas, then follow you to the Hungerford exit and then down to de Savary's," John explained.

I was about to ask John the directions to the M4 when he turned and called the group together.

"OK everybody, this is your road captain, Richard La Plante, you'll be following him to the motorway, then on up to the exit and off to the camp ground, so everybody stay in line and rely on Richard to set the speed and the direction," he explained.

I had a premonition of a major fuckup even as John spoke, but the video camera was rolling and it was too late to resign, and way too late to get a map and take a look to see where the hell the M4 was. Meanwhile, all the HOG-patched chapter members had started their bikes. Assembled and poised, they were ready for their road captain to take his position.

The cameras rolled as I shimmied the Springer into the front of the lineup. And away we went. Me following Mark, sitting backwards, camcorder in my face, following the second unit crew in the Ford Estate. John Warr was at the back of the group and Bro Si somewhere in the middle. The procession headed down the King's Road, blocking both pedestrians and motor vehicle operators.

"Does the guy in the car know where the fuck we're going?"
I shouted above the roar of engines.

"The M4!" Mark shouted back.

I grunted, nodded, and shut up. I didn't want to look too
confused, not during my debut as the Wild One of Chelsea and
Fulham.

I breathed a sigh of relief when we hit the M4, at least now
it was a straight run to Hungerford. By Heston, everything was
going well. A couple of bikers hadn't bothered making the stop
and obviously weren't interested in their featured parts in *Easy
Rider II*, but the rest of us were all staying together, and I had
forgotten that I wasn't exactly sure of where we were going. I
had even started a bit of impromptu drag-racing with Proops,
who must have had the notion that because he'd had his new
Springer custom-painted a sort of metallic mauve it could compete with my Branch heads. He kept stealing up from the back
of the pack, slipping in beside me, challenging me by revving
his engine, then taking off with me in hot pursuit, until I had
caught up and passed him, then slowed down enough to let
him ride up beside me. And we'd be off again, and again, as
the cameras rolled.

And then the rain began.

The Ford Estate slowed down, and Mark and Jonky slipped
out from the front of the line and dropped back to film the
procession from the rear. And the rain came harder.

And I, the Road Captain of HOG, Fulham and Chelsea
Chapter, didn't have a clue where I was or where the hell I was
going, and, because of the last half-hour's road-racing with the
now invisible Proops (he'd dropped back with the camcorder)
I'd lost all conception of how far we'd gone. All I knew was that
Hungerford was somewhere up the road: I couldn't actually
remember if the turn-off was marked. The rain was now dictating
the "Tilley Technique" of riding with one hand while wiping
the aviators with the other, and, under my expert guidance, the
group had slowed to less than thirty miles an hour.

So I panicked and took the nearest exit off the motorway.
I discovered midway that it wasn't an exit at all, but an on-ramp.

I rode till the end, then pulled over to the side of the road and shut off my engine.

John Warr arrived, amidst a block-up of automobiles trying to go the right way, and looked at me in utter amazement.

"I don't know where the fuck Hungerford is!" I shouted above the horns. John shook his head, turned his bike around, and led a handful of charter members back on to the M4. The rest went their own ways, sneaking into the one-way system and disappearing in all directions. Bro Si and the Digas vanished.

I was ashamed, humiliated, and angry: with the weather, with John Warr for appointing me road captain, with myself for accepting, and with Mark for losing his license. I sat another few minutes then decided to go on, trusting that one way or the other I'd get myself to Littlecote.

A couple of hours later I arrived. It was still raining and the camp grounds resembled a battlefield already: people with buckets baling out water-filled tents, people digging in with shovels, people cursing. Most of the chapter had already arrived and I—captain of the *Bounty*, post-mutiny—was greeted with varied laughter and comments. There was already a rumor circulating that John Warr was interviewing other patch-wearing members for my post. I accused Proops of distracting me; it was my single defense.

The ride-out was as disastrous as my brief tenure as road captain. About one hundred bikes, led by a rubber-suited de Savary and a similarly slick companion, headed through the great iron gates of Littlecote. The Chelsea and Fulham contingent constituted at least seven of that number (the rest were either headed home or holed up in the saloon bar of the nearest hotel). Bro Si, the reverse-seated Digas, and I were amongst the die-hards.

We lasted two miles. By then the rain was coming down so hard that it was impossible to see, let alone film, and, one by one, we pulled off the road. Only the Full-Dressers with their walkie-talkie hook-ups and wraparound windscreens managed to finish the course.

On our way to our hotel we were sadly reminded of the downside of riding a motorcycle: a Sportster lay in the road directly in front of the hotel's parking lot. There was something about seeing it like that, on its side, wheels off the ground, handlebars twisted, tank bent inwards, that sent a chill through me. It was a completely unnatural sight. Because the rider was no longer at the accident scene, I conjectured the worst. If the bike could look so vulnerable, what had happened to the rider? I knew that it could have been me, my bike, lying still and broken; that knowledge, however buried, is always there and when the reality stared me in the face there was no place to hide.

I discovered later that the man had been badly injured. Apparently he had skidded in the wet and broadsided an oncoming truck. On top of the weather, the accident threw a shroud over the day.

By the time we'd parked in the hotel lot, and checked in—I was rooming with Bro Si, Mark with Jonky—the rain had evolved from drops to a solid sheet. Even the sprint from the room section of the hotel to the bar, the congregating point for most of the rally, resulted in a thorough soaking. But the majority of the Chelsea and Fulham contingent were already there, along with a hundred or so other partiers, ranging from HOG patch-wearing bikers from as far north as Southport to several rougher-looking bros of unknown origin.

I had come prepared to pose in an old Harley T-shirt, the logo so faded as to be almost invisible and the arms cut way back to reveal the fresh ink. Johnnie Walker was the first to notice, saying, "Watch out, it's Rambo," as I prowled the room. Proops was more complimentary, doing everything but putting on his jeweller's eyeglass to make certain the blue crane was not a transfer. Finally he declared it a work of art, tasteful and not too big, and admitted to wanting one himself. Someone else asked me if the crane was the logo for the Nat. West. bank. It should have been, with the money I owed them, but the comment hurt anyway. In fact it began a reaction that continued well into the next riding season and kept me thinking of certain enlargements to the pattern.

The rain never let up and by the time we struggled through the mud to the camp ground it was fairly obvious that the only wet T-shirt competition that was likely to take place was walking around in front of us: one hundred percent male, and highly water-logged. The marquee was there, so was the famous gnarled oak, minus the celebrity tooter, but the log fires were so saturated that they couldn't be ignited, and the band hadn't showed up. Jonky continued to film, travelling from hotel room to hotel room, camera in hand, doing spot-interviews with the water-logged and disgruntled. Bro Si and I made the best of a bad situation. We purchased several copies of *Tattoo Review*, now we had earned the privilege of commenting on the various levels of "demographics," and retired to our room with a fifth of Scotch and whatever other mind-alterers we could get our hands on.

By eight o'clock we were wandering around our six by ten double-bedder in a substantial state of inebriation, checking out each other's tats, comparing them to more heavily inked bros in *Tattoo Review*, and vowing a return to the Den of Skulls. By nine we had decided to visit the Digas and see if he was up for a side-saddle ride to the fairgrounds.

The bikes, meantime, looked the same way they had on the second night of the Marbella Run, miserable and getting worse.

The Digas was holed up watching television, equally intoxicated and complaining about the sore ass caused by his peculiar riding position. His chauffeur was in the bar filming, and Bro Si volunteered to transport him via his "pussy pad." We headed out into the downpour and sloshed our way to de Savary's.

There were a few partiers on site, but too few to actually party, although I did spot one naked reveller dancing madly in the mud, beside his one-man tent, the Rolling Stones' "Satisfaction" being pumped from a cassette player inside. Most of the Chelsea and Fulham contingent had headed back to the King's Road and were by now probably well into their third cappuccino at the Dôme. We hung around till we were soaked, shivering, and certain that the sky would never clear.

"I wonder if there's anything good on TV?" Mark asked.

It had come to that.

I think we were all asleep, heavily sedated, by midnight.

It rained all night and into the next day.

We departed at noon, groaning and hung over, on saddles that felt like wet sponges. It was a one hand on the bars one hand wiping the aviators ride to London.

"Hey, Boy, Do You Know How to Dance?"

The weather cleared, as much as it ever does between October and May, and the HOG meetings at the Arizona continued. Membership was growing and the rumor that I had been replaced as road captain was confirmed, although the replacement had not been named. There was also talk that the Hell's Angels were coming down to check us out on the next Thursday gathering.

It didn't make much sense to me; I hardly considered Johnnie Walker, myself, or the Digas much of a threat to the Jeep patrols at the Bulldog; although on the other hand the Chelsea and Fulham chapter of HOG could provide a bit of light entertainment. I had fantasies of various scenarios of humiliation, on the order of the old Western movies, when the real cowboys pulled into town, headed down to the local saloon, and "invited" the local dudes to "dance," providing the rhythm by pointing their six-guns at their feet and firing away. . . . I could imagine Proops doing an inspired quick-step.

"No, nothing like that," Bro Si assured me, "Charger and Snob have been coming in here for a few months; they're great guys. You'll love 'em."

Charger? Snob? I ran the names through my head a few times, hoping I'd be spared the silver-bullet quick-step by virtue of my ink, however humble.

The big night came. It was crisp and dry, and the moon was full. I rode down to the Arizona, powered by a "nitrous cocktail," five tabs of guarana and a shot of tequila. There were about twenty of Chelsea's finest in attendance, and the slammers flowed. Kathy viewed my new ink, spurred on by Bro Si, and asked, "Where is it?"

And the slammers flowed.

And no Hell's Angels showed up.

It got to be ten o'clock. This was late by Chelsea and Fulham standards, particularly for men like me, retired road captains in continual training for events that never take place—films, TV series, life or death battles.

And then it began, like a low thunder on the night horizon.

"Here they come," Bro Si whispered.

I had long had one particular image of the Hell's Angels, ever since the early '70s, when I was stoned on acid, hitch-hiking across the Golden Gate Bridge in San Francisco. A solo Angel had appeared on the crest of the bridge and roared down in my direction, a Highway Patrol car, lights flashing and siren screaming, in pursuit. The Angel was riding a chopper with bars so high he seemed to be standing on the bike, cut-off denims and colors flapping behind, long hair trailing him like a banner. He'd looked back once, given the cops the finger, opened up his bike and shot past me like a bullet ... a wild flash of danger, color, and roar.

Now I watched as about ten bikers rounded the corner, revving their engines and cruising the crowd which had gathered in front of the restaurant. Some were wearing their full colors, the famous Hell's Angels patch with its winged death's head and the letters MC below and to the right side and London, signifying the name of their chapter, arcing upwards beneath it. Some had only the word London on their jackets, and I found out later that these were the "prospects," men on probationary status before being accepted as full members of the club.

Their bikes were generally older than ours; out of the ten, there were only three or four Evolution engines, the rest were Shovelheads, and each bike had been altered in some way. Tiny saddles, high ape-hanger handlebars, drag pipes. They didn't, however, look like factory customs—perfect paint work and high-gloss polish—more like they had been customized by their owners, adding bits and pieces along the way.

The Angels rolled their bikes back against the curb opposite ours, forming a perfect line-up in one swoop. Then they got off and looked over at our group. By then I was nervous, feeling a touch of fear. I wasn't really picking out individuals; more wondering what they were going to do and how I would react. Bro Si broke the ice. He grabbed hold of me and led me forward to meet Snob.

Snob was standing by his bike, a flamed Softail that looked as though it had been stretched and raked, with the front fork extended and the angle of the front end raised, making the bike longer and lower.

"Richard, meet Snob," the master of ceremonies commenced.

Snob and I shook hands.

He was younger than me by a good ten years, taller than my five ten and looking broader across the shoulders, with dark hair and a wispy beard, plus brown eyes that glowed in the dark.

"How do you do, Richard," he said as we shook.

I was struck by his voice; he sounded like he might teach elocution in his spare time.

I stood for a moment without a lot to say, a bit awkward,

then I did what usually comes naturally in these situations. I asked him about his bike.

"A gift from a brother in New York; he had it done up over there; I didn't change much, re-jetted the carb, polished the heads."

I studied his bike for another minute then pointed out my own.

"I hate the pipes." Snob was obviously not a man to mince words.

"Yeah, but they work; the bike flies."

Meanwhile, the rest of the Angels had either joined the crowd or headed in to the bar.

"What have you had done to it?" Snob asked.

"Branch heads, Screamin' Eagle cam and carb," I answered.

Snob fingered his beard and nodded his head; he didn't look totally convinced.

"Take it out for a run," I suggested.

"Only if you'll take mine."

I looked across at the flamed Softail; I'd never ridden a bike with a stretched frame and wasn't so sure I wanted to make my debut in front of the London chapter of the Angels.

"I've had too much to drink, I wouldn't trust myself on it," I answered.

"Fair enough, we'll save it for another time."

Right about then we were joined by a tall, good-looking lady pushing a baby carriage. "Richard, this is Fiona, and that's Daniel, my son," Snob said, introducing us. Fi was full of life and Snob melted over his son, lifting him from the carriage and nuzzling him like a big friendly bear. But there was an edge to Snob, something in his eyes and manner, as there was to the rest of the club. They were friendly, to a point. Beyond that, non-members weren't invited.

They stayed another half-hour or so, drinking and chatting, occasionally taking a look at one of the Chelsea and Fulham bikes, then, in unison, they left. As ordered as they had arrived. Two by two, perfect formation.

Before he took off, Snob handed me a business card:

Ultimate Performance U.K. Harley-Davidson Specialists
"We Build Horsepower, Not Horseshit"
Unit 6, Sandringham Mews, Ealing, London

He invited me to stop by any time; "We'll talk about making that bike go a little faster. . . ."

A Natural Showman

A couple of things motivated me to take Snob up on his offer. The first was the old Hog fever. Snob's departing line about making that bike go a little faster rekindled questions about just how fast my bike could be made to go, and by now I'd had the Branch and Screamin' Eagle set-up on long enough to be used to it.

The second was curiosity. I was interested in the Hell's Angels Motorcycle Club. To me, they represented the real thing, their colors, their style, their sense of brotherhood. The fact that I had gotten on well with Snob and that he operated a legitimate business gave me reason to turn up at his shop; it wasn't like I was gate-crashing the club house.

So the following Saturday I rode the Springer to Ealing, down the Broadway, turned right into Sandringham Mews, and parked in front of Unit No. 6. The doors to the shop were wide open, and I saw Snob standing with a couple of other men, staring down at the Shovelhead engine of an old Sportster, listening as he cranked the throttle, building the revs, then letting it back off, using a screwdriver to make adjustments to the carburetor. His sleeves were rolled up, and he had two armfuls of tattoos, from club insignias to twin-cylinder bike engines. I walked closer and stood in the doorway. No one looked up and for a moment I considered backing out and departing, like an uninvited guest, thinking, Maybe this *is* club territory.

Finally Snob saw me. "Hold on, Richard, I'll be with you in a second!" A few minutes later he shut the engine off, nodding to the fellow holding the handlebars to roll the bike out of the shop.

Talk about a crucifix position, the ape-hangers on the Shovel were so high that the rider looked like he was hanging from a parallel bar, ready to perform some gymnastic exercise.

"They're the kind of bars you should have," Snob said, glancing from the Sportster to my Springer.

"What else do you think you can do for it?" I asked, as the Shovel blasted off, back wheel throwing gravel as the bike rounded the corner at the top of the alley and disappeared.

"He wants to know what we could do for it, Arn?"

A bearded man with several earrings, half a dozen finger rings, and sparkling eyes walked out of the garage, followed by a dark-headed boy who looked about fourteen. They circled the Springer.

"What do you think, Pee Wee?" Snob asked the boy.

Pee Wee smiled.

"What are you trying to tell me?" I asked.

"I'm trying to tell you that we could do anything you wanted, if you knew what you wanted."

"Well, hell, I just spent a load of money having it customized."

Snob laughed. "That's what I loved about you guys the other night, all your mates there at the Arizona, standing around looking at each others' bikes. . . . Staring at your gold eagles and fish-tail exhausts." There was no malice in his tone, just simple amusement. "You guys are all riding stock bikes. Even yours has just got some bolt-on parts added. Right out of the box. That's not a custom bike."

It was the first time I had heard the term "bolt-on parts."

"I mean do you want your bike raked, stretched . . . ?"

Thankfully I was well versed on my *In The Wind* literature.

"No, I want to keep the frame standard, those springs and that twenty-one inch tire are dodgy enough without a stretched front. If anything I want some performance work." I was talkin' the talk. As usual with no concern for cost.

"Come on inside," Snob said.

We went down the stairs at the back of the workshop. It was like a wine cellar down there, a maze of underground rooms with shelves and bike parts and stone walls and the right chill factor for a good Chablis. Snob's office was heated and had two desks, a fax machine, and a wall full of pictures of Snob with his arm around various other members of his club. Some of the shots looked like they were taken in England, others New York, or maybe LA. I was minding my manners so I didn't ask. There were also a couple of brothers installed in the two available visitors' chairs.

Snob made some brief introductions, and we sat at the adjoining desks. "It all depends on what you want to spend on it," he began. "A couple of hundred will get you an S&S carb, and another couple'll get you an Andrews cam. They'll make it run better than the set-up you've got. After that it gets real expensive; you're talking about rebuilding the engine, upping the ccs."

Meanwhile I was not thinking about how much money I had in my account, or how much I owed, or about the letter that my bank manager had written me that morning, but about that old American Express gold card account and whether I could squeeze it for another grand.

There was something *real* about Snob's place, and I figured I needed a little of it on my bike.

"Why don't you ride it first, then tell me what you think I need?" I replied.

"I don't have time right now to ride it. Do you want to leave the bike here?"

"I can't do that, I use it too much . . . Just take it for a quick one. I think it runs pretty good." Just that hint of a challenge.

Snob looked at me and nodded. "All right, all right. Pee Wee!!! Get me my lid!"

Pee Wee appeared with Snob's helmet while he pulled on his riding jacket and colors. He put on his gear like a knight climbing into his armor, and I began to see that Snob was a natural showman.

"Arn, will you take a look at Charlie's bike," he said, indicating one of the seated Angels, "while I take a spin on Messieur La Plonk's machine. I won't be long." Then we headed for my Springer.

He pressed the starter button, then let the engine idle, all the time giving me a lecture on the importance of allowing the engine to warm up. My grandfather used to give me the same lecture about my '57 Ford. I was starting to feel at home, particularly after Snob had departed and I was standing next to Charlie in the workshop.

Charlie, a.k.a. "Crazy" Charlie Batten, had been in the club for a long time, right back to the late '60s. When London got its charter, the first overseas charter from the American Hell's Angels, Charlie was a founding member. Gray-bearded, with the eyes of a sage, Charlie's seen a lot of people come and go; he's been off his bike as many times as most people have been on—on one occasion pronounced DOA at the hospital, only to self-resurrect after two months in a coma—and he's the only Angel I've ever met who is not tattooed (apart from a small club insignia on his left forearm). He is also a street poet. And as Snob's echo faded in the distance Charlie took hold of my arm and began a recitation.

I can't repeat his delivery, which rivals any Southern Baptist preacher, but I can quote an example of his work.

> *That which seems like an impossible dream of heaven*
> *Which we have in this world, which gets more like hell every day*
> *Can only come nearer as a result of our mutual exchange without*
> *   price*
> *On condition of* Truth, Trust, *and* Respect.
> *That Kingdom we pray for can only come when God's will has been*
> *   done on earth.*

*We must fully practise that commandment, supreme amongst the
    others,*
*"Love one another," without having to beg, borrow, or steal from
    each other.*
We must help each other, and give of ourselves that which we can.
We must forgive others, before we can expect them to forgive us.
*We must never lead another astray, but rather set an example for
    them to follow if they will. . . .*
It can only be if we are totally together with each other
that we will be able to really begin to see
that God's kingdom is all around us.
*Only when we are totally united regardless of race, color, or previous
    creed*
that we will be able to realize the required power to live even longer
than to the end of this century, if we manage to survive that long.
But if we can, then, forever, we will be able to share God's glory. . . .

                                                              So be it.

I was staring into his eyes, listening with one ear; the other was
tuned to the sound of the traffic, trying to hear the echo of my
pipes—I was, as usual, praying. Then Charlie delivered his final
verse;

I know that to many, I am regarded as an asshole,
but then I also know that although I may be, at least I try to put my
    shit where it belongs.

After which Arn suggested I go down and sit in Snob's office
while Pee Wee made me a cup of tea.

Another fifteen minutes passed, and my nerves were making
me sit rigid and silent. Then I heard something, almost like
my motorcycle, maybe just a little bit louder, approaching the
garage. . . . Finally I heard Snob's voice and breathed a sigh of
relief.

Until he came down the stairs.

"I'm going to have to rebuild that bike for you."

It was the way he said it. Not like "Do you want me to rebuild it?" but "I'm going to *have* to rebuild it."

"I came off," he added.

I saw that his blue jeans were shredded at the thigh and knees and there was blood seeping through them. He also had a rip along the sleeve of his jacket.

It's strange the way my mind worked. Even though I was seeing the evidence, hearing him say it, I still thought he was sending me up, testing me. The old paranoias cut in full throttle: it was all a set-up to see how I would react. So I didn't.

"I'm really sorry," Snob said, walking into the office.

I stared at him; the blood looked real enough.

"I wasn't going fast, maybe thirty; I hit a manhole cover and that front wheel just went." He sure as hell didn't sound like he was having me on.

"Are you all right?" I asked.

"It's not me I'm worried about," he answered.

I think we were both embarrassed; there was still part of me that didn't believe he could have come off the bike and it caused me to put a hold on my emotions. "Are you sure you're OK?" I asked again, looking at his knee; it seemed swollen.

"Yeah, yeah, I'm fine. . . . But I feel terrible about your bike."

"Let's go take a look at it," I said.

On the way up the stairs I felt like I was in a hospital, going to visit a member of the family who was on the critical list. Arn and Pee Wee were very subdued. For a moment I questioned myself. Is this where I was supposed to erupt like an animal, enraged that my precious creation had been dropped and broken . . . ? I didn't feel that way at all. In fact I felt like I had been asking for this for a long time. Why did I always insist that people ride my fucking bike. . . . ? This had been bound to happen, sooner or later.

The Springer was sitting outside the shop. At first it looked fine and the thought of a put-on returned to me. But as I got closer I could see the front forks were bent, the tank was scratched, and the rear right tail-pipe was minus a muffler. The boys gathered round like mourners at an open-casket viewing.

"You think I can get it home?" I asked.

"It's not safe to ride, not with the front forks bent like that," Snob answered.

"Fuck, what am I going to do?"

It was all very somber.

"Don't worry, we'll get it back together for you, no problem," Arn assured me.

"Yeah, but I use that bike every day."

"Let him have the Fat Boy," Snob said, pointing to a new silver Harley-Davidson parked across from the shop.

The Fat Boy was not my idea of a mean machine. The Fat Boy, I believed, was Harley-Davidson's answer to the '90s. Something based on their tried and true Heritage, but just that little bit innovative: lower handlebars, shot-gun style exhaust-pipes and two solid wheels, no spokes, with a yellow trim around the heads of the standard 1340 Evolution engine and a sculpted front and rear mudguard, all painted silver. *HOG* magazine had reviewed it as a "remarkably tasteless motorcycle, made up of a dozen different bad ideas." It was a silver blimp, and I was in motorcycle purgatory as I rode away from Ealing and towards home.

Used to having people give my Springer the once over at traffic lights and nod their approval, I was amazed when the same thing happened on the Fat Boy, amazed that anyone could find the bike attractive. But the more I rode it the easier it seemed to become. It always takes time to get used to a new motorcycle. To adjust to a new saddle position, different handlebars, brakes, etc. The Fat Boy was the easiest adjustment I had ever made. By the time I'd reached Richmond Park I was throwing the bike around. Maybe it was the two sixteen-inch wheels—as opposed to the Springer's twenty-one-inch front—or maybe it was the low, wide handlebars, but suddenly I could corner.

I whipped it inside my garage, looked it over again. I still hated the sight of it. Went inside and phoned Snob.

He'd already checked with Fred Warr about the availability of parts and figured he could get me back in my own saddle in a week or so. Until then, he added, "Treat that Fat Boy like you own it."

I did.

That evening I performed a major polish.

A week later I was carrying my first pillion passenger since Johnnie Walker, my theatrical agent, Duncan Heath, *en route* to a meeting with another recent Harley convert, Mike Ryan.

"God, I love this bike. How much did you pay for it. Is it easy to ride? Do you think I could ride it?"

"It's the easiest bike I've ever been on; it's called a Fat Boy," I answered.

"A Fat Boy, what a great name.... I just love this Fat Boy...."

"Right, let's get down to business," Heath began, taking immediate control as he eyed everything from Mike Ryan's hairline to his new silk waistcoat.

Fifteen minutes later, business concluded, we got on to motorcycles.... Mike's Shovelhead was nearly on the road, I was on the Fat Boy, and Heath was pissed off . . . he didn't own a bike.

"And if you had one, you wouldn't ride it," I said sarcastically.

"That's not true.... If I had that Fat Boy—"

"Do you want to buy it?"

"Absolutely.... Is it for sale? How much is it....? How much?"

I knew by the perspiration on his forehead that Heath had the beginning of Hog Fever. Price would be no object. He was destined for the Fat Boy.

I made the necessary phone call and Snob agreed to let the

bike go for £8,900, about five hundred less than new, which worked out at about a pound off for every mile on the bike. Two hundred of which were my own. And Fat Boys were hard to come by; there were only a few in England.

I called Heath and told him the price.

"I don't have any money," he said. Fine. That didn't bother me at all; I wasn't that wild about the idea of losing my "new" ride anyway. "But I've got to have that Fat Boy," he went on. It was that old Hog Fever talking.

"I'll call you tonight. . . . Let me have till six o'clock."

By then, I assumed, if I knew my Hog Fever symptom Heath would have jimmied and shimmied every banker's card and overdraft, even the big gold card account, until he had figured a way to steal the money.

At six, on the dot, the phone rang. It was Heath. On time for one of the few times in his life.

"Give me that Fat Boy."

I don't know where he'd found it, but he had. Ready to produce a "banker's draft" and take possession of the silver blimp.

Then I asked the million-dollar question.

"Duncan, do you know how to ride a motorcycle?" From what I remembered his entire experience in the saddle had been two miles from Kensington to Sloane Square, in 1969. Silence. "Have you got a license?"

At times like these, when the fever has taken complete control of everything from your balls to your bank book, things like money, the ability to ride, or owning a driver's license, are trivial.

"I want that Fat Boy," he growled down the line.

"Yeah, but Duncan, you're not going to be able to ride it legally." That coming from the man who had operated two Harleys without a license.

"All right, Dickster, listen carefully, here's what we're going to do. . . ." I waited. "I buy the bike and you keep it for me until I get a license. Ride it all you want."

I liked the idea; I estimated that would give me a couple of years with the Fat Boy. At least time to get my bike customized.

From a Crane to an Eagle

With business concluded and the Fat Boy as good as my own I decided to let Snob hold on to my Springer and do that bit of performance work that would separate me from the growing number of Screamin' Eagles at the Arizona.

Meanwhile, back at ICM, Heath was threatening to go on a rider's training course, one of the ones that guaranteed a pass on part one of the test and refresher courses until the trainee managed to obtain a full license; but it went on like that for several months. Heath would threaten to learn to ride, Snob would tell me to be patient.

By then I was a frequent visitor to Ultimate Performance and spent a lot of time with Snob. He was an interesting man. Product of a middle-class upbringing, proper English public schools, and a doting, if somewhat neurotic, mother, Snob has been a member of the Hell's Angels for nine years.

I asked him what got him into the club.

"Public schools," he replied, "the old English 'bully' system. When the senior boys decided to beat the shit out of the younger ones, and it got to be my turn, not just once but lots of times. Until I got tired of being bullied. . . . So, under the guidance of my friend, Tigger, I joined a group of juniors who banded together and returned a bit of the treatment. . . . It taught me early that there was strength in numbers, particularly when it came to opposing what we considered a misuse of authority. Then, when I was older, I saw an interview with Sonny Barger, one of the American presidents"—of the Oakland, California Hell's Angels—"and he was talking about the same thing, banding together, looking out for yourself by looking out for your brothers. What he said made sense to me, because I'd already proved it to myself. So I got to know some of the guys in the London chapter, became a hanger-on for a while, decided that the things they stood for were the things I believed in. Finally I became a prospect and then a member."

Snob was not typical of the Angels that I've met, but then in my experience there are no typical Hell's Angels. Between Snob and Crazy Charlie there are three generations of club members, all of them governed by the rules of their organization and united by their colors but each separate in personality. The club members that I met, I liked, and the fact that Snob was a Hell's Angel (currently President of the London chapter) became incidental to our friendship.

I paid a visit to Ultimate Performance on the day that the internal wiring was being orchestrated, fed through holes drilled in the handlebars by a man from Reading known as "Steve the Plumber."

By now my motorcycle had been converted from the stock belt to chain drive—the O-ring steel links are less likely to slip or break from the power surge of the 95 cubic inch engine— and the extra-wide tire and solid chrome back wheel had replaced the stock tire and wheel. The steel skeleton was filling out and it looked mean; lean and mean.

One of the reasons it looked so lean was that it didn't have an engine. That piece of the jigsaw was being handled by Snob, personally, downstairs in his engine room. Occasionally he would call me down to view his creation: nitralloy crankcases housing the famous Sputhe big-bore cylinders, an Andrews EV7 camshaft (Snob had called it a "wild cam" and said he was using one in his own engine, and I told him to put one in mine,

I liked the term "wild" in spite of the fact that he thought an EV5 might be more suitable to my riding style. . . . ("Fuck the five, let's go for the seven," I said), and Crane roller rocker arms. None of which I understood, no matter how many times he explained to me what each component did, but all of which, he assured me, were the best money could buy and would make my bike very fast with loads of torque at the bottom end.

When I got tired of examining the inside of my newly cleaned heads or peering into the Sputhe barrels, or making the pistons go up and down like a baker kneading dough, I would return to the upper floor and watch Steve the Plumber in action.

He was wearing a T-shirt and, being a recent connoisseur of ink, I couldn't help but notice that he was "wall-to-walled," with some of the best-looking skin art I had ever seen: a dragon running up his arm, flames, and an Indian head, all beautifully colored and detailed. I complimented him on his tattoos and he stopped long enough to lift his shirt and reveal a half-finished back piece. At first sight the piece looked somehow biblical, like one of those ceiling murals in a Roman chapel, but as my eyes honed in on the canvas I could see that the tattoo was contemporary, depicting a gang fight in progress. A man had been thrown to the floor in the center of a circle of bikers. One of them hovered above him, chain in hand, while their leader was giving the thumbs down sign. It was a painting of modern gladiators, somewhere between *The Wild One* and *West Side Story*; the detail of the work was incredible, graphic, yet somehow alive.

"Fantastic. Who did it?" I asked, suddenly inspired to have my crane turned into an eagle.

"Ian of Reading," he answered.

"Does he have a shop?"

"If you want, I'll give you his phone number."

Half an hour later, Ian of Reading's number in my pocket, I rode home. The following Saturday I Fat Boyed to Ian's and added to my wildlife collection. The pony-tailed biker tattooed a Celtic eagle around my left forearm, done in turquoise and

The Softail

The Fleet

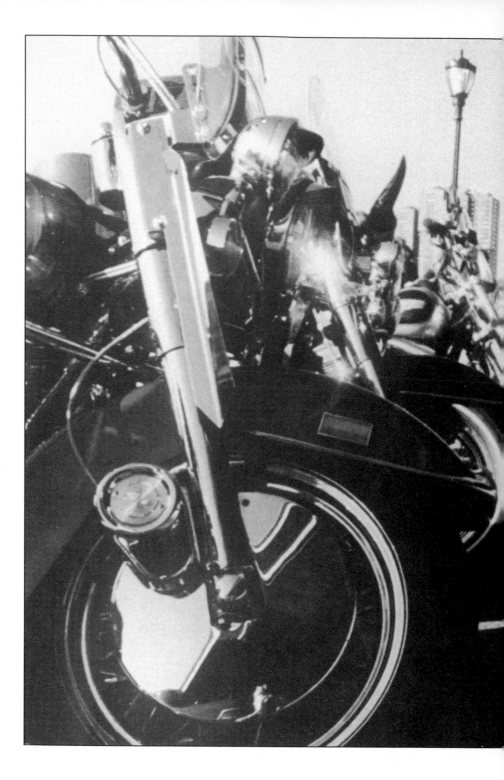

The Manhattan Lineup

Captain Bandana on the Prototype

The Illusion of Speed

The Connoisseur and the Tortoise

Service call in Kansas

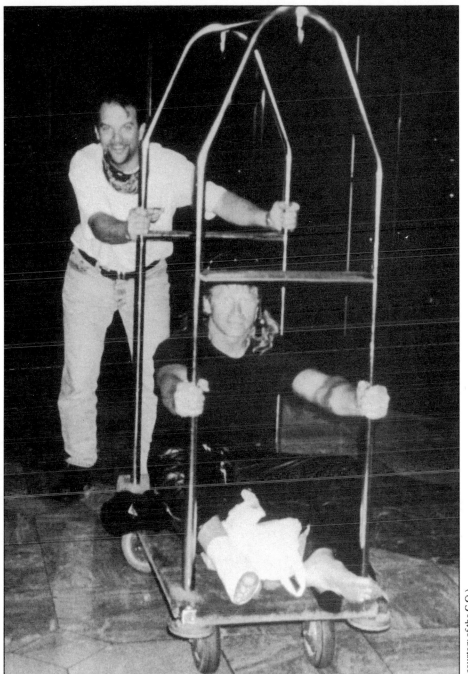

(courtesy of the C.O.)

A dignified arrival

Every inch the heavy bro

with such intricacy that it looked like a piece of jewelry. I was now a two-tat man. I was evolving.

Meanwhile, the London Harley scene was also evolving. About three years behind Los Angeles, where—before he ran a red light and ended up in the hospital—Billy Idol was already into chopped Harleys and ape-hangers, and actor Gary Busey into wheel-stands, prior to some serious damage to the back of his skull by virtue of a failed wheelie in front of Bartels'.

Bro Si had sold the Arizona, and the HOG meetings had been moved to the Hard Rock Cafe, whose owners had agreed to give all Harley riders free admission, a free drink, and complete run of the downstairs room.

I remember the first Harley night at the Hard Rock, rounding Hyde Park Corner and riding the Fat Boy down Piccadilly, expecting to see the usual dozen or so bikes that had been showing up in Camden Town at the Arizona and seeing, instead, over a hundred Harleys, lining the pavement in front of the Hard Rock, being photographed, videoed, and generally ogled by the fans.

All the regulars were there, Huggie, Johnnie Walker, Adrian, Proops, Mark, Bro Si, Richard Young, Martin, John Warr, the twins, Fred Warr, even Dave, plus just about every face I had ever seen come in or go out of Warr's, including Paul Young, the rock singer, and a couple of Harley-owning DJs and rock stars. There were some fabulous motorcycles, immaculately restored old timers, including an original 61E, a 36 HP 61 cu. in. (1000 cc) machine with a sprung front end—which the modern Springer is based upon—a Knucklehead engine, and gear levers mounted on the side of the tank. The 61E was manufactured between 1936 and 1952 and a modified version set the mile speed record of 136 MPH in 1936. The "E" is still a very sought-after bike. The owner of this one had restored it himself—keeping everything as close to stock as he could and ridden it down from Nottingham.

"How about the gears; it's got to be a bitch shifting by hand," I commented.

"It's no fun in town," he admitted, "but once I'm out there on the motorway, that old bus just rolls along, smooth as silk."

I could take one look at him—he was in his mid- or late fifties and had rally badges all over his leather jacket—and understand how much he loved that bike. It was that way with most of the people at the Hard Rock that first night, riding everything from American police bikes—with flashing lights and sirens still functioning—to racing Buells and Full-Dressers: a lot of people who genuinely loved their Harleys, who had not come to pose, as Harley people are often accused of, but to look at and talk about the objects of each other's obsessions. . . . Maybe a little posing on the side.

A few folks asked me about the Fat Boy. Did I like the way it handled? Did I think it was worth the nine and a half grand. I answered them as well as I could, all the while feeling like I should be wearing a placard which read *My other bike's a custom Springer*. It wasn't that I didn't like Duncan's bike, it was just Duncan's bike, the bike that he saw as the most beautiful motorcycle in the world. It wasn't mine. That is where the Harley-Davidson becomes so personal; the more you do to it right from that first eagle, the more personal it becomes. And the Springer was becoming very personal.

The next time I saw it the handlebars were wired and in position. A set of sixteen-inch apes, formerly owned by Arn and ridden, he testified, at least thirty thousand miles, added a bit of character to the chrome, and gave a high-rise effect to the "scarecrow" appearance of the bike.

A rear mudguard had arrived from the States, shorter than stock, and tighter to the wheel, with much smaller struts, and the gas tank had come back from Dream Machine.

Here is where a very personal touch came into being.

I am crazy about cats, and in my first book, a fantasy fiction, I had a woman who metamorphosized into a panther. The cover artist had designed a back piece for the book that had the head of the cat, the upper half of its face hidden behind a gold mask, only the eyes coming through. Very surreal. I'd liked it enough to have my cousin, a silversmith, make me copies in sterling silver and gold. I used them as key rings.

So what I did was take the key rings into John Sylvester, a Richmond silversmith, and asked him to make copies, so they could be screwed on to the sides of my gas tanks, replacing the Harley logos. They looked great. Silver and gold against lacquered black. I couldn't wait to get the tank back on the bike.

But what about the engine?

There was a lot of cursing from the bowels of Ultimate Performance, down in the engine room. Dr. Snob wasn't getting the valve clearance he wanted, or something to that effect, and Crane still hadn't sent the pushrods, or they had sent the pushrods but the wrong pushrods.

Now Snob can be a bit temperamental at times, and when he starts in on one of his artistic tantrums it's a good idea to clear the premises. There's always a lot of eye to eye contact between Pee Wee and Arn, a few nods of the head, and then the raging bull appears from the basement, roaring up the stairs. By now, the bike was not only personal to me, but also to Snob. I may have been the guy who was going to ride it, but Snob was the creator.

A couple more Thursdays at the Hard Rock—with me on the Fat Boy—and there began some discreet inquiries as to whether I was ever going to get the Springer back. Snob had gone on temporary strike, saying that he couldn't continue until the bloody Americans sent him the parts that he had asked for. Parts did keep arriving, but the wrong parts. . . .

So, for a period, the steel skeleton-scarecrow—with its wide back tire, O-ring chain, and extra-low rear mudguard, plus Arn's soulful ape-hangers, stood like a custom effigy in the back of Snob's workshop. Many, including myself, came to pay homage, but few ventured to ask the creator when the fuck it would be on the road.

Until Fiona, Snob's willowy lady, did me the ultimate favor.

She had a blazing row with the maestro which prompted him to depart their automobile in mid-roll, hail a cab, and take up residence in his office at Ultimate Performance. Right next to the workshop.

He telephoned California, demanded that they ship the parts he needed by overnight express, and then, for three days and three nights, he labored, completing the power plant. Forged out of love and anger.

The call came on the fourth day. . . .

"Come and get it!"

My sheer excitement was tainted by severe embarrassment. I was, at that moment, a little strapped for cash.

During the twenty-minute cab ride to Ultimate Performance I conjured a hundred variations on what the Springer would look like, and what I would say to the maestro. What I saw when I opened the door of the workshop exceeded all of them. The bike had been transformed. Chassis low to the ground, bars to the sky, upswept fish-tail exhaust-pipes—check out Peter Fonda in *Easy Rider*—and those cat's eyes staring at me from the side of the tank.

Performance Machine brakes, the Ultimate Performance engine, an S&S super E carb, and Sportster rocker covers—a Snob original—that gave it a tight, compact look.

"It may have a few teething problems," he said, as we viewed the creation.

Let me on it, was my only thought before we went downstairs to settle up. The parts list with its accompanying bill was as long as my arm. I cringed.

"I know I took a long time, and I know you were patient, so on a lot of this performance stuff, I'm only charging for parts, no labor," Snob said before he tallied it up on his computer and read me the bill.

"Snob," I began, "if you had caught me a month ago, before

my last trip to LA, I'd have been fine, but right now, well, I'm a little tight . . . No, that's not exactly true. I'm nearly broke."

"No money. You've got no money?"

"Maybe a grand. . . . And if I stay in the movie business I won't have that. I'll end up having to sell the bike and my house."

Snob considered. "I didn't build this bike to have you sell it. I built it so you would ride it," he said, finally. "Give me what you can and pay me the rest in time. . . ."

You couldn't get any fairer than that. It was more an act of friendship than business. I thanked him and we went back up to the workshop. I stood in front of the maestro's creation.

"Let me on it." Hog Fever was churning like a tornado in my gut.

It was one of those freak afternoons in late winter. The sun was shining, the sky was blue, and the wind was coming gently from the south. The temperature was about fifty degrees, an oasis in a land of gray, and a prelude to spring.

I took it easy for the first couple of miles, getting used to the crucifix position, and the fact that there were no longer any indicators or mirrors—why wreck the lines of the beast?—and that the Springer now had enough grunt at the bottom end to lift the front wheel from the ground. Also I knew Snob, Arn, and Pee Wee would be listening to my departure—and believe me the Springer had about a two-mile listening range—making sure I didn't abuse the new engine before I had properly run it in.

By the time I had cleared Ealing, out of earshot, I was getting into the new riding position (the apes did give the bike its look although they lacked the control of the drag bars) and by the time I passed beneath the flyover, *en route* to Kew Bridge, I was in the wind. The bike bucked at the lights, full of torque, and pranced like a race horse when I accelerated, lean and light. I was singing by the time I rode into Richmond Park, a medley of hits from my highway jukebox, circling the park twice, just to lay into the bends in the road. Then down Kingston Hill straight by the entrance to my house and out on to the A3. No way anybody could catch the Cat—because that is exactly what I was riding, a fast, sleek black panther. Eating up the road, carrying me past the gates of Hog Fever and right into highway heaven. . . .

"Oh yeah, oh yeah . . . Oh fuckin' " —*sput, sput, sput*— *"no."*

Teething problems? Yes, there were a few.

"It needs to go on a rolling road," Snob explained, "that's the only way you can get a perfect balance between the engine, the carb, and the pipes."

In layman's terms, a rolling road is a treadmill hooked up to a computer. The front tire of the bike is held stationary while the back is attached to the mill, then the bike is run; it doesn't go anywhere, but the full range of its performance is graphed from the low end right through the upper range of its revs, and a good engineer can diagnose any imbalance in the system by reading the graph.

Snob had a rolling road, but at that time it wasn't functioning. So I took the Harley to the tuning specialists Rally and Race in Edmonton. They strapped it down, turned it on, and broke my heart.

"It's your tail-pipes, they're starving the engine, like breathing through straws."

My beloved Peter Fonda fish-tails were too long, upswept, and thin to allow the big engine to breathe properly, choking it out at the top end of its performance.

"We can build you some that will balance the engine."

And wreck the look of my motorcycle, I thought. But I couldn't stand the idea of Snob's engine being starved for oxygen; it was a pose versus practicality situation. I chose to make the bike work, and three weeks later it did. All 100 HP of it (the standard 1340 is estimated at 40 HP measured off the back wheel). I threw gravel and left a trail of rubber all the way from Edmonton ("Put the pipes on Access, please") to Snob's shop in Ealing.

"I preferred the look of the fish-tails," the maestro said, saddling up, "but these sure as hell work," he stated ten minutes later, after a reported 110 MPH in fourth gear.

In fact the pipes were beautiful, like extra-wide stainless-steel drag pipes, turned out at the ends and connected to each other by a balance pipe, adding back pressure to the system. They just weren't the perfect pipes, aesthetically, for the ape-hanger bars and chopped look of my motorcycle; it appeared, to me, as if two bikes had been hammered into one, a drag bike and a chopper. But, because of money, and the fact that my bike had been off the road more than on in the past six months, it was a look I was determined to live with. And the bike did *go*. Tried and proved at an abandoned airstrip, over a quarter-mile, topping 110 MPH. Until I was apprehended by the law. . . . The airstrip was not actually abandoned and a light plane was trying to land.

"Hey, Bro, It Ain't a Harley Any More"

During the next riding season I paid Snob the money I owed and almost got to accept the look of my motorcycle. Almost, until I saw the cover bike on a copy of *Heavy Duty* magazine. It was an Arlen Ness creation, and Ness is the undisputed king of the California custom scene. The bike looked about twenty feet long, low and sculpted, as if it had been aerodynamically shaped in a wind tunnel. The accompanying article gave the owner's name as Jeff Duval, of Battistini's Custom Cycles in Bournemouth. I was there the following Saturday, to examine the Ness bike in the flesh. Jeff Duval was there also and so were Rikki Battistini and his brother Dean.

"We can do most of that work right here," Rikki assured me, as I got on my hands and knees to examine Ness's art. The bike had been hand-crafted: fenders and tank molded to sit low against the extended frame, painted in red and trimmed with gold leaf, its forward look accentuated by the pulled-back drag bars and lowered head lamp. It looked too pretty to ride.

Meantime, Jeff Duval was examining my bike. "These pipes are fabulous," he commented, "I would love to see a one-piece tank wrapped around your engine and the bike lowered a couple of inches; it would clean the lines up and blend better with the lines of the pipes." He said it like an artist, not a salesman.

"And lower the handlebars, maybe a set of drag bars—" I began, the next incarnation beginning to shape in my mind.

"Yes, pull backs, and drop the front end." Jeff was a step ahead of me and on the same wavelength.

I left for London, the bike stayed at Battistini's. My parting words were. "Do whatever you think it needs."

Five weeks later, Rikki arrived at my house; he was driving a van.

"We went a little further than we originally planned," he explained as he opened the van's back gates. "I hope you like the result."

I waited as he disappeared inside; I could hear him removing the ties that held my motorcycle in place, then movement.

"Do you need a hand?"

"No, let me do it, I don't want you to see it till it hits the light," Rikki answered.

I held my breath as he rolled my bike backwards down the ramp, black lacquered paint and chrome reflecting the morning sun. He placed it on its stand and stepped away. Hog Fever hit me like a tidal wave: I wanted to jump on the motorcycle, ride it, polish it, and stare at it, all at once. Then the fever broke, leaving me calm and clear. I walked closer to the bike.

My motorcycle was finished. It was me. No longer (strictly speaking) a Harley-Davidson, but a completely unique custom motorcycle. It looked about half the size of the stock Springer, tight and low, with pulled-back drag bars, lowered front end, and that wind-tunnel appearance that had first attracted me to the Ness bike. My cat heads were mounted on a one-piece tank that sat low, literally wrapping around the rocker covers, and Snob's engine nestled like a steel fist beneath.

I knew, intuitively, that the bike was complete; that I would never alter its design again. It was as if something had been dredged from my subconscious and taken material form. A composite of the many hours and minds that had gone into its creation, yet guided by my own innate idea of my perfect motorcycle.

I had finally cured the fever.

THE AMERICAN RIDE

My right foot is in London, England, in a
splint, and my Harley Davidson is in Wichita,
Kansas, U.S.A., a very un-Zenlike separation
of man and machine.
"Shit happens," that's the old biker's
proverb. And it does. And it did.

I've got to confess. I did not cure the fever; I lied.
As soon as I had enough money to pay off my American Express
account, I dipped in again and bought another Harley. This
one was used, by a friend of mine, Jimmy Maloney, a man with
enough rally badges on his cut-offs to make him bullet proof.
Maloney knows bikes, and his Softail had a great engine. The
rest of the bike I turned over to Battistini's, in Bournemouth. It
came back long, low, and black. After the initial transformation I
took it down to Martin and Bill, at Fred Warrs, for a mechanical
once-over. It came back fast.

In fact, my new Harley was so far from stock that U.S. customs
refused to admit it into the country. They couldn't figure out
what the hell it was.

Finally, after signing affadavits, getting it bonded, singing
the "Star Spangled Banner" down the telephone, and swearing
allegiance to the United States of America, they released my
motorcycle.

It arrived, at my New York residence, in a wood crate, in
the back of a van.

The driver and I couldn't figure how the hell to get it from the van to the ground. It was a serious problem. Two hundred-and-seventy-pound men with a six-hundred-and-fifty-pound piece of metal sculpture in a hundred-pound crate, and a four-foot drop between the tailgate of the van and my dirt and gravel driveway. I spotted my wife staring at us from the window; I knew she'd have a solution—she generally does—but somehow, I didn't want to hear it. This was biker business.

We finally settled on sliding the crate down a couple of rotting fence poles, positioned like a ramp against the tailgate of the van.

It was a nervous five minutes, with a lot of, "hold on, it's shifting to the left! Wait, we're gonna lose it! Don't drop the fucking thing!" as, inch by inch, it made its descent.

My wife watched from the window, shaking her head.

The driver stuck around while I cut through the steel-reinforced tape with a kitchen knife, then tore the wood apart with my bare hands. He wanted to see what Customs had made such a fuss about; I was in a viewing frenzy.

In the New York sunshine the Harley looked like the Mona Lisa of two wheeled travel. A gleaming work of art.

There was a reason I shipped the bike to America; I planned to ride it cross-country.

The American Ride, cross-country; I'd been dreaming of doing it since I first hit the roads on my Norton Electra in 1966 but, between the psychedelic sixties, a few years lost in Mexico, and a move to London, I never made the run.

The idea, however, remained in my mind, lingering, like an acid flashback, painted in red, white, blue, black, and chrome. The Blue Ridge Montains of Virginia, the flat plains of Kansas, the desert highways of New Mexico, dry roads, sun pouring down. Oh, yeah. . . .

My chance came in early June, 1994. I was invited to ride cross-country with The Club.

* * *

The Club is a very exclusive group. Some very high rollers. Business men, politicians, entertainment moguls, fashion icons, property tycoons, these guys are serious. And, they love motorcycles.

One of the members is a wine connoisseur. I met him at a tasting and discovered we had a mutual interest in Harley Davidsons. He mentioned the Club, and their cross-country ride. I immediately suggested that I join up. He balked, informing me that it was not entirely his decision as to who rode with The Club. I persisted. It took a lot of wine, but, eventually, the Connoisseur became my Club sponsor.

Leather Stud

June 2nd, 1994

I rode in to New York City, this afternoon, covering about a hundred and thirty miles, from Springs, near the tip of Long Island to midtown Manhattan. The ride featured some of the most godawful potholes known to civilized man. By the time I hit the Triborough Bridge, leading into Manhattan, I'd spent at least half of my time in the air.

Along the way, I pulled into a custom bike shop and let "Crazy Ace" change my oil. That's where I bought my second helmet, one of those Prussian models, tight to the crown and turned up around the edges; they're not Department of Transportation (DOT) approved, but you can't beat them for style— See Marlon Brando in "The Young Lions."

It is now the night before the American Ride, and I'm holed up in a third floor room at the Drake Hotel, on Park Avenue, in New York City—a far cry from the two dollar a night, mosquito-infested "Hostels" that housed me through my European tour.

As opposed to previous Runs, when I carried my entire travelling kit—toothbrush and spare socks—in a small, leather tool bag (or stuffed down the front of my pants), I've packed heavy for this one. Leather pants, blue jeans, plenty of underwear, spare shirts, spare cowboy boots, a waxed rain jacket, and an extra helmet, all stuffed inside a suitcase and carried in a "Chase truck."

I've never been on a ride as well organized as this. Never been sent maps, itinerary charts, hotel locations, day-to-day breakdowns, a list of "essentials"—like wet weather gear—and I've never had the benefit of a Chase truck—carrying suitcases, spare parts, and spare motocycles. But this is the longest ride I've been on, nearly four thousand miles of highway and back roads, from New York City, to Las Vegas, Nevada. And, this is the most elite Club I have ever ridden with.

I met the Members earlier this evening, at the pre-ride dinner, and, frankly, I was a little concerned. They appeared incredibly civilized, real gentlemen, soft spoken, a few business suits, a lot of button down, oxford cloth shirts, and several pairs of highly polished shoes. Maybe a shade too sedate for me. Not much wine consumption. In fact, during the main course, the Club's road captain, looked over at me and said, "This ride might be a bit tame for you, Richard."

He was probably right.

Currently, I'm staring at myself in the Drake's bathroom mirror. I've got the new Prussian helmet on, along with a set of shades, my underwear, a new set of fingerless riding gloves, and a pair of black, suede cowboy boots.

It's past midnight, and I look like a pervert from *Leather Stud*, or some similar "gentlemen's magazine."

I think I'll drop a valium and see if I can sleep.

Death Race 2000

DAY 1

The following morning, at seven o'clock, we lined
up. Oxford cloth was replaced by T-shirts and Levis, and a night's
growth of stubble hardened formerly smooth faces. Thirteen of
the fifteen bikes were Harleys, mainly dressers and touring bikes,
plus a customized Low Rider FXR, a silver Fat Boy ridden by
a reknowned Stunt Pilot, a new Harley Road King, and the
Connoisseur's vintage FLH. Then, there were the accessories:
windshields, walkie talkies, and wrist mounted radar detectors.
The other bikes were a Ducati 900 Supersport and a Yamaha
FZR Rocket Sled.

At seven forty-five we pressed the starter buttons and roared
to life. Out of Manhattan and into the American Dream.

I didn't know it then, but I had just entered the millionaire's
version of "Death Race 2000."

"Pass every car on the road, and let no car pass you. That's
the main rule of The Club," a member informed me as we
exited New York City. I thought he was joking. I was wrong.

I knew I was in serious trouble when the Club banked right
to connect with the Garden State Parkway, and winging along
at eighty miles an hour, I discovered that I had no rear brake—
a direct result of Crazy Ace's oil change.

* * *

Me: "Are you sure you know how to get that oil filter off, it's right next to the brake line?"

Crazy Ace: "No problem, man, I've built two hundred custom bikes, this is nothin' new, leave it to me!" After which the guard chain went up, barring me from Ace's workshop, as his wrench slammed into my brake line, and the deed was done.

"I got no back brake! No back brake!!" I shouted across two lanes of asphalt at the bandanaed Road Captain.

Somewhere, in the recesses of my ego, I thought everyone would stop, while I sorted out my problem.

"Use your front!!" Bandana suggested casually, as he accelerated to a cruising speed of ninety, leaving me sputtering in the dust from his back tire.

"Christ," I thought, "Isn't that the same guy, who, last night, decked out in his ivy-league khakis and a wide smile, had layed the 'this could be a bit tame for you,' line on me?" After which, I'd settled smugly into my filet mignon, and pushed up my sleeve to reveal my blue, celtic tattoo. I was a man whose riding fame had clearly preceded him.

Now, here I was, bouncing like a pogo dancer, on my wafer-thin, street-cred saddle, shouting about having no brakes, and faltering on the first lap of the race.

"Right, fuck it, I'll pump the front break for four thousand miles," I decided, hitting a pothole which left me airborne for the two seconds that it took the Yamaha to fly by in the outside lane.

They may have looked like Dudes at dinner, but, on the road, they were Speed Monsters. And I, with my 88 cu. in. of power and a motorcycle that had been built more for the drag strip than a cross country adventure, wasn't about to fall behind. I vibrated to a hundred and held steady, checking my odometer. We'd covered thirty miles. That left only four hundred to go before Charlottesville, Virginia, our first stopover. I was already having spasms in my shoulder muscles, due to wind resistance, and my Everlast weightlifting belt—always a must for lower lumbar support—had vibrated upwards against my diaphragm, constricting my breathing.

"Comfortable?!" A voice to my right inquired, as another full faced helmet, shadowed by fairing and a windshield, eased by.

I grimaced, showed teeth, and wagged my head manfully.

"Comfortable?" Oh yeah. The five inches of elongation to the front end of my bike, which required a riding position equivalent to the yogic back stretch posture—where, seated, you grip your toes with your fingers and pull your head to your knees (preferable at speeds below one hundred)—was sublime.

Anyone who believes that America's fifty-five mile an hour speed limits are taken as gospel has another think coming. Cars, trucks, and milk wagons all rolled along at seventy-five. My images of a sedate crossing, banded together with my fifteen road bros at sixty MPH, breathing the country air and taking in the scenery, were replaced by Jimi Hendrix's rendition of "All Along the Watchtower," trailing from the speakers of the cream and black Touring bike in front of me, occasionally punctuated by a thundering "yee-haw!!" from its rider. "Death Race 2000," with the sounds of the sixties.

New Jersey was a blur.

We regrouped at the ferry—which crosses the Delaware Bay, from Cape May, New Jersey, to Lewes, Delaware—stowed the bikes, and floated away.

Without the Chase truck. That was driven by Gary, the club's mechanic; it was his thankless job to drive the fifty foot Ryder rental truck, and follow the hounds.

Impossible, since the truck's top speed was sixty, and maneuverability was limited to a straight line. But Gary was hardcore, complete with biker tattoos and a great drawl to his voice.

"Fuck it, I'll get there, when I get there," he'd declared at a gas station, about a hundred miles back along the highway.

An hour later, and three miles on the Delaware side of the ferry, I broke down. My road bros kept riding.

"Bastards," I thought, watching them disappear.

Then, the rumble of pipes, and two bikes circled back.

"Keep going, I'll wait for Gary," I urged my rescuers. I was already getting paranoid about lunch gatherings, without me, on the open road.

"Where's LaPlante?" The Road King would ask.

"Couldn't keep the pace," Captain Bandana would reply.

Then, turning to my sponsor, the Connoisseur, "what the hell did you bring him along for, anyway? Jesus, have you checked out his bike? It looks like a proctologist's examination table."

"You guy's keep going," I repeated, opening my gas cap, and looking in. There was the swirl of gas and the hiss of air; I screwed it back down, pressed the starter, and, miraculously, the engine roared.

"Vapor lock," the Ducati owner said, nodding his head, "keep the gas cap loose and let it breathe."

Back to business. Being the tail end of the afternoon, and following some hard combat to establish lead positions, my half of The Club slowed to seventy. With my front hand-braking technique mastered and my vapor lock vented, I started getting into the ride. It was the first time in my post-midlife biking career that I had ridden American highways, and they do ride good. Flat and wide, and, once outside of New York City, relatively free of pot holes, and those ski-jump joins in the asphalt, that can launch a Stretch into the stratosphere.

We ambled through the small towns of inland Delaware and across the Chesapeake Bay Bridge. Climbing high, above the silver-blue water, I was sitting on top of the world.

Then, onto a section of Interstate 495, otherwise known as the South Washington Beltway. Designed to circumnavigate the nation's capital, the Beltway is, instead, a navigational nightmare.

We hit it at rush hour, and within minutes I was following the strains of Jimi Hendrix's guitar, as we bobbed and weaved through the smoking metal.

Half an hour later, and it was just me and Electric Ladyland, alone on the loop. I watched the needle on my speedometer dance at a hundred and twenty as I fought to keep up. Finally, Hendrix pulled off, on the soft shoulder.

"Have you got any idea where we are?" he asked, stroking a chin so black from road soot that it looked like a beard.

"I think I've seen the same sign for Annapolis about three times. We might be going in a circle," I offered.

Hendrix grumbled, then looked down at his on-board road map, pinned to his console; he shook his head and eyed the traffic in front of us. "If we keep going south, we've got to get to Virginia." Not much conviction in his voice.

We set out again, cutting in through the stalled traffic, then out, then up, and through the middle. All my city driving skills were exercised to the max. The only thing missing was a couple of oxygen tanks, to compensate for the pure carbon monoxide we were forced to breath.

The sign "Welcome To Virginia" welcomed us like a mirage.

After that, the riding was good, just me and Hendrix, travelling along cool, country roads, through small towns and hamlets, past wood framed houses, and white painted churches, places that looked as if they'd been "time wrapped" at the end of the Civil War. Then, miles of country, interspersed with the occasional concession to modern man, the shopping mall, planted like vast, concrete latrines, along the barren landscape.

* * *

I figured that between vapor locks and the Beltway, Hendrix and I had to be the slowest duet of the day. Until I saw the two police cars and an assembly of Death Racers by the side of the road. Members of The Club. Nabbed for illegal use of lanes. I felt an instant loyalty; it lasted ten seconds, the time it took to remember that I was on the most illegal bike in America. No mirrors, no indicators, and no back brake. Plus an expired British license plate.

I rode by. Following Hendrix on to some nice, curving roads, grass so green on either side that, through my sunglasses, it looked blue. My bike was running smooth, and the slow, rolling hills rocked me like a baby.

Hendrix was a couple of bike lengths ahead of me and, I noticed, he kept glancing in his rear view mirror, while dropping his speed. I slowed, looked over my shoulder, and spotted a bike and rider, closing fast.

Another hundred yards and I could make out that the bike was a Harley—a silver Fat Boy—and that the rider was one of ours. It was the Stunt Pilot—reputed to one of America's best. He was six feet two, with arms like tree trunks, riding that Fatboy like he was flying a plane. Helmet slung back, off his head, held to his throat by its chin strap, he roared up beside Hendrix. I heard traces of their conversation, spilled by the wind.

"We've been lost on the beltway—five hours—haven't seen the Road King since—saw the other guys going in the opposite lane—"

Then, the sound of a police siren behind us, and the blinking lights.

We pulled to the side of the road, and shut off our engines, the patrol car right behind us.

"You boys know we got helmet laws in this state?" the officer began, staring at the Stunt Pilot, while hoisting his beefy frame from the car.

"I'm sorry, sir, but I've been lost for nearly eleven hours, and I'm so damn hot—" The Stunt Pilot sounded convincing.

Meanwhile, the policeman was headed for my bike.

"Aside from helmets, we require mirrors, and indicator lights, and, what's this?" Eyeing my plastic, yellow plate.

"I'm from England," I replied, stepping off, and away from the machine, "so's the bike. It's an English Harley."

"Damn, never heard of an English Harley," the cop answered, circling.

"Sit on it, go ahead," I urged.

A second later the overweight cop was in the yoga back-stretch posture. "Christ, how the hell can you ride on this thing?"

I was hoping he didn't try the foot brake.

The policeman was wide in the ass, and most of it hung over the edge of my saddle. He looked too big for the bike. It made a nice picture, and Hendrix was already lining it up.

"Don't do that, don't do that," the cop protested, blocking his face with his hands, struggling to dismount. "Hell, I'll lose my badge if they see me on this thing. Especially in uniform."

Hendrix reholstered his camera, and the cop waved us off. "You boys take care now, ride safe." He was still eyeing my bike and shaking his head.

I didn't leave the other two riders till we hit Charlottesville. I knew where the hotel was, and I needed gas. My bike was getting about a hundred and twenty miles to my sculpted tank, compared to their hundred and fifty, so I liked to be topped up.

Fueled and tired, after twelve hours of saddle time, I drifted to a stop at a red light, about five hundred yards from our hotel. A red pickup truck coasted to a halt beside me.

"Hey, Easyrider?" The voice was sharp, but not aggressive.

I turned to see a tattooed arm extend from the window of the truck. There was a familiar smell, and smoke coming from the fingertips.

"Suck on this, bro," the voice suggested.

The joint was long, and thin. One of those that the late rock singer, Jim Morrison, had referred to as a New York toothpick.

I accepted the toothpick, and took a heavy hit before returning it.

"Have a good one," the tattoo smiled, then pulled away.

I was stoned. Totally. One hit, and I was a goner. "They must grow it strong down here," I thought, making my way, at six miles per hour, towards the hotel gates.

Most of The Club was already in residence, at the hotel, gathered outside, polishing their rides, or sipping beer. They all knew each other, had ridden together before, skied together, partied together. Everyone but me. Two things struck me as I parked up, dismounted, and mumbled some hellos. The first was that they were all surprisingly tall, and the second was that they were all very quick witted. They shared the kind of repartee developed from several group experiences, on the road, or on the ski trails. I, on the other hand, stuck behind the paranoid haze of a Virginia Slim, was proportionately short, both in stature and mind. Very nearly inarticulate. I followed numbly behind as they made way for a local restaurant.

Wine was ordered, food was ordered, and road stories exchanged, a general recant of the first day. How many speeding tickets, how many lost on the road, how many still missing. I tried to gulp enough wine to dull my marijuana heightened consciousness, and laughed whenever anyone looked in my direction.

Gary arrived before the main course, and the Road King—breaking in his new bike by becoming the phantom cyclist of the Washington Beltway; I think he'd done the loop four times—made it before the second bottle of wine. All present and accounted for, I was finally coming down enough to talk. I also seemed taller. Actually, I concluded, swilling my fifth glass of red, these were some of the greatest guys I'd ever known.

I kept that thought right through the walk home, and into my midnight attempt to operate the antique Jacuzzi, located on the platformed side of my bedroom. I was exhausted, partially stoned, completely loaded, and I nearly drowned in the half inch of gurgling water. After which, I crawled to the bed and slept.

Blue Ridge Custom

DAY 2

I pulled on my leathers at seven o'clock the next morning, concluding that, in spite of the heat, when racing cross-country, heavy leathers were a must. Besides, my appearance in my English riding pants would serve as testimony to The Club of the fact that I meant business. I'd intended to throw a fast polish on my sled, then wait for the stragglers to get out of bed.

I walked out, into the Virginia sunshine, to find ten obsessive-compulsive Club members, armed with chamois cloths and torn towels, polishing like there was no tomorrow. I was truly humbled, squatting silently beside my bike to join in a ritual I thought I had invented, the pre-ride polish. Perhaps, after wandering the highways of two continents, I had finally found my tribe.

A quick glance around and I noted there were also assorted sets of leathers, ranging from Yamaha's cowboy chaps, to Ducati's full "Italians," featuring a fully gussetted, elasticized waistband.

"I'm going to try and get my knee to the ground when we hit those mountains today," the Ducati explained, noticing me checking out the thick pads on the downside of his pants.

"That bike's meant to corner," I answered; I hoped he didn't think I was a crotch spotter.

* * *

Before we kicked off, Captain Bandana handed out road maps, our routes highlighted in felt tip, and breakdowns of our itineraries. The last sentence on the page read: "Points of Interest— A dry county, but we will be equipped."

I took a quick glance at the directions, noted the section on Points of Interest and decided that, come hell or high water, I'd stick tight to one of The Club; I'd never find Corbin on my own. Not today, anyway.

We gave Gary—the Chase truck—a ten minute head start, revved up, jockeyed for pole position, then roared from the hotel gates.

Mothers with children, old men on zimmer frames, adolescent females: all huddled back along the shop fronted sidewalk as The Club rolled forward—in what was, probably, the only time of the day we would ride together.

The Wild Ones were leaving town, with their grizzled faces and lantern jaws. Disguised by sinister, dark glasses, a Prussian helmet, an adjustable gusset, and assorted leathers, the cowering civilians never suspected that they were watching a parade of heirs, moguls, wine connoisseurs, politicians, stockbrokers, ski instructors, fashion designers, a corrections officer, a stunt pilot, and an aging novelist.

Fifteen miles later we entered the Blue Ridge Mountains. Mountains: steep roads, and lots of tight curves, an aspect of the trip that had me concerned. I was, after all, riding the equivalent of a stretched limousine. "Five inches over (a stock frame)" may not look like much on paper, but swing it round a mountain bend, with a knee dragging Ducati on your tail, and it's the difference between life and death.

That's what I had anticipated. In truth, my stretch handled well. The Yamaha flew past, and I could hear the sound of Ducati's knee pad scraping from many bends ahead, but I was definitely holding my own. Forty miles into the mountains, and I was having a ball, catching some of the finest views in America from the mountain peaks, valleys and mist, then swinging the stretch into the dips and round the bends.

It was virtual reality with mountain air and kaleidescope colors.

Captain Bandana was winging along behind me, riding his sled like a jet ski. I accelerated, then congratulated myself for losing him on the bend.

Only to find out later that in fact he had lost it. Hitting some gravel, he'd cartwheeled his bike. Luckily, he was thrown clear, and his motorcycle settled about thirty feet away.

His handlebars were bent, but with help he righted his bike and continued, as if it was no more than a mild tumble on the Aspen slopes.

Sixty miles into the Blue Ridge Mountains, and I was singing my heart out, relaxed in the saddle, and as happy as I've ever been, anywhere, at one with the road, and completely oblivious to the slight change in surface that heralded a rough patch. A pot hole—probably transplanted from the Cross Island Parkway—changed all that. When my ass reunited with the saddle, I noticed my ride was considerably harder, and my bike was vibrating like a joy stick.

I slowed down, but kept on rolling, out of the mountains, and onto the Interstate. Even with a smooth road, I was still aware of a particular bruising sensation in my posterior. It wouldn't quit, and I was becoming concerned, when Hendrix cruised up beside me, and shouted, "There's smoke coming off your back tire!"

We pulled into the next gas station. Sure enough, my rear fender had split and dropped down, onto the rear tire, burning the rubber and flattening the tread.

My custom strech, covered in dust, minus its front brake, and now running a bashed fender and a tire that resembled a racing slick, was turning into a jalopy. I grieved a moment, then flashed on an idea for further customization.

"If we could only saw that rear fender in half, and lose the bit that's hitting the tire," I mused to Hendrix. "Hell, I've always liked that short fendered look."

The Chase truck pulled in, followed by Captain Bandana, riding his own, off-kilter rendition of a Blue Ridge Custom. Behind him came the Road King and a small crowd of locals, drawn by the action.

Within minutes, it was party time at the gas station. The locals were on the bike, underneath the bike, pushing up and down on the bike. "Your shock absorbers are gone," a tattooed, bikeless bro announced.

I nodded my head, not certain as to the implications of riding without shocks, then countered by asking who did the Harley Eagle on his right bicep, "Mary, my wife, first tattoo she ever did," he answered, looking towards the cab of his four wheeler, "Mary, come on over here."

A six pack of beer later and I was displaying my own art work, while discussing the possibility of pushing my bike over to my new friend's garage, for some temporary repairs.

"No. It's best to load it on the van, and fix it in Wichita," Gary's voice cut through.

The idea of abandoning my sled was devastating.

"Isn't there some way around this?" I asked.

"Not unless you want to pull off the whole rear fender and ride your ass on the tire," Gary stated.

We loaded my former show bike, onto the back of the Chase truck and rolled out two spares. One for me, and one for Captain Bandana, who happened to own a bike shop in Wichita. Both bikes were custom touring bikes, and mine, complete with windshield—an accessory I had vowed never to ride with—were shop creations.

"You're going to sit a lot higher in the saddle on this," Bandana explained, pointing to my cream and black "Hybrid" (as he called it).

I was used to a saddle height of about twenty-two inches; in other words, I was accustomed to my ass nearly touching the ground. The Hybrid felt like a high chair, and very well upholstered, including a studded saddle and saddlebags. As I shinnied up into riding position, touching my toes to the ground—just to make sure they'd reach—my self-image as Bronco Billy, the authentic American Hero, evaporated in the heat of the afternoon. Easyriders II became City Slickers III, as I waved my tatted friends goodbye, and floated down the road.

The Hybrid was one hell of a motorcycle, a merging of the ridged framed Softail and the rubber mounted engine of the FXR. There was hardly any vibration (because of the rubber mounts), and the suspension was like a Cadillac's. Also, having never ridden behind a screen, I soon figured out why The Club bros could cruise all day at ninety. There was no wind resistance, and, consequently, no shoulder spasm.

The road was gently banked, and the Hybrid dug deep into the corners, then flowed into the straights. I hated to admit it, but within fifteen minutes, I was a convert to the type of motorcycle I had formerly decreed as an armchair for old men, the Touring Bike.

The Hybrid went straight to my ego. I nipped in and out of the three other bikes, until I had assumed lead position. After that, I twisted the throttle and cruised. It was as if I had been given wings. I caught glimpses of Captain Bandana in my rear view mirror—another feature (mirrors) I had stoically lived without. He was riding his Prototype, a modern version of the Connoisseur's vintage, 1969 FLH.

Bandana's Prototype was designed, externally, to look like the old FLH, but it featured an Evolution engine, modern suspension, and all the conveniences (wiring, tightly sprung saddle) of a new Harley. This was the Prototype's test run, and Bandana appeared to be slipping behind.

The winding road segued into a four lane highway. I accelerated, and outran the three guys who had been kind enough to wait while I'd trashed my stretch. Before long, they'd vanished from my mirror. I pulled to the side of the road, looked back, and waited. Nothing, no one.

Finally, I made a U-turn and followed the highway in the opposite direction, keeping an eye peeled for route signs. I had no idea which section of the Day 2 Travel Plans I was currently riding, but I was definitely on a solo voyage.

A few more miles and I spotted them. Of course, by now, they were riding towards me, in the opposite direction. They looked very relaxed. I waved as we passed on the highway. Apparently, they hadn't known we were racing.

Humbled, I swung another U-turn, and trailed the Road King into Corbin.

All of the other Club members were already in residence at the hotel, which was a pretty elaborate affair, cut into the side of a mountain, overlooking a river.

Now, the Points of Interest section of the Day 2 Itinerary came into effect. My sponsor for the run, the Connoisseur, had his own travelling wine cellar, located at the back of the Chase truck, but, in this instance—a Dry County—transported to the coffee table of his hotel room. His window adjoined the main patio, and he was serving wine and mixed drinks to the gathering Bros.

A whiskey and water settled me right down, opened the gates to my personality, and got me to the point of near hysteria, listening at tales of wrong turns, lonely mountain cruises, road-side encounters with various lawmen, and the general disintegration of several of the bikes: smoking carbs, flat tires, floating saddles; I wasn't alone.

I was beginning to get into the spirit of the ride. It was a type of solo-group adventure. Sometimes you were on your own, sometimes you were riding with The Club. As long as you had a road map and a hotel reservation, all you finally had to do was arrive. These were high pressure people, and they needed a high pressure ride to relax. Obviously, so did I, since I relaxed enough to conduct an impromptu physical fitness seminar for Hendrix, on the chinning bar—a water pipe—inside his room. The Stunt Pilot, resplendent with his eighteen inch biceps, encouraged us from behind a six-pack. Many repetitions later, I retired for the night. I was having a ball.

Premonition

DAY 3

This was a big one, from Corbin, Kentucky, all the way to West Plains, Missouri. Over five hundred miles.

One of The Club, the Stockbroker, had left at the crack of dawn, on the back of the Correction Officer's Dresser (leaving us his Low Rider FXR, as a spare bike), to catch a plane back east. There was talk of a ten-million-dollar deal for the Stockbroker, and a thousand mile day in the saddle for the Corrections Officer.

From the off, the C.O. had reminded me of the martial arts actor Chuck Norris, and now the thousand solo miles confirmed his heroic stature. He was solid, The Club's backup man.

Outside, we checked the bikes over and prepared for take-off. I noticed Yamaha snapping pictures, and asked if he'd get one with me, standing next to the Hybrid. He obliged, but between lining up the shot and closing the shutter, a fellow guest at the hotel—and not one of The Club—rambled into frame. He was wearing a white T-shirt, and had a gut that preceded him by several feet. Aesthetically, he didn't do much for my picture.

Snap! I heard the shutter close.

I looked at Yamaha, then towards the gentleman with the offending belly.

"Did you get him in the shot?"

Yamaha, glancing towards the uninvited, photographic guest, "How the hell could I miss it?"

"Well, it'll give us some authenticity," I answered.

Meanwhile, the Gut was at least twenty feet away, and, we assumed, out of earshot.

"I heard what you said, I heard ya'," he unexpectedly retorted.

We turned, as, both hands placed on his hips, the Gut stared us down, "Where I come from, I drive a bus, and there's nothing I like doin' better than riding over you bikers, leavin' ya' flat in the road. Kinda' like a hobby with me."

"And where do you come from?" Yamaha countered.

"Atlanta, Georgia."

"Well, we'll have to remember not to ride down there," Yamaha replied.

The Gut huffed and puffed, then joined his equally corpulent wife in a Dodge Ram. He reversed and rolled down the window.

"Y'all have a nice day, now."

I couldn't figure out if he was suddenly being forgiving, or simply setting us up for the kill. In any case, we gave him a few minutes head start before pulling out.

Once beyond the hotel gates, secure that we weren't being followed, and reminded how easily things can flare up from nowhere, I settled back into the comfort of the Hybrid. If the bike was good yesterday, it felt great that morning. The country road that linked us with Highway 90 was wide and winding, and the group naturally divided into three sub-groups. Yamaha, Ducati, Hendrix, the Politician, and the Stunt Pilot were up front, while I was riding behind Captain Bandana, with the Connoisseur right behind me. A third, more leisurely group, including the Road King and the Ski Instructor, followed us. The Connoisseur held with us for ten miles or so, but the spring-mounted saddle of his FLH caused him to float at dangerous angles while cornering, sort of like a man hiking out over the side of a sailboat while tacking into the wind. Gradually, he dropped back to the leisure group, as we roared ahead.

The great illusion of speed was demonstrated at the first gas station. After hammering our bikes for the better part of two hours, and leaving the Connoisseur along the winding gravel many miles back, it was a bit disconcerting to have him, along with "Leisure Group," arrive at the gas station before I'd even finished filling the Hybrid. By pushing it, we must have gained less than five minutes, which probably correlated to the fact that if the Death Race 2000 was run at legal speeds, we'd make it across America, and arrive in Las Vegas for dinner, not lunch. But where's the adrenaline in that?

The way, I decided, that people got to know each other on this trip was by riding together; I'd gotten to know Hendrix by drifting behind assorted rock classics, blasting from his on-board speakers—volume automatically controlled by his throttle—at a hundred and ten it was sort of an "Apocalypse Now" type of effect (when Robert Duvall's chopper flew in to drop the napalm, its on-board loudspeakers belting out Wagner's "Ride of the Valkyrie"). Hendrix's bike was a power-fortress, fairing and panniers, windshield, digital clock and gauges, wraparound spreakers. If the occasion warranted, he would don a full-faced helmet. "Whatever was necessary to complete the mission," I surmised. He was also very organized, as his console mounted map testified, yet humble enough to allow me to instruct him on the fine points of doorway chinning. I rated him as a man destined to continue both his muscular and spiritual growth. Come hell or high water, Hendrix would make Vegas.

The Yamaha and the Ducati were fast-laners. Quick of both wit and throttle, and highly maneuverable—as their Blue Ridge knee-to-the-ground riding style confirmed—they were probably already in Vegas, or at least a Vegas state of mind. In fact, too classy for the slot machines, I speculated that they had transcended Vegas as a geographic point and were more likely locked into a certain Vegas kind of moment, that clatter of chips, in front of you, as your cards come up

"21" at the blackjack table. No one could outrun these two. Except:

The Stunt Pilot. Mounted on his silver Fat Boy, which was the aerodynamic equivalent of the Hindenburg, the Stunt Pilot rode like he flew, fast and low to the ground. The only wind resistance came from his herculean biceps, which he kept tucked neatly to his side, using them more for balance than brute power. He soared and swooped.

The Road King was understated. Stock but secure; he could keep up with the best of them, or drop back with the leisure riders without any noticeable slip of ego. A gentleman cruiser, he'd take Vegas in stride.

The Ski Instructor was breaking in his bike like a set of new skis, holding it high around the corners and taking no chances on the straights. Cautious but steady, it was the tortoise and the hare syndrome. Many set out ahead of him, grinding their rides till they dropped, only to look up from the side of road to see the tortoise crawl by.

The Politician was competent, persevering, and a true gentleman, the kind of guy who was happy to be a few bike lengths behind the group leader, yet, with enough muscle in his throttle hand to overtake if necessary. Not a pressure rider, there was something very vice-presidential about his style.

Captain Bandana was an athlete, a daredevil, and an organizer. He rode like he was skiing "off-piste," at Aspen. Fast, but controlled—with the exception of the Blue Ridge Incident—Bandana was capable of taking the lead at any moment, yet retaining enough self-control to keep The Club together. Even in moments of high-tension road work (a six car pass at ninety-five on a single lane), Bandana was known to control his bike with a single hand while operating a hand-held camcorder with the other, recording both his road skills and the efforts of those riders, risking their lives, to keep up with him. He'd hit Vegas on a roll, hose down his ride, then win a few hundred thousand at the tables.

The Connoisseur was quiet, but with a wicked wit. Wearing a jaunty red scarf and riding his vintage sled, he kept a keen eye on his travelling cellar. Although his motorcycle was reputed to go no faster than seventy-five, somehow in spite of his floating saddle, I expected him to roll into town in the first wave of riders, and set up a wine tasting.

And I'd be there, glass in hand, Prussian helmet, and polished Stretch, Viking features etched in neon—

Or would I?

We were six days and two and a half thousand miles from Las Vegas when the first rain began to fall. And in the sudden darkness and chill, I had a premonition. "I won't be making it to Las Vegas." It was that fast, and that simple. All my hype and machoism deserted me for a brief, hollow moment. I slowed down. The Connoisseur caught up, and pulled along my side.

"Everything okay?!" he shouted across.

"Yeah, I just need a rest, you go ahead," I answered.

I let him glide by, then laid back for a while, trying to redredge the strange, vacuous feeling—my premonition—from my subconscious. It had existed in a space all its own. I wanted to bring it back, analyze it, nullify it, but, it was gone. "A premonition? More likely a flash of paranoia," I told myself, as I dropped down behind the Hybrid's windshield and accelerated.

"I wouldn't take that back road to West Plains if I were you," the lady proprietor warned, pointing to the more rural of the two roads. "My daughter's a biker. Damn good rider, but that crosswind caught her, and blew her straight off that old road. She broke her leg. Nope, it's gettin' dark, and the wind's kickin' up, maybe some more rain, I wouldn't be takin' that road."

I could tell by the glint in Bandana's eyes that he was sold. He had to have that old road. Rain, crosswinds, dips and corners, all good positive stuff. As for myself, I was thinking more in terms of a hot bath, and a dry pair of jeans.

I waved Bandana and the Politician goodbye and headed off on the highway version of the fork. I was approximately sixty miles from West Plains, Missouri, and it was the first time on the trip that I had, voluntarily, ridden alone.

It was dusk, and the sky was patchy with scattered rain clouds, but the road was wide, winding and dry. There was something good about riding alone, so far from anything familiar. Just me and the Hybrid, out there on the American highway, in the wind, with the sound of the Big Twin engine, the flat blue-gray color of the sky, and an empty road that rolled forever. I was temporarily disconnected, from people, from business, from everything but the bike and the road. Twenty-five years ago, I had walked and hitched across America, living rough. I had that same feeling then, lost to the world, but found, inside myself. The bike trip was bringing it back, stirring those old feelings of independence and self-reliance, giving me back to myself.

With the exception of Bandana, the Politician, and the C.O., The Club was all there, parked in the back lot of the West Plains Ramada Inn when I arrived. Plus, there were two new faces, the Southern Gentleman—who rode up from Missisippi—and his younger brother, Junior, who had followed by car. Junior was busy washing windshields.

"Junior, here's a new one," the Southern Gent called out as I parked up.

Before I could get off the bike, Junior was squirting away, claiming that whatever he had in his spray can would cause any rain to bead up. "Just like wax on a car," he promised.

"Do you ride a bike?" I asked, feeling I should at least make polite conversation while he labored on my screen.

"Never have," he answered in his thick, southern drawl.

"Ever been on one?"

"Ya' mean, ridin' bitch?" Junior inquired. Something in the way he said "bitch," indicated that "bitch" was not a very dignified way for a man to travel.

I looked at him. He was wearing bottle thick glasses, and had a smile that tilted slightly to the left. He reminded me, both in looks and demeanor, of the Jack Nicholson character in *Easy Rider*, slightly naive, smart, and very genuine. Impossible not to like, a Southern Classic.

"Nothin' wrong with ridin' bitch, if you ain't got a bike," I answered.

He looked at the Hybrid, looked at me, threw a quick glance at the Southern Gent, as if asking for silent approval, then smiled as if we'd just concluded a secret arms transaction.

"I wouldn't mind."

By then, Bandana and the Politician had arrived, and Junior had other screens to clean.

I got my bath and my dry jeans, and after dinner Junior got to ride bitch. I insisted he wear the Prussian helmet.

Later in the evening, Junior entertained us with a selection of the Rolling Stones' greatest hits, pumped from the juke box of a local redneck bar. The locals preferred country music, and after several death threats, The Club departed. Junior was placed under armed guard.

Exhausted as always when I hit the bed, I still couldn't sleep. It was near midnight, and the C.O. was still out there, somewhere, on the road. Being a natural drill sergeant, and, by now, feeling a bond with the other riders, I was having a hard time dozing off until all of the unit was present and accounted for. So I lay there, listening for the sound of exhaust pipes.

About an hour later, I heard them, coming from far away, along the road. I leapt out of bed, wrapped myself in a towel, and opened the door. Sure enough, the C.O. had made it.

"Where the hell have you been?" I called out, waving the remains of a six-pack in my right hand.

"At the wrong Ramada Inn, about sixty miles back," he answered.

"Here, have a beer," I offered.

The C.O. came in, and we talked about the ride.

"A lot of these guys only see each other once a year, for this ride," he explained. "They're some pretty strong personalities, with some heavy business responsibilities, and this is how they relax. One way or another, we all need this ride."

Amen.

The C.O. was different from the others, and from me, in that he wasn't so fast with the New York repartee or the quick one-liners. He had a sense of humor, but at the same time he seemed grounded, as if his personality was the safety net that allowed the rest of us to raise a little hell. He respected the others for who they were and what they had accomplished in their lives, but he also respected himself. I thought of him as the kind of guy who'd keep an eye on your back if there was trouble. I trusted him.

We finished the beer, and I rested in peace.

```
┌─────────────────────────────────────────┐
│                                         │
│              Joe's                      │
│                                         │
└─────────────────────────────────────────┘
```

DAY 4

Only 376 miles, with a party at Bandana's place in
Wichita to celebrate the halfway point in our ride. Points of
Interest: Massage available on request at Captain Bandana's.

By the time we rode from the parking lot of the hotel, I'd
already mentally booked myself onto the massage table. I'd
need all the lower back relaxation I could get before reboarding
my Yoga Stretch Machine.

Above, the sky was dark, and the wind was howling. We were
entering the middle of America, the flatlands, tornado country.
In fact, I'd heard on the early morning T.V. weather forecast
that there were tornado watches in effect for most of Kansas.

I was going to be happy to clear this half of America, and
get into the desert highways of New Mexico. I'd wanted to ride
those big, flat western roads since I'd first owned a motorcycle,
and it had taken me half a lifetime to get this close.

We rode into our first big storm of the day about thirty miles
from West Plains, a cold, dark, sheet of rain, blown into our
faces by a strong wind. Thank God for the windshield, or I
would have kissed the others goodbye, right there. As it was, I
put my head down and twisted the throttle, blasting through
at ninety. We'd entered the storm together, but the rain was so

intense that, within minutes, I was only aware of Ducati ahead of me, and Yamaha and the C.O. behind. Then, I caught the flash of red in my mirrors, and Yamaha was a prisoner of the highway patrol. In this part of the country, the penalty for going thirty-five miles an hour above the legal limit was a trip to the county jail. I rode another couple of miles, pulled over, and shut the bike off. The C.O. pulled in behind me.

"I think Yamaha's on his way to prison," I said, looking back, through the rain. "A cop just pulled him over."

"I'll go back and see if I can help," the C.O answered.

I watched him disappear, then decided to ride ahead, slow enough that whoever was behind would catch up. I pushed the starter button and nothing happened. Again. Still nothing, the Hybrid was dead. I got off, bent down beside the bike, and saw that the cable, which led from the voltage regulator to the alternator, had disconnected. My battery was flat. I stood up in time to see Yamaha race past. I waved. Then the C.O. I waved again. I had decided to sort this trouble out on my own.

Across the highway, about a hundred yards ahead, I saw a sign which read JOE'S GARAGE. I eased the Hybrid off its stand and began to push.

Joe was all smiles. He admitted that he'd never worked on a bike, but, what the hell, he had a wrench and a battery charger. Plus a urinal that was the nearest thing to the Black Hole of Calcutta, this side of LA. It was a narrow passage, pitch black, and had a hole at the far end. One step too many, and I would have drowned. Afterwards, I grabbed a six pack of Budweiser from the nearby convenience store, and camped out on Joe's front bench.

"Every day at three o'clock, we close up shop, sit down, and watch it all go by," he informed me, as I settled back. "Vegas?" I thought, "who the hell needs Vegas?" These roadside stops had an inertia all their own. They were like islands where time stood still, and "Vegas" became a city man's hallucination.

I had just begun to consider an application to become Joe's personal assistant when I heard the sound of Harley pipes.

It was the C.O., on a reconnaissance mission. I waved him

into Joe's parking lot, then pointed him towards the black hole.

"Dangerous in there," he commented on his return, then joined me on the metal bench.

The rain had passed, the sun was shinning, and the one horse town, which ran for about a hundred yards to either side of Joe's Garage, appeared luminescent in the golden haze.

'I could stay here forever, "the C.O. said, his voice suddenly lazy.

"I'm not so sure about this battery," Joe called over.

The C.O. and I eased our way from the metal bench, and walked to the Hybrid.

"It doesn't seem to be holding the charge," Joe explained. The meter on the battery charger was bouncing around like a geiger counter.

"Can we get the bike started," I asked.

"Try it."

I hit the start button and the Hybrid roared to life. I looked at the C.O.

"I guess we'd better see if we can get it to Wichita."

We said goodbye to Joe, who refused any money for his services, and somewhat reluctantly hit the road.

"You're going to have to keep the engine running all the way," the C.O. cautioned. I was more optimistic. I figured the problem was cured.

I was wrong. At the first gas station, I shut off the Hybrid to fill it, and that was it. Dead, again. We took turns pushing, trying to jump start it. Ninety-six degrees in the sun, and both of us sweating.

"I should have listened to you, I should have listened," I confessed, when it was the C.O.'s time to push. No luck, we couldn't get the engine to turn over. On the verge of exhaustion, we were rescued by a couple of hombres in a Dodge pickup, with battery cables.

"Hurt him for this, hurt him bad," the C.O. encouraged, trying to catch his breath. Twenty dollars of hurt later, the Hybrid came to life.

```
┌─────────────────────────────────────────┐
│                                         │
│                 Prayers                 │
│                                         │
└─────────────────────────────────────────┘
```

Now the prayer section of DAY 4 began. Me, looking
down at the gas tank, "come on, don't stop now, get me to the
massage table."

Between prayers we were trying to follow the detour signs
which pointed towards Highway 96 West, the road to Wichita.
Somewhere, we slipped up, and hit the Oklahoma border. I
looked across at the C.O.

"We're going the wrong fucking way."

Midway through my U-turn, and twelve miles from any semblance of human life, the Hybrid stalled.

"No!" I shouted, revving like a banshee. A dying banshee.

Then, silence from the Hybrid.

I rolled the six-hundred-and-fifty-pound customized steel
carcass to the shoulder of the road. The C.O. did the same
with the Dresser. The temperature had climbed into the low
hundreds.

We stared at each other; I hoped my nose wasn't as sunburnt
as his. Difficult to tell, since I'd lost touch with my entire face
about fifty miles back. I was overheated, filthy, and angry.

Then, the roar of exhaust pipes, and, for a moment, the
hope of reprieve.

Until the dropped, chopped Chevy roared into view. This red four wheeler featured X-tra wide rear tires, like truck tires, and a totally ventilated engine—in other words, the hood had been removed to reveal the 450 horsepower block of steel. The monster roared by, the brakes screeched, and the Chevy reversed towards us at approximately the same speed it had passed. It slid to a second stop. The door opened, and Conan the Barbarian stepped out, with a full body suit of tattoos, neck to fingers.

Always a tricky moment, ingratiating yourself to the locals. Especially when Conan's lead line was, "You boys better take care of them cycles; they steal'm pretty quick round here. I got seven of'm myself."

"How bout a fresh battery; you got one of them?" I asked, meeting eyes that flickered like a hawk's.

The C.O. was leaning casually against his bike.

"Usually carry one, but not today," Conan said. "Why, you in trouble?"

"No," I answered, "just my battery's low, and we're gonna' do some night riding."

"Where to?"

"Wichita."

"Wichita's that way," he pointed west, "'bout two hundred miles. You're a long way from Wichita."

I looked west, nodded my head, then, deftly changed the subject.

"Man, that's a hell of car," I said, eyeing the Chevy.

"She'll do under ten seconds for the quarter mile," Conan beamed, the edge suddenly gone from his voice.

I walked around the Chevy, and kept nodding my head.

"A hell of a fucking car," I repeated.

"Sure is," he agreed, slipping in behind the wheel, and starting it up, so I could appreciate the full kick of the engine.

"Thanks for stopping," I said.

"No problem." He looked a last time at the bikes. "Just don't leave m' sittin' there by'm selves."

"We won't."

Conan hit the pedal, and squealed into Oklahoma, trailed by four hundred yards of burnt rubber.

I turned to the C.O. "Why don't you ride back to that last town and see if you can get a service truck with some cables."

"I'm not going to leave you here with a dead bike," he answered.

"I'll be all right," I assured him.

"I'll stay, you thumb a ride."

"I'm not leaving you with both bikes."

"Go ahead, nobody'll touch them," he promised.

"It's my responsibility, I'll stay," I insisted.

"No." The C.O. stood firm.

"What's the matter, man, you don't think I can handle it?"

"I'm not saying that."

"You don't have to nursemaid me," I went on.

"I'm not nursemaiding you."

"If you took off, and came back in three months, I'd still be here, I promise," I reinforced my stance.

The C.O. was silent, and I thought it might be time to lighten up.

"Hell, I lived on the road for a year in the early seventies. Half the time, I'd get picked up by women, and end up spending a few days with them. If you leave, I might get lucky."

We both laughed.

"I'd still feel better if you went to town," he repeated.

By then, there was a van ambling west down the road, and I was through arguing. I stuck out my thumb, and the van stopped.

"Have you got battery cables?" I asked.

The driver shook his head.

"How bout' a ride to the next gas station?"

The door opened, and I was gone, sharing a can of Coke, and hearing about the furniture auction that the driver and his workmate were en route to attend.

I ended up in the service department of a Ford dealer about

fifteen miles south. The manager, Mike, owned a Harley and a sympathetic ear, and, within minutes, we were headed back to the bikes.

Mike's cables were shot. So we tried, the three of us, to lift the Hybrid onto the back of his truck. It was impossible.

"I get off work at five-thirty. I'll get some live cables and come back," he promised.

The C.O. and I fried up the side of the road for another hour and a half.

Mike showed at six, cables in hand.

"Hurt him for this, hurt him big," the C.O. groaned.

Thirty bucks, and the promise of two Harley T-Shirts from England, got us rolling.

"Go down the road eleven miles, hang a left at the post office, and that'll take you into Highway 96, go straight on 96, maybe three hours and you'll see signs for Wichita," Mike instructed.

The shortest ride of the trip had turned into an endurance contest.

The C.O. led the way.

We turned left at a traffic light; there was a white building on the corner. It could have been a post office. I had a brief flash that we'd made the wrong turn, but the road was new and wide, and I was concentrating more on keeping the bike alive than following directions.

The C.O. accelerated to sixty, and I stuck with him, cruising to the inside of his motorcycle, about two bike lengths back. There wasn't another car on the road, and the breeze cooled my face. I started to relax.

The next few seconds seemed to take place in slow motion. The kind of "slow" you can't stop.

First, I noticed the C.O. signaling with his left hand, pointing down with his index finger. Was he turning, stopping, or signaling me forward? I wasn't sure. I maintained my speed, until my front tire was even—on the inside—with his rear.

"What's happening?" I shouted.

Before he could answer, I saw what he had already seen.

The road ended abruptly, dropping down, onto dirt and gravel, with a ditch to the far left.

The C.O. veered, trying to avoid the drop, directly in front of me.

I ploughed into him, at fifty.

First there was a bang, then the sound of sheering metal, then a cutting feeling in my right foot. After that, I was on the gravel, braking, trying to keep the bike up. Finally, it stopped.

I turned to look for my right foot. I really thought I'd see it lying in the road. The rubber top of the Hybrid's foot board was there, flat against the asphalt, along with the leather saddle bag, sliced straight through the strap.

I looked down; I was wearing my heavy leather pants and a pair of black leather and suede cowboy boots. My foot was numb, but still attached to my leg.

"Are you all right?" The C.O. shouted.

"I broke my foot," I answered. I knew it, simple as that. I'd had enough kicking injuries in karate over the sixteen years that I'd practiced to sense the difference between a sprain and a break. My foot didn't feel attached. I started to get off the bike.

"What are you doing?" The C.O. had parked up and was running towards me.

"I've got to see if it still works."

I held onto the Hybrid and put my weight on my foot. My ankle was sore, but solid, and I could wiggle my toes. The real pain was coming from the top of the foot, along the instep. I limped a couple of steps, and thought a moment of removing my boot, before the swelling made it impossible, then reconsidered. Maybe the boot would act as a cast, or splint.

"What did I hit?" I asked.

We turned, looking at the Dresser. The crash bar—which is a rounded, hollow steel tube protruding from either side of the motorcycle behind the front forks, forming a circular protection to the legs of the rider, and the engine—was bent backwards, by about four inches on the left side. We stared at it.

"That was one of the worst sounds I ever heard," the C.O. said.

"Lucky, I've still got my foot," I replied.

The C.O. looked down at my boot, which was already starting to expand at the sides, and nodded his head.

"What do you want to do now?" he asked.

We were, again, in the middle of nowhere. No hospitals, no ambulances, and neither of us had a mobile phone. While I was considering my next move, a truck drove towards us, along the unpaved section of road, kicking up a cloud of dust as it slowed down. "They steal'm pretty quick around here." I remembered Conan's words. I felt like a lame duck. Helpless.

"You fella's lost?" The driver's voice was curious.

I straightened, and tried to look at ease, like, maybe, we'd just stopped for a breather.

"This isn't Highway 96 West?" the C.O. asked.

The driver smiled. "96 West is back down that way," he pointed in the direction we'd come, "to the main road, then, two miles to the left." He started to get out of the truck. "You look thirsty, I've got beer, coke, water."

We had a coke, and I rested by sitting on the saddle of the bike, still too cautious to announce my injury or ask about hospitals. After a few minutes the driver was on his way, stopping once to retrieve the rubber foot pad from the running board and the cleaved saddle bag, which were lying in the road. He walked them back, and handed them over.

"They must have vibrated loose when I hit the stones and gravel," I suggested.

The C.O. stuffed them inside the free saddle bag of the Hybrid.

After that, the trucker was gone, and the swelling had started to make my foot throb—at least there was life. I reached into my pocket and found three aspirin, downing them with the last of the coke.

"Let's see if we can make it to Wichita," I said.

Lucky Break

We got on the bikes; my luckiest "break" of the day was that the Hybrid had remained upright, and, miraculously, running.

Back to the main road, then left, and finally, onto the real Highway 96. I tried not to concentrate on my foot. By now, it was so painful that I could no longer use it to brake. Fortunately, I'd solved that problem with the stretch. Rear brakes were for pussies.

"How do you feel?" The C.O. shouted across at intervals.

"Like a million bucks," I answered. Somewhere, I was still contemplating Vegas.

Midway between nowhere and Wichita, trying to fill my gas tank, while simultaneously hopping on one foot and attempting to keep my engine revving by twisting the throttle with my free hand, the Hybrid died for the fourth time. It was a very sad sputter, compounded by the fact that there were no battery cables at the gas station.

We waited for help to arrive, while the C.O. disconnected my lights. In accordance with U.S. law, they had been wired to the ignition, to insure that they go on when the bike is started.

By now, mine were so dim that they were useless, plus, they were draining what was left of Hybrid's battery.

Another twenty minutes, and another twenty dollars, and another size increase in my right boot, which had begun to take on an oval shape, and we were back on the road.

The sun had set, and the temperature cooled. When I managed to shift my consciousness from whatever was taking place inside the leather and suede at the bottom of my right leg, the ride was beautiful. The land was flat, with shrubs and trees to either side, and the road wound gently. I had enough gas in the tank to make Wichita.

We'd covered more than half of the two hundred miles before it got dark, and then the real nightmare began.

I had no lights, and we were riding a truck route. Cross-country truckers make most of their time at night. Less traffic, and fewer police. They were barreling right along Highway 96, in both directions. I was doing my damnedest to keep up with the Dresser, and use its lights as my own, and the C.O. was doing his damnedest to keep me in sight, but the darker it got, the harder that became. He couldn't see me in his mirrors and, if he got ahead by more than a few yards, it was hard for me to catch up because I couldn't see the road.

We had just been overtaken by a ten-ton diesel, and as I felt the Hybrid pushed by the draft from the passing truck, I remember thinking that this was about as far as I wanted to push my luck. If I got squashed, it was my own fault. I was invisible. I slowed down and looked to the side of the road, and, for a few seconds, considered pulling over and sleeping beside the bike. It was all getting to be too much. The C.O. must have read my mind. Understandably concerned, he slowed down and urged me on.

"Oh yeah, I feel good!" I shouted. Screams from the asylum.

We rode on at about fifty miles an hour. I tried a bit of silent prayer: "Lord, if you get me out of this one, I'll never get another tattoo."

Fifteen miles from Wichita, and, about a hundred yards from

an all night gas station, the Hybrid began another death dance, shaking and farting.

"No, please, not now. Not when we're so close," I begged the backfiring bike. "Come on, motherfucker, I've had enough!" Just in case the Hybrid liked it rough.

Splat. Silence, as the C.O. disappeared over the next hill.

I rolled to the shoulder, put the kick stand down and tried to climb off. I couldn't even touch my right foot to the ground. It felt like an open wound. So I sat, half on, half off the bike, watching the C.O. circle round and ride towards me. I felt like saying "shoot me," but refrained.

He loaded me onto the back of the Dresser, and rode me to the gas station, where I collapsed in front of the Coke machine. Leaving the Dresser at the station, the C.O. double-timed, on foot, back down the highway, and pushed the Hybrid to safety. If I got a Purple Heart, he definitely deserved a Medal of Honor.

Once again, we tried to find a battery cable and a willing truck battery. No luck.

Then came the rescue.

"Mister, you look like you need a hospital," the voice said from somewhere above me.

I groaned appropriately and looked up. Into a broad face, with wide, forgiving eyes.

"My name is Bubbles T. Klown," she said.

"How do you do," I answered.

"I'm headed into Wichita, and I'd be glad to take you to the emergency room at St. Joe's."

I thought of the Hybrid. Fifteen miles from home; I didn't want to abandon her here.

"Let me help you to my car," Bubbles T. insisted.

I looked at the C.O. and winked, *Remember what I told you back there, about when I was on the road. Well, looks like I've still got the old charm.*

He laughed and grabbed my other arm. The C.O. was a big man, but not as big as Bubbles T. She was a good six feet tall and built like a linebacker.

Together they draped me across the front seat of her Plymouth, between a couple of empty gallon containers of buttered popcorn, and a few cans of diet coke.

"How 'bout the bike?" I asked.

"The manager of this place says we can lock it up behind her chain linked fence, till morning," The C.O. answered.

"Done," I said.

Bubbles T. climbed in, and we wheeled in her impromptu ambulance towards Wichita. *En route,* I learned how she had become a professional clown, by attending training courses in Salt Lake City, Utah, and reading all the available text books on the art of clowning; she explained which type of facial makeup was most effective for hot, afternoon garden parties, grand openings, and balloon banquets, and what type of footwear was most conducive to clown dancing in full costume.

I pressed my face against the window of Bubble T.'s rescue vehicle and caught the attention of the C.O., who was riding, like a police escort, beside us. I mouthed the words, "Help me."

A Medical Marvel

The truth was that Bubbles T. Klown was an angel. She got me to the emergency unit at St. Joe's, and waited while the C.O. parked up, and appropriated a wheelchair.

I made a seated entrance to emergency.

Welcomed by Wes and Blaine.

Wes was the resident doctor, and Blaine was in charge of security, with a nice little sideline in boot removal.

"Hell, that's a fine pair of boots, seems a shame to cut one of'm up," Blaine said, eyeing my suedes.

"Let's see if we can get a picture of the foot through the leather," Wes suggested.

They rolled in the portable X-ray unit, and fired away. Between leather, cotton (my sock) and swelling, the pictures were vaque, to say the least. Of the twenty-six bones in the human foot, about five of mine were visible: The metatarsals, the long bones which run downward from the phalanges, or toes. And, they were all in one piece.

"Looks good, from what I can see," Wes announced.

"I ain't pulled on anything in a long time," Blaine growled from the corner of the office, limbering up.

Enter the Connoisseur, complete with camera. Alerted to

my whereabouts, following a phone call from the C.O., the Connoisseur had rushed to the hospital, to document the event.

He leveled the camera, while Wes and Blaine, a former kick boxer with the Professional Kickboxing Association, assumed their pulling positions.

Wes held my leg steady, while Blaine, using skills developed through years on the pugilistic circuit, began to ease my boot over my watermelon sized foot.

Wes held, Blaine tugged, The C.O. stood back—prepared to step in, if more muscle was required—and the Connoisseur snapped away.

"Ahhh!!!" I howled.

Blaine froze.

"Cut him," Wes advised.

"Damn nice pair of boots," Blaine lamented, before reaching for a set of surgical scissors.

"Cut along the seam, I'll have'm restitched," I promised.

Blaine cut like a seamstress, nice and neat, right down, along the shank of the boot, and across the foot, then slid it off. Finally, with a delicacy belying a warrior of his stature, he slipped my sock off.

"Jesus, look at that thing!!"

The C.O. stepped forward, as if to examine a prize trout, the Connoisseur flashed, and the medical men marveled.

Wes pressed a button on his intercom, "Better bring the X-ray machine back here."

The second set of X-rays were not much better than the first. I'd been a size nine, prior to the crash-bar incident. By my own estimates, I was now sporting a size fourteen. "Big Foot." My toes had merged into a solid unit and the rest of the flesh, which was an electric blue-purple in color, was rounded, like a sausage about to burst on the grill.

"I still don't see any breaks, but I'd like the radiologist to take a look," Wes said, examining the pictures.

"You mean, this could be a sprain?" I asked.

"Could be."

"Oh yeah!!" I shouted. From somewhere, I conjured images

of healing overnight, and riding my own sled the next morning. It was a victory all around. The C.O. was laughing, Wes and Blaine were grinning, while the Connoisseur continued to record the show.

Wes presented me with a gift-wrapped set of X-rays, and a prescription for Ibuprofen, the over-the-counter, anti-inflammatory drug found in Advil and Neurofen. I slapped hands with Blaine, climbed back into my wheelchair and exited St. Joe's.

The Connoisseur had commandeered a Jeep, and, again with the C.O. riding escort, we headed for the Marriott. *En route*, to fully celebrate my good fortune, the C.O. guided us into the parking lot of Hooters, the local strip club.

The C.O. and the Connoisseur carried me from the vehicle, and towards the building. We were about to enter when the door exploded outwards, two bodies in mortal combat, one male and one female, entangled, followed by the club's bouncers. I hopped gallantly on my single functioning foot, wondering what the hell to do, while the C.O. and the Connoisseur grabbed me—one under each arm—and whisked me away from the battle zone. It was by now two o'clock in the morning, and we'd been at it since six A.M. yesterday. Non-stop action. And still, somehow, I believed I would heal adequately by morning to ride.

Once at the Marriot, my two friends mounted me on a luggage trolley, fixed my helmet, and shades, in place, and paraded me through the lobby, hands in riding position, right leg extended, sausage held forward, ready for the grill.

A bucket of ice from room service, a couple of beers shared with the C.O. and the Connoisseur, and at three o'clock, I settled back, preparing to spring out of bed four hours later and ride.

Four hours later the phone rang. It was the hospital. Could I come in and see the radiologist? Right away.

My foot had, during the night, gone to a size sixteen, and looked set to continue its astounding growth. It hurt to even touch it with my fingers.

I was fucked, and I knew it.

The Drip

"I want to CAT-scan this foot, it doesn't look right to me," Doctor Kater, the radiologist explained.

It was all downhill following the scan. The cuneiform bones, small triangular platforms that support the metatarsals and form the transverse arch and are responsible for adjusting the balance of the foot when walking on a tilted surface, were pulverized, thereby causing the other bones, including the metatarsals, to be dislocated. To repeat what I suspected when I woke up, I was fucked.

"You need to have this foot reset, and soon."

Between the gloom of the CAT scan and my appointment with the orthopedic surgeon and his assistant in the operating room, I managed to get into town, on crutches, to see the healthy members of The Club depart.

I watched from the side of the road as they roared away. I felt like crying.

The surgeon's name was Doctor Eyster, and his assistant was Mike Ramsey. I'd opted for a nerve block, as opposed to a general anesthetic, and I got the added treat of a valium drip, spiked with thiopentone, a modern derivative of sodium pentothal, the old truth serum. By the time they started manipulating my foot, I was back in the saddle, riding to Vegas.

I was on one side of the dividing sheet (to keep me from seeing my own reassembly), hands held high, as if I was holding on to a set of apehanger handlebars, making motorcycle sounds with my mouth, and shouting, "Oh yeah, give me more of that shit (the drip) I'm swingin'!"

On the other side of the sheet, Eyster and Ramsey worked furiously on my foot. It did not want to go back into position. They were seriously concerned.

I kept rearing up—sit-up fashion—trying to see over the dividing curtain, yelling, "How's it going fellas? Any mobility yet? Oh yeah!!" I was having the best ride of the trip, or drip.

After an hour and a half of tugging, and turning, plus an incision, to get a lever in to help with the repositioning, my foot snapped back into place. I heard a cheer from beyond the cotton barrier, saw Eyster and Ramsey smack hands, high-five style, and heard Eyster say, "Let's pin him."

All this technical, life-and-death stuff existed, to me, in sort of a dream plane. I was still riding.

And I continued to ride, as they slipped the stainless steel pin through to hold the bone and connective tissue in place, then rolled me into the recovery room, and, finally, up to my hospital bed. My drip-induced ride lasted through a barage of phone calls home." Having the best time of my life! I love these guys. Absolutely brilliant! Wouldn't have missed this part of the trip for the world."

My new riding buddy was a ninety-one-year-old from Wichita, Hollace Shaffer. Hollace had been pulling stuff off his garage shelf for a yard sale when he'd slipped and broken his hip. He was pretty near deaf, so my attempts at communication were fruitless, although his wife and daughter reported that he'd been a top country dancer before the fall.

I was still hooked up to a couple of drips, and was getting shots of anti-inflammatories and antibiotics by the hour. On top of which, my blood pressure and pulse were regularly taken. While The Club was checking motorcycle fuel levels and oil pressures, I was being similarly monitored.

That evening, the C.O. phoned from Cimarron, New Mexico.

"How are you?"

"Having a ball," I answered, sincerely.

"You may not be here, but you're still on the trip," he assured me.

I checked my bedside gauges, felt the residue of valium pumping through my fuel lines, and answered, "Oh yeah, I know, I feel it. I'm still tripping."

I hate hospitals. Pissing in bottles, spilling food down the front of my ass-displaying gown, listening to the moans and groans of the fellow afflicted. Many sponge baths were requested—by me—but none received. After a day, I wanted out.

"Not till we're sure there's no infection," my nurse replied.

Within two days I was obsessed with the religious channel on my cable television. Modern prophets predicting the demise of western civilization, the end of mankind, and the second coming of the Saviour. All thoroughly documented by current world events. It made a believer out of me. On top of which, it was my only source of entertainment, with the exception of trying to alter my blood pressure and pulse by yogic breath exercise, and answering the telephone for Hollace, who couldn't hear it ring.

A campaign to keep my upper body muscle tone, by means of doing chinups on my overhead drip-feed bar, resulted in a spilled urine bottle, and an emergency sponge bath. Finally.

On the third day, I phoned Captain Bandana's wife and announced my imminent departure for Las Vegas. I was checking out.

She was blonde and beautiful, and had been married to Bandana for one year. She handled me with all the care of Florence Nightingale and wheeled my chair through two airports *en route* to the Neon Strip.

We arrived in Las Vegas, at the M.G.M., on the morning of the last day of the ride. I'd missed the part I had looked forward to most—New Mexico and the desert highways—but I had no intention of missing the last supper.

I checked into a suite that was roughly the size of a twin bedroomed house. Its sheer size made it hell on hospital crutches for navigation. Having a bowel movement or taking a shower became a military maneuver of major significance. First the distance covered, then finding the right angle to lever the body and getting the correct saddle position on the throne, and finally, when cleaning up, making sure that no water hit my stapled, sutured, and pinned foot. The ride was over.

Dinner was at six.

The Club was sun bronzed, shaved, and freshly starched. Much the same in outward appearance as the group that had started; they'd simply added four thousand miles to their travel clocks, and acquired a half dozen speeding tickets.

We drank, we laughed, we recalled golden moments of the last eight days. There was some great food, and many champagne toasts. I had just begun to feel that I had, somehow, managed to arrive by motorcycle and not by crutches, when the Road King tapped me on the shoulder.

"Richard," he said softly, "I think your rig's at the door."

I followed his eyes and saw one of the hotel security men, waiting with my wheelchair. A sorrowful sight. But, by no means, my last ride of the trip. There were still many airports—I was upgraded from a wheelchair to an electric cart—and the flight back to England.

A month later, and I'm walking.

"What do you think of getting back on a motorcycle?" people ask.

"I can't wait."

GENERAL		PAINT & PLATING		Oil Tank	Stock
Owner	Richard La Plante, London	Painter	Terry Spencer	Seat	Dave Batchelor/P&D Svcs.
Make	Harley Davidson	Color	Black	Sissy Bar	Nottt!..........
Model	FX STS	Type	2 pack	**FORKS**	
Builder	Dean Battistini	Mural/Detail	—	Type	Springer
Time	3 months	Molding	Terry	Builder	HD
ENGINE		Chroming	—	Extension	Stock
Year	1991	**FRAME**		Yokes	Ness Top Yoke
Model	Evolution	Year	1989	Special Mods.	Kuryakyn Lowering unit
Rebuilder	Alan Fisher/Ultimate Perf.	Builder	HD	**WHEELS**	
Capacity	95ci	Type	Softail	FRONT	
Cases	Nitra-alloy (Sputhe)	Rake	Stock	Make	PM
Crank	S&S	Stretch	Stock	Size	19″
Rods	S&S	Swing Arm	Chromed	Tire	Metzeler
Pistons	Sputhe	Shocks	Billet Front	Brake	PM & Ness s/s Disc
Barrels	Sputhe	Other Mods.	—	REAR	
Heads	H.D./Jerry Branch	**ACCESSORIES**		Make	PM Solid
Cams	Andrews EV5	Bars	Ness Pull Back	Size	18″ x 4.25
Lifters	Adjustable Pushrods	Risers	Ness Top Tree Conversion	Tire	Metzeler 170/60
Ignition	MC Power Arc	Grips	Ness	Brake	PM & Ness s/s Disc
Carbs.	S&S Super E	Front Fender	Ness	**OTHER SPECIAL MODS**	
Air Cleaners	As Above	Rear Fender	Ness	Ness Regulator by Accel	
Pipes	Stainless Custom	Electrics	Dean	PM hydraulic clutch	
Mufflers	By Rally & Race	Head Light	5 inch lowered	Ness Offset Sprocket Kit	
TRANSMISSION		Tail Light	Ness Cateye		
Year	1991	Indicators	None		
Type	5 Speed	Speedo	Battistini		
Clutch	Barnet	Front Footrests	PM with Kuryakyn		
Primary Drive	Chain	Rear Footrests	None		
Final Drive	O Ring Chain	Petrol Tank	Battistini	PRICE £	